The Creative Magician's Handbook

The Creative Magician's Handbook

A Guide to Tricks, Illusions, and Performance

MARVIN KAYE

MADISON BOOKS
Lanham • New York • Oxford

First Madison Books edition 2001

This Madison Books paperback edition of The Creative Magician's Handbook
is an unabridged republication of the edition originally titled The Stein and Day
Handbook of Magic and first published in New York in 1973. It is here supplemented
with an updated appendix and is reprinted by arrangement with the author.

Published by Madison Books
4720 Boston Way
Lanham, Maryland 20706

12 Hid's Copse Road
Cumnor Hill, Oxford OX2 9JJ, England

Distributed by National Book Network

Library of Congress Cataloging-in-Publication Data

Kaye, Marvin.
  [Stein and Day handbook of magic]
  The creative magician's handbook : a guide to tricks, illusions, and performance /
Marvin Kaye.
      p. cm.
  Originally published: The Stein and Day handbook of magic. New York :
Stein and Day, 1973.
  Includes bibliographical references.
  ISBN 1-56833-229-7 (pbk. : alk. paper)
    1. Magic tricks—Handbooks, manuals, etc. I. Title.

GV1547 .K33 2001
  793.8—dc21

                                                            2001037054

⊖™ The paper used in this publication meets the minimum requirements of
American National Standard for Information Sciences—Permanence of
Paper for Printed Library Materials, ANSI/NISO Z39.48–1992.
Manufactured in the United States of America.

To my favorite dealer,
Russ Delmar,
and to the memory of my magical mentor,
Alwyn Stevenson

Contents

Acknowledgments

All professional magicians performing or writing today stand in the debt of a host of conjurers they have most likely never met. I am no exception. Out of the long roster of important contributors to the literature and craft of magic, I would single out half a dozen "idea men" who influenced my personal style and philosophy: Theodore Annemann, Tony Corinda, Bruce Elliott, Dariel Fitzkee, the wonderfully inventive U. F. Grant, and that master of macabre *mise en scène*, Tony Shiels.

I am especially indebted to Bert Easley and Eric P. Wilson for writing the *only* indispensable text on children's magic. And as a child of the nineteen-forties, I warmly recall that encourager of fledgling conjurers, A. C. Gilbert.

The performers whose showmanship I admire without qualifications are few, but would certainly include Harry Blackstone, Sr., Bud Dietrich, Joseph Dunninger, and Marvyn Roy.

Some of the most important lessons a magician can learn are taught by his professional assistants, and I have been fortunate to have worked with several particularly fine ones, including William D. Bonham and my wife and puppeteer, Saralee.

One of the special delights of working on this book was preparing the illustrations with Al Kilgore, a pleasure much enhanced by the hospitality and superb cuisine of his wife, Dolores.

Finally, deepest gratitude and love is here expressed for Florence Duray, whose excellent hospital shows in New York enabled me to polish techniques and try out many new effects. Her encouragement, advice, and friendship are perhaps the greatest rewards of my magical career.

The Creative Magician's Handbook

Introduction

There is a vast difference between telling how a trick is done and teaching how to do it. The existing treatises, with few exceptions, do the former only.

> "Professor Hoffman" (Angelo Lewis),
> in *Modern Magic* (c. 1875)

There are over fifteen thousand magicians in the United States, and about three times that number throughout the rest of the world. Conjuring has become a thriving hobby. But in the century that has elapsed since Angelo Lewis penned the above declaration, few magicians—whether amateur or professional—have paid heed to his warning.

Countless teen-agers and adults invest their money and time learning difficult digital maneuvers and acquiring expensive apparatus. Yet few of these would-be mystifiers ever master the much more vital techniques of *entertaining* people with magic.

As a result, the average conjuring buff spends some time in front of a mirror practicing hand and finger movements, memorizes some ghastly jokes out of a long-outdated book, and then—with no knowledge of timing, delivery, or the other essentials of entertainment—proceeds to treat a hapless gathering of victims to his many dull tricks. His audience forms a low opinion of magic as a whole and would probably agree with the Great Masoni, who says in *Showmanship out of a Hat*, "I do not think there is anything more boring than a bad magician."

The primary purpose of this book is to show the unpolished performer how to become a magical *entertainer*. Far too many magicians are ignorant of the basic principles of showmanship, and the majority of magic texts, dealing primarily with the revelation of "secrets," are of little help to them in this respect. Even the otherwise reliable Dariel Fitzkee errs in *Showmanship for Magicians*, when he suggests that a magician should have his act reviewed by a theatrical director, who "has specialized experienced technical knowledge which you can't possibly possess."

The Stein and Day Handbook of Magic puts the fundamentals of showmanship within the grasp of any reader. This book explains the individual skills of performing, one by one, and gives suggestions for practice and further study. Even those tricks that have been explained elsewhere serve to elucidate discussions on showmanship and staging. Unlike most conjuring texts, this one is designed not to be skipped through but to be read sequentially.

A major fault of many magic texts is that they encourage magicians to perform the authors' routines, including long blocks of "canned" speech. There is nothing so inartistic as a copycat, yet many magicians execute their tricks in dreary similarity to thousands of others. This tendency is vigorously discouraged in this book, and everywhere the reader is aided to develop a nonimitative personal style.

Sleight of hand (see glossary) is a more difficult problem, since there is nothing fundamentally wrong with manipulative prowess—provided it is not achieved at the expense of other, more essential, skills. Unfortunately, too many magicians concentrate on "finger work" far beyond its basic importance. Consequently, this book undertakes to make a new assessment of manual manipulation, and all but the most indispensable "secret moves" have been eliminated.

The tricks themselves have been set forth in a way designed to avoid the indecipherable language of the instruction sheets that accompany much commercially marketed magic. The way the trick looks to the audience, the equipment necessary to accomplish it, the basic secret and method of working, and tips on presentation—all are treated in an easy-to-follow format. Lucid illustrations further simplify the explanations.

A special feature of *The Stein and Day Handbook of Magic* is a section on entertaining "special" audiences—children, hospital patients, the aged, the disadvantaged. Until now, little or no information has been available on these difficult shows. Yet every magician, at some time or another, has probably been called on to give such a performance.

Another feature of this book is an appendix which tells where further literature and magic apparatus may be purchased, augmented by brief reviews of available merchandise at the ends of most chapters. Difficult or special technical terms are defined in a glossary supplement.

It has been said that a good actor can become a good magician, but few magicians can become good actors. The reason for this is simple. Most magicians, both amateur and professional, are ordinary people who perform magic simply because they like it. Showmanship is not a natural talent in them; it is a concept to be studied, examined, sniffed at suspiciously, adopted with caution.

But to the experienced actor, the ability to entertain and be at ease with an audience comes naturally. This book aims to teach the same skills to any magician who cares enough about his craft to learn its most important aspect: showmanship.

M.K.
New York City, 1973

Modern Magic— Its Rise and Fall

1

It is better for a man to honor his profession than to be honored by it.

Robert-Houdin, in
King of the Conjurers

Magic in the modern world has a split personality. The dictionary defines the word two ways: first, as witchcraft, wizardry, and all the attendant mumbo-jumbo of mysticism; second, as the theatrical art of illusion and psychological deception.

Each kind of magic has the same apparent goal—the temporary suspension or control of natural laws. But whereas the witch or warlock professes to exercise supernatural powers, the performing magician merely attempts to divert his audience with skillful shows of carefully developed abilities.

Both "magics" share a common ancestry. The earliest necromancers no doubt employed the same dodges and manipulations practiced today, though they probably did so to achieve temporal power.

The literature of the occult teems with such unsavory terms as "necromancy," "voodoo," and "demonology," while show magic is beset with such demeaning synonyms as "trickery," "humbug," and "charlatanism"—or, at best, mechanical descriptions such as "legerdemain" (meaning "light of hand") or "prestidigitation" ("rapid finger work," a term coined in 1815 by the French magician Jules de Rovere).

For all this, the magical art is not without honor. Its early practitioners, seeking methods to work their deceptions, often discovered scientific phenomena and natural laws. In a modest way, these explorations contributed to the histories of religion, philosophy, and the sciences.

Archeologists have conjectured that magic may be as old as prehistoric times, for certain smooth stones found in caves could have been used as conjuring devices. Magical entertainment in ancient Egypt is documented in papyrus records that describe court wizards turning wax effigies into live crocodiles or cutting off the heads of geese and restoring them. Scenes painted on one Egyptian tomb depict a primitive form of the cups-and-balls trick—which has been described as the oldest deception in the world. This modest bit of magic, in which a performer makes small stones or other objects appear and disappear beneath three cups, has proven more durable than nations, dynasties, and world visions. It is still performed today.

The Orient has long been associated with magic. Early Japanese history tells of sorcerers pulling ropes through their throats, while in China, the modern Linking Rings act, in which several metal hoops connect and separate at will, has long been performed.

India boasts one of the most famous illusions in the world, the so-called Indian Rope Trick. A guru hurls a rope up into the air, where it remains suspended. A boy climbs to the top and disappears; his voice is heard refusing to descend. The performer, knife in teeth, climbs and also vanishes. Screams are heard, then the bloody parts of the lad fall from above. The performer climbs down, relents, and restores the assistant to life.

Many magicians have rashly claimed that the Indian Rope Trick is pure fiction, but Harry Price's scarce book, *Confessions of a Ghost Hunter*, offers a plausible explanation. The illusion takes place, he says, in an open area where the bright rays of the midday sun dazzle the spectators' eyes. After an hour or so of preparing his audience psychologically and physically, the performer tosses up what appears to be a rope, but really consists of sections of bamboo or bone. Through this cylinder a central pole is thrust from a pit concealed under the rope's large receptacle urn. The disappearances occur with the top of the "rope" directly in the sun's path, and are further hidden by a white smoke screen, secretly produced by the magician. The performer carries up the stained rags that pass for the boy's corpse under his voluminous robes and smuggles the assistant back down in the same manner.

Like the Indian Rope Trick, early European magic shows were first performed outdoors. The conjurers wore special aprons that identified them as magicians (and also no doubt had convenient pockets for concealing things). When it became apparent that the revenues from street shows would be limited by the amount of space available for onlookers, magic began moving indoors to barns or onto the backs of wagons that converted into miniature stages.

Though an ancient art, show magic developed slowly through the centuries, primarily because of the dearth of written material on the subject. Either through illiteracy or because they were reluctant to expose their secrets, magicians did not pass their methods on, except by word of mouth to suitable apprentices.

The first book of magical secrets was probably *The Discoverie of Witchcraft* by Reginald Scott, published in 1582. Repulsed by the persecution of alleged witches and wizards, Scott reasoned that magic had to be executed through indetectable maneuvers or little-known natural principles. He set out to study the methods of conjurers with the humane purpose of discrediting the charges of demonic assistance often leveled against them. James I quickly banned the volume—and it became a "best seller."

The first book of magic secrets published in America was a reprint of an older British text, *Hocus Pocus: or the Whole Art of Legerdemain, in Perfection.* It was printed in 1795 in Philadelphia by Mathew Carey.

More and more magicians began to appear in the eighteenth and nineteenth centuries, but most of them relied on suspicious-looking apparatus and frequently wore Merlin-like robes and peaked hats. The first important conjurer to break with tradition was Jean-Eugene Robert-Houdin, often called the father of modern conjuring. He scorned mummer dress and appeared on a sparsely furnished stage in evening clothes. Robert-Houdin combined manipulative prowess with mechanical marvels. Formerly a watchmaker, he included a variety of clockwork figures that could execute intricate movements. But as he grew surer of himself as a performer, he reduced the mechanical portion of the program and added illusions which he himself invented.

Robert-Houdin's imitators were numerous, and included Joseph Michael Hartz, who began a professional career as a magician in 1859. Hartz soon found his own style and began to devise an unusual type of performance; he used only apparatus made entirely of glass. By 1864, he was known in London as the Crystal Illusionist.

Another important nineteenth-century magician was Alexander Herrmann, the most illustrious of a family of conjurers. Known as Herrmann the Great, he was a compulsive entertainer, and found excuses everywhere for performing his tricks. He would tip porters with "materialized" coins and often fished jewelry out of friends' dinner plates. Perhaps his most mystifying feat took place at the old Whitechapel Club in Chicago. Indicating a nearly invisible crack in the club's ceiling, Herrmann hurled a playing card more than twenty feet and lodged it in the crack, where it remained until the club went out of existence.

Henry Kellar, whose career spanned the turn of the century, was a thorough showman and a perfectionist. He was an incessant rehearser, as was the man he named as his successor, Harry Thurston. The latter magician was so fanatical about presenting new material that he spent the bulk of his huge profits each year on designing ever bigger and grander illusions for succeeding seasons.

Similar to Thurston in his ability to stage a big show was the ultimate showman, Harry Blackstone, Sr., who filled his stages with elaborate equipment, numerous assistants, and chorus girls. The fast-paced Blackstone extravaganza was often as much spectacle as it was legerdemain.

The man whose name is most often linked with magic is, of course, Harry Houdini, a specialist in hair-raising escapes as well as an accomplished magician. Other conjurers have sometimes scoffed at Houdini's abilities, pointing out that his brother Hardeen was the superior manipulator. But the fact remains that Houdini was a master in the one area that matters: showmanship.

Second only to Houdini as the greatest magical showman of the twentieth century is Joseph Dunninger. Though he began as a vaudeville conjurer, Dunninger soon confined his act solely to mind-reading effects. In the early days of television, he established a national reputation by appearing weekly with the ventriloquist Paul Winchell. Dunninger's portion of the show was spiced with a strong sense of drama as he read the thoughts of audience members and, on at least one occasion, the projected mental impressions of the *viewing* audience. Perhaps the most spectacular feat he staged was reading the mind of a subject flying in an airplane high above the studio from which the program was broadcast!

All masters of magical entertainment are noted for the unique personal styles of their presentations. Today, all too few magicians possess this distinctive quality.

Contemporary magicians seldom perform large illusion shows. They are often restricted to acts in private clubs with relatively small equipment, or even more intimate table-side demonstrations in nightclubs, casinos, or ship lounges. On TV, magicians are generally conspicuous by their absence. A few of the more gifted performers may appear on variety programs or late-night talk shows, but by and large, agents and talent bookers have little respect for magicians.

This unfortunate attitude is mostly well deserved; the present state of magic is deplorable. Many so-called professionals are incompetent, while amateurs, though numerous, are often misled by their own enthusiasm. Says Edward Maurice in *Showmanship and Presentation:*

> I have known performers of six months' experience getting to work with letterheads, etc., and advertising for (and obtaining) paid engagements. This procedure has doubtless been the cause of many professional performers expressing the view that magical societies do more harm than good.

The fact that there are estimates of as many as a thousand magic "clubs" all over the United States only confirms the hobbyist nature of today's average magician. It would be incomprehensible to envision a similar national social movement of professional comics. The clubs are no disgrace in themselves; it is only when novices try to pass themselves off as performers that harm is done.

The beginning magician is not solely to blame, however. Retailers often mislead customers by telling them a trick can be performed within minutes after purchase—a simple invitation for the amateur to make an ass of himself in public. A magician should never present any equipment to any audience, large or small, until he has worked with it exhaustively.

In addition, the general condition of magic catalogs is shameful. Tricks are described in misleading language that promises more than the apparatus can deliver. One mental-magic supplier even lists the same piece of equipment under at least two entirely different names, leading the shopper to believe he is reading about two distinct gadgets. Because magic buffs are a relatively small retail market, such practices have thus far escaped attention from consumer groups. But the time is surely coming when the magic business will receive a long, hard look from such investigators.

The worst abuse perpetrated by dealers is one generally condoned by magicians: the enslavement of the buyer to the *secret*. A novice buying magic equipment generally does not see what he has purchased until he takes the merchandise home. If this apparatus is unsuitable to his skill (and he is sensible enough to be aware of the fact), he may try to take it back—only to be told that returns are not permitted.

"We are only selling secrets," the magic dealers protest. "If our customers knew how a new trick was done, they would not buy it. Their curiosity is an all-important marketing device for us."

This excuse is no longer valid. The retailer's role must be more than movement of product. In what other merchandising field is the customer forbidden to examine the goods before he buys? The "secret" apparatus that works a trick is just so much hardware, and the customer has a right to know what it is.

"The secret hoarder is *not* a magician," writes Fitzkee in *Showmanship for Magicians*. "He never will be a magician from the standpoint of being an interesting entertainer. These secrets aren't so damned valuable. There are few of them that can't be reasoned out by a man of fairly logical analytical ability."

There is only one concern with which magicians should be involved, and that is showmanship. The best professionals look on secrets and apparatus as mere blueprints for the construction of a pleasing magical entertainment.

But what is showmanship? Masoni calls it the way a magician sells himself and his tricks—in that order. A woman who has often served as a magician's assistant defines it as "the ability to step out onto a bare stage in ordinary dress and have nobody in a packed audience cough."

Showmanship is a complicated subject that defies simple definition. It involves mental analysis by the magician of the material going into his act, but is also concerned with the manner in which the selected tricks are performed. It involves the mastery of theatrical speech and stage movement, timing and routining, selection of personal style and material, and the handling of audience volunteers and trained assistants. Showmanship also implies the ability to adapt one's playing style to different staging setups and special kinds of audiences.

Showmanship. That's what the rest of this book is all about.

2

Why Do People Like Magic?

Any relationship between the illusions you like to present and those that your audiences like to watch is purely coincidental.

Henning Nelms, in
Magic and Showmanship

More than 850 different tricks are described in a recent catalog of Louis Tannen, Inc., one of the world's largest magic suppliers. This figure (which by no means reflects the firm's entire stock) comprises tricks alone—no books, accessories, or stage illusions.

It stands to reason that there must be a wide range of quality in such a plethora of merchandise. Some tricks would work well for any competent performer, while others would only be suited to certain conjuring styles. Still other effects are probably dreary, no matter who employs them.

Unfortunately, the beginning magician is not experienced enough to decide what kind of magic is best suited for his entertainment skills. What is worse, he often makes the mistake of buying apparatus just to learn the secret behind it—and then is stuck with it. Perhaps he puts together an act which consists entirely of such ill-chosen goods. Eventually, he perpetrates a few performances and is surprised to be greeted with a less than enthusiastic response.

At this point, the veteran showman would quickly review his material to see where he went wrong. But the novice all too often refuses to accept the blame. Instead, he decides that the spectators did not have enough taste to appreciate the terrific show he gave them.

Audience disrespect is an unpardonable sin. The magician who protests that his act is too clever for the audience is merely confessing that he is too poor a showman to select the right routine for the occasion.

The basic problem is that most magicians have a distorted concept of the performer-audience relationship. Ask the average entertainer why he takes bows, and he will probably say he does it in order to give the audience an opportunity to applaud him. Viewed historically, this idea is quite erroneous. The curtain call originated as a method of allowing the *performer* to express gratitude for the audience's attentiveness. Thus, bows were first conceived as gestures of humility, not the puffed-up effrontery they have since become.

There are no bad audiences, only bad magicians. The first rule of good showmanship is: *respect the audience.* Do not blame it for a poor show, but find out what went wrong and try to correct the mistake next time. To do this, a magician must first understand the reasons audiences like magic—which will probably differ from his own. For example, many amateur magicians enjoy the purely physical challenge of mastering sleight of hand—that is, secret hand maneuvers. Being able to execute a complicated card concealment is as thrilling to them as picking up a seven-ten spare would be to a bowler. However, this manual deftness is out of place during performance. If finger work is not concealed from the audience's vision, the magician becomes simply a juggler.

Undoubtedly, many magic buffs are attracted to the gadgetry and bright coloration of some of the equipment on the market. To some extent, this visual appeal may be shared by the audience; but more often, people simply grow suspicious when the wizard trots out some odd-looking object never used in everyday life. This delight in magic apparatus is really a kind of fascination with toys—it's all right as long as the playthings are kept at home. But when inappropriately used in performance, such apparatus becomes a liability. It is almost as if an actor playing Hamlet suddenly became so delighted with Yorick's skull that he began playing catch with it. Good actors regard props as necessary tools for creating a performance, but they do not allow themselves to be upstaged by them.

In the January 1965 issue of *Genii* magazine, John Booth cites a few other motivations for becoming a conjurer. There is the intellectual attraction of practicing a slightly nonconformist hobby. Then there is the emotional reward afforded in attaining new self-definition and expression.

What about the audience? Like the magician, the spectators must be intrigued by the ability of magic to gratify the imagination. In childhood, we all want to do impossible things—to fly or disappear, to read thoughts or make desired objects materialize. As we grow older, we reluctantly set such dreams aside. But a magic show gives us back a tantalizing promise of longed-for powers. Ultimately, it hints that the harsh natural laws governing our lives may themselves be illusions—and if so, nothing is impossible.

Of course, most people realize at heart that this stretch of the imagination is only brought about by artifice. In this sense, magic is also a type of escapism—a commodity which is always needed in our anxious civilization.

Basically, most people really like—perhaps even need—to have their perceptions shaken up now and then. They want to be surprised and fooled. A good magic show holds them in delicious suspense, teases them with the questions, Can the laws of physics really be abridged? Will the performer be able to convince us that the impossible has happened?

There are exceptions, of course. Some individuals (especially children) view magic as an intellectual puzzle, a mystery to be solved. But most adults do not take magic as a challenge. If an entertainer is truly accomplished, he will find his audiences generally content to sit back and accept his paradoxes in good faith. Such a courtesy is similar to the willing suspension of disbelief by the reader of a convincing ghost story. Though he is rationally aware that vampires and ghouls do not exist, the reader allows his critical faculties to doze in order to enjoy the tale. By suspending his skepticism temporarily, he permits the author to perform his own type of magic.

Another reason people like magic is the aura of glamour and mystery it shares with circuses, carnivals, and even amusement parks. Like these other kinds of entertainment, magic seems to beckon with vague promises of other worlds just waiting to be explored.

Yet in the last analysis, audiences like magic because it is a legitimate form of show business, subject to the same rules that all good entertainment follows. When magic is presented well, people like to watch it simply because it is *fun*.

The magician's real job should now be apparent: to find out what kinds of magic his audiences like to see, and then perform accordingly. He must put himself in the spectator's place and say, "Even though I like this trick, would it really amuse me if I were watching someone else do it?"

Before he can analyze what his audiences prefer, the magician must genuinely like and respect people. When he makes his entrance, he must smile and mean it. He should be able to look at his spectators from time to time as if to say, "It's a real pleasure entertaining such a nice group!"

This kind of admiration is a two-way street. When Robert-Houdin learned one night that only three persons had bought tickets for his show, he agreed to go on anyway. At the end of the evening, he invited the trio onstage for a surprise dinner which he had earlier instructed his assistants to prepare. Both audience and magician had a marvelous time, and Robert-Houdin made three lifelong friends.

There are several basic appeals which the showman learns to rely on when selecting tricks to please audiences—music, comedy, drama, color, flashiness, and so on. But in a larger sense, finding out what kind of magic people enjoy seeing is a continual educational process for the magician, and each show is a new lesson. There are many variables to take into consideration when putting together an act: How old are the individual members of the group? Is there a mixture of ages? Is the audience predominantly male or female? What economic and educational levels will be represented?

Given these factors, the magician must then rely upon taste and experience to choose entertaining magic for each audience. After giving a show, he must honestly evaluate the reception of every trick; if an effect did not go over well, was it due to its inappropriateness for the audience mix, to the magician's incompetence in presenting it, or to the trick's lack of worth in *any* show? It takes time to develop criteria of judgment for such decisions, but if the performer does his best to respect his audiences and abide by its decisions he will soon be able to judge the worth of his routines with reasonable accuracy.

But before a magician can begin to analyze the tastes of his onlookers, he must first comprehend precisely what is meant by the term "audience."

A large group of people gathered in one theater or room is not an audience. Take the nightclub show as an example: the customers sit in small groups at separate tables like so many private islands. Each social circle is isolated, a distinct clique interested chiefly in enjoying one another's company. The performer must weld these disparate communities into a single entity; otherwise much of what he tries to perform will be greeted with indifference or even resentment.

A true audience is one in which the personalities of the members have been submerged in a conglomerate identity. This corporate body will act and react to the performer as a single unit. Its members will feel joy or fear or tension together, laugh and applaud together; they will share a collective consciousness.

When a magician is performing alone, it is his responsibility to transform the various members of the group sitting out front into a true audience. The process by which this is accomplished is called *polarization,* a term more familiar to the theatrical director than to the variety artist. It is a system for turning a disparate body of people into an audience, then directing the attention of the unified body to the playing area. Polarization takes place *before* the show begins.

Various elements may be employed in the polarization process: seating arrangement, music, speech, lighting. Essentially, individual conversations in the room or theater are canceled and everyone's attention is turned to the place where the magician is about to do the show. Technically speaking, polarization temporarily cancels each spectator's personality long enough so he can become part of the collective entity we call an audience.

In a small room, polarization may be accomplished simply by being introduced, or by walking on while speaking in a commanding tone. But if the room lights are flashed or dimmed, or if music is played on a phonograph or cassette or live, it will be that much easier to gain the group's attention. (If an audience is improperly polarized—especially at a "problem" show such as a nightclub or children's party—the opening moments of the show will be greeted with talking and little respect.)

In a stage show, the polarization process begins when the customer takes his seat. Walking into the theater, he is part of a large crowd, and his angle of vision encompasses much of the theater, many people. But upon sitting, he finds his circle of attention diminished; he can see only a few nearby people. Further, the direction in which his seat is mounted forces him to look at the stage.

As the play begins, the lights in the theater fade out. Music may start to play, or perhaps some kind of sound effect—drumbeats, street noises, etc.—is heard over the sound system. Darkness invests each spectator with some measure of anonymity, while the music or sound effects discourage private conversation.

A spotlight appears on the center of the front curtain—a finger of light drawing the eyes of every spectator. The curtain rises.

It is time for magic.

3

Fail-safe Magic

> Try to get a few good self-working tricks and stick with
> them until you get some experience in front of an
> audience.
>
> James Reneaux, in
> *The Professional Technique for Magicians*

Confidence is all-important to a magician, but it can only be built
by performing successfully time after time before audiences. The
beginner who attempts illusions beyond his skill will be so afraid of
making mistakes that he will be unable to concentrate properly on
his style of presentation.

Therefore, it is wise for the beginner to include in his repertoire
several tricks that work automatically, or are at least extremely
easy to do. These tricks will build the confidence of the fledgling
entertainer by allowing him to perform with little or no fear of
failure.

Such tricks might well be called "fail-safe magic." Several
examples fill the following pages, along with analytical commen-
tary, where appropriate.

THE NONBURNING HANDKERCHIEF *

How It Looks: The magician borrows a hanky from the audience
and drapes it over his upturned palm. He stubs out a cigarette on

---

* The name of this trick (and all others) is given solely for the sake of reference. A
magician should never employ trick names in performance, since they would remind the
spectators that they are not witnessing miracles but only a skillful series of dodges,
maneuvers, and devices.

the cloth, but the material does not burn. When the ashes are brushed off, the handkerchief is intact.

What You Need: A handkerchief borrowed from a spectator. A quarter or a half dollar.

How It Works: The heat of the ember is drawn away from the cloth by the metal coin underneath.

How to Do It: The magician secretly hides a quarter or half dollar in his hand. When he drapes the handkerchief over the hand, the coin is beneath the cloth at the palm's center. He presses the butt onto the coin through the cloth. (Be sure to flick off excess ashes first, and keep the cloth taut.) After discarding butt, flip hanky and brush to remove ash marks. Slip coin into pocket.

Tips for Presentation: 1. In a small room, perform casually, with little preamble, as if it were a prank.

2. A necktie may also be used if only one thickness of cloth is involved.

3. In larger rooms, build up the trick by humorously dwelling on the likelihood of failure, and by making a few false starts. Care should be taken to stage the effect so the actual burning can be seen.

4. Perhaps a confederate can put his hand (and coin) beneath the center of the hanky, while his other hand and one of the conjurer's hands grasp the edges of the hanky. If this is done, the confederate's "nervousness" at the possibility of getting burned will add to the effect. Pace may be slow until the burning is accomplished; then the windup should be very brisk and snappy.

"Divination," or "second sight," is the pretended ability to see concealed objects. The next trick may be shown as an example of this bogus power, or as a simple test in mind reading.

Like the Nonburning Handkerchief, this trick uses a confederate—a secret assistant who aids the magician without the audience's suspecting he is in on the act. Throughout this book, three terms are employed for persons who take part in performing magic tricks other than the magician: confederate, *the secret helper;* assistant, *a person who is known to be part of the act; and* volunteer, *an audience member called up to help during a trick. For more about assistants and volunteers, see chapter 14.*

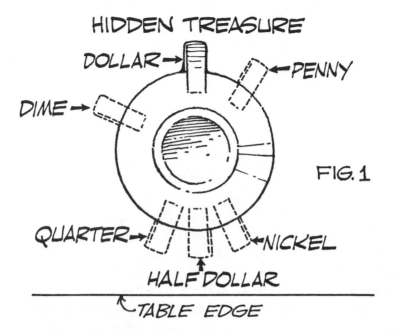

HIDDEN TREASURE

DOLLAR→ ←PENNY

DIME→

←NICKEL

QUARTER→

HALF DOLLAR

FIG. 1

TABLE EDGE

HIDDEN TREASURE

Basic Illusion: The value of a hidden coin is revealed.

How It Looks: The magician claims that he can see or sense hidden objects, then leaves the room. In his absence, a coin is placed beneath an inverted coffee cup. The magician returns. He neither touches nor moves the cup, but succeeds in telling the audience whether the coin is a penny, nickel, dime, quarter, half or silver dollar.

How It Works: A simple positional code is employed by a confederate (secret assistant).

What You Need: A table. A cup with handle. Coins borrowed from audience, or supply your own. An assistant.

Preparations: Magician and confederate must practice and learn the positional code.

How to Do It: The magician's confederate pretends to be just another member of the audience. Before the magician leaves the room, he picks the confederate to place the coffee cup over the coin. In so doing, the confederate takes care to point the handle in a direction which tells the magician the identity of the coin by prearranged code. *(Fig. 1)*

For instance, the magician and his confederate might agree that a silver dollar under the cup would require pointing the handle on an imaginary line perpendicular to the table's edge; it would seem to point to midnight. A penny might mean placing the handle at one o'clock; a nickel at five o'clock; a dime at ten o'clock and a quarter, perhaps, at seven o'clock (2 + 5 = 7). The position for the half dollar or silver dollar could also be arranged, although these latter coins are rarely available.

Tips for Presentation: 1. The magician might claim that he can look through objects under certain conditions. Such an assertion must be made lightly, with a hint of spoofing—first, because it saves the magician from being challenged to see uncoded objects; second, because it takes the trick out of the class of fraud.

2. Hidden Treasure may be presented as a case of mind reading. To do this, the magician asks the entire group of spectators to concentrate on communicating the coin's identity to him.

3. No matter which presentation is employed, the performance plan stays the same. The magician begins by pretending he can see or sense a concealed object; as a "random" example he suggests using a coin and follows through by introducing the cup as a mode of concealment. He delegates his confederate to borrow a coin from some other person and put it beneath the cup. After this is done, the magician reenters the room and *takes his time* in revealing the denomination of the coin. He might talk casually and naturally to the company and/or close his eyes to "concentrate"—or whatever other action is natural for him. But the one thing he must *not* do is look directly at the cup. Instead, he must gradually and indirectly approach it. Thus, all eyes are drawn to it with his, step by step. (If the performer were to look immediately for the handle position, he might well give away the method.)

4. The actual revelation of the coin's identity should be stretched out for dramatic effect. Squinting, furrowing the forehead, acting as if obtaining the answer were a great mental strain—these touches heighten the drama of the act.

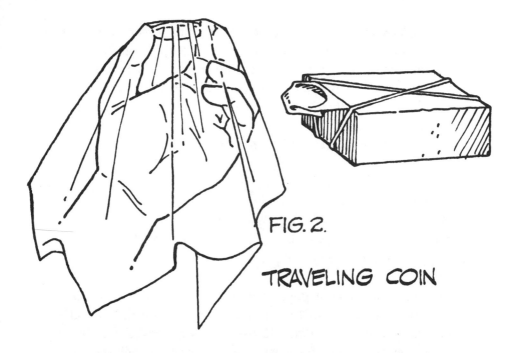

FIG. 2.

TRAVELING COIN

5. Though this trick is normally shown in a parlor or other small room, under certain circumstances it might be used in a bigger room as part of a more formal show. In such a case, it would probably be best to make it part of a series of mental tests to be set up while the performer is blindfolded or out of the room. The confederate would sit in the audience and be called "at random" to come onstage and assist.

6. Hidden Treasure is a "repeater" trick—that is, the same effect can be done again immediately. Most "repeaters" look no more magical on a second showing, but this trick is an exception. The second time a coin is divined, the stronger the effect, since the results of two trials are less likely to be due to chance. A third repetition, on the other hand, would be boring and might well tip the method to a shrewd observer. If performed as part of a larger set of mental tests, one divination would be sufficient, since the elimination of luck as a factor would be accomplished by the other tricks.

In Hidden Treasure, the magician relies upon a secret assistant. Some amateurs consider the use of a confederate vaguely unethical—a ridiculous attitude. If a method genuinely entertains or contributes to a pleasing effect, it is valid. Some illusions produce stupendous results that would be virtually impossible without a secret helper or two.

The next trick uses a confederate to great advantage.

THE TRAVELING COIN

Basic Illusion: A coin disappears from the magician's hand, though manipulation seems impossible. It reappears within a series of sealed containers.

How it Looks: The magician borrows a coin from the audience and marks it with a felt-tip pen. He reads out the date for the audience to remember, then holds the coin by the edges, parallel to the floor, with the palm of his hand beneath it; his thumb is on one side, his index and middle fingers on the other.° Then, with the other hand, the magician drapes a handkerchief over the coin and fingers *(Fig. 2)*. The magician stretches the arm holding the coin all the way out, with the elbow locked; a spectator grasps this wrist and forearm to prevent the magician from performing any secret moves. A few spectators feel under the cloth to make sure the coin is still there. One spectator reaches in the magician's pocket and removes a small box sealed with rubber bands. The volunteer holding the magician's wrist and arm lets go, simultaneously removing the handkerchief. The coin is gone. When another volunteer opens the sealed box, a second box is found inside, also closed with elastic. In it is a cloth bag with a rubber band sealing the neck. The marked coin is in the bag.

° Many magic books cause confusion when referring to the fingers of the hand. A consistent system will be employed in this book: proceeding from thumb to pinky of either hand, the fingers will always be referred to as the thumb, index finger, middle finger, ring finger, pinky.

How It Works: A confederate takes the coin while supposedly checking to see if it is still beneath the cloth. He loads it into the nest of boxes-and-bag with a secret chute.

What You Need: One confederate. A coin (penny, nickel, dime, or quarter). Either a Magic Coin Box or Nest of Boxes (both are inexpensive, standard supplies that can be purchased from almost any magic dealer).

Preparations: Train an assistant by rehearsing him several times in the necessary moves until they can be smoothly executed. Put a handkerchief, preferably a dark-colored one, in the breast pocket. Set up the Magic Coin Box (or Nested Boxes) with the coin slide protruding *(Fig. 2)* and place it in an outer pocket of the jacket, slide sticking straight up.

How to Do It: The principle of the Magic Coin Box is well known to most magicians, as it is one of the first tricks (and one of the best) that the beginning magic lover usually buys. Essentially, it consists of a chute which is preset in the boxes and bag so that a coin may be dropped down into the cloth bag at the center of the nest. When the chute is pulled out, the rubber bands which have been stretched apart by the chute snap back in place, shutting up the neck of the bag and the tops of the boxes. (The Nest of Boxes, a slightly more expensive version of the same trick, uses a smaller chute. It consists of a series of plastic pillboxes whose lids snap into place when the chute is withdrawn. Each box fits very snugly into the next bigger one, and the effect is so astounding that even magicians who own the Magic Coin Box are not always aware the Nest of Boxes works the same way. Either version, however, is worthy of performance. In Fig. 2, the Magic Coin Box is depicted.)

After placing the Magic Coin Box into his jacket pocket, the magician borrows a coin (a quarter is the largest size that can be used in the chute). He marks it and has the date noted by the audience. Then he puts it in his hand and stretches the arm as far away from his body as he can manage. With his other hand, he drapes the handkerchief over coin and fingers. He then has a spectator hold his wrist and upper arm tightly. Inviting two or three other spectators onstage—including the confederate—he has each feel the coin through the cloth. Then he asks each to reach beneath the cloth and feel the coin directly. The confederate feels the coin last *and takes it away in his hand when he does.* The magician's fingers, spread apart, still maintain the space the coin is supposed to take up under the cloth. The magician asks the confederate to reach into one of the performer's jacket pockets and take out whatever he finds. The confederate puts his hand in the proper pocket, loads the coin into the chute, pulls the chute out with his fingers, and drops it into the pocket. He then takes the sealed box-bag nest out and puts it on the table, as the magician tells him. He is now directed to whip away the cloth. As he does, the magician stretches out his fingers and, with the fingers spread apart, slowly turns his hand backward and forward to show it is empty. He asks another spectator—*not the confederate*—to open the boxes and bag and find the coin, which is verified by date and marking.

Tips for Presentation: 1. The magician must always handle the coin slowly and deliberately with as much of its surface protruding beyond the fingertips as possible without dropping it. Fast moves must be avoided, for they will cause suspicion.

2. If possible, find a particularly brawny individual to grasp your arm and tell him to do so tightly. The effect will be worth the discomfort.

3. After producing the Magic Coin Box from his pocket, the magician should stay as far away from it as possible—and stress his distance from it. Tell the volunteer to remove each rubber band deliberately and drop it some distance away. When he is ready to open the bag, the volunteer should hold it a few inches above the table and let the coin drop out. The sound and the sight of the dropping coin adds to the effect.

4. The magician should never have his confederate take the coin out of the box. Someone might know there is a relationship between the two of you, but no one is likely to be able to figure how it helps if the confederate stays far away from the sealed box.

5. There is a slightly more difficult but remarkable way to perform the Traveling Coin. By using an Asrah device, the disappearance of the coin can be delayed until the box is actually on the table.

An Asrah counterfeits the shape of an object which is about to "vanish." To make one for this trick, place a coin on a piece of cardboard, draw its circumference, and cut out the shape carefully. Paste the cardboard circle to the center of a handkerchief with double-edged sticky tape. Push the cloth into the breast pocket so the gimmick will be the last thing felt through the fingers when the hanky is withdrawn. Be sure to borrow a coin the same size as the gimmick and place it on the center of the hanky—right on top of the cardboard circle, taking care to hold it at enough of an angle so the audience doesn't see it. Turn the cloth over so it hangs down and covers the coin (and gimmick). In this case, the fingers hold the hanky in just the opposite manner from that shown in Fig. 2: they grasp the edges of coin and gimmick, palm downward, through the cloth. It is now easy for the confederate to feel the coin from beneath and, under cover of the cloth, bear it away. Yet the cardboard gimmick still shows the coin's outline. Now have another spectator *lightly* rest one fingertip on the cardboard circle through the cloth. Grab one of the corners of the hanky that are hanging down and flamboyantly whip it away in one direction. (Practice for a graceful, impressive movement.) No one will see the gimmick adhering to the cloth because of the movement. Stick the hanky back into the breast pocket and tell the spectators to begin dismantling the sealed box.

It will be noticed that the props utilized so far have been either commonplace or at least not particularly extraordinary in appearance. Coins, cups, and handkerchiefs are all things which do not arouse suspicion. But even though the things the magician touches are everyday items, he must examine them from every angle and get to know their feel. He must look at the trick from the spectator's viewpoint and decide whether he is showing off the props to the best advantage. In the Traveling Coin, the confederate must practice often enough to remove the coin casually and, when putting it in the chute, must know instinctively what the end of the gimmick feels like.

The following trick, though extremely easy to perform, requires much practice to develop the precise feel of the props—a cup and a paper napkin.

THE PENETRATING CUP

Basic Illusion: A coffee cup penetrates the table from beneath a napkin.

How It Looks: The magician wraps the cup in a paper napkin and taps it a few times on the table. Suddenly he smashes the napkin down flat. The cup is gone. He removes it from beneath the table.

How It Works: The magician fashions an impromptu Asrah device from the napkin, then steals the cup from inside it.

What You Need: A paper napkin. A cup. (A glass will also work.) A table.

Preparation: The magician should be seated at a table.

How to Do It: The magician wraps the cup in a napkin, taking care to leave the bottom open—in other words, he encloses the object in a paper shell. By twisting the napkin gently around the inverted perimeter of the cup, the magician can make a cone of paper that maintains its shape. A little practice will show the right technique, which is mostly a matter of rolling the paper around itself like a very loose tube.

The magician shows the cup inside the napkin and then turns it down, allowing the object to slip out onto his lap. In the same movement, he places the napkin shell as near the center of the table as his arm can reach. He then pretends to tap the cup on the tabletop. In reality, his finger or thumb stops the napkin from touching the table. Meanwhile, the other hand raps the cup upward against the bottom of the table surface. The rapping coincides with the downward movement of the paper shell. At the third tap, the hand proceeds suddenly downward and smashes squarely against the paper, crushing it flat. The other hand then reaches underneath the table and seems to produce the cup from the underside of the table center.

Tips for Presentation: 1. Since this trick must take place at a table, it is well suited to the dinner table, when there is a natural reason for magician, cup, and napkin to be there.

2. If the table is the magician's, he may hang a C-shaped hook beneath the table and simply hang the cup handle on it. Then he can rise and show his hands empty, reaching for the cup only after this point has been established.

Here is still another trick that uses cups and coins. It is another repeater, and one of the few that can be done as many times as the audience requests without revealing the secret. Once more, though, the performer is cautioned not to repeat it to the point of boredom. It was shown to me twice by a magician who challenged me to figure it out on a bet. I lost a weekend's sleep trying to solve it—as well as the wager.

FIND THE BALL

Basic Illusion: A ball is hidden under one of three cups, which are moved about to confuse their position. The magician infallibly reveals which cup hides the ball.

How It Looks: The magician places three playing cards—an ace, a two, and a three—face up on the table as markers. He then puts three cups on the table, one above each card. *(Fig. 3)* A ball is placed near the array and the magician turns his back.

Now the magician invites a spectator to put the ball beneath the cup at position one or two or three, whichever he wishes. When this has been done, the magician asks the subject to switch the positions of the two cups that do not hide the object. (For example: if he puts the ball under the cup just above the ace, he switches cups two and three.) The magician points out that he has no idea which two cups have been switched, nor which one houses the ball. To further confuse the matter, he asks the spectator to shift the cups some more, moving them two at a time—*but he now must tell the magician which two he is changing.* For instance, if the spectator switches the "ace" cup and the "two" cup, he says to the magician,

FIND THE BALL
(STARTING POSITION)

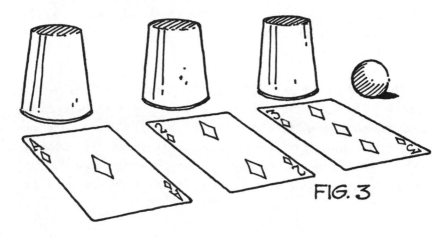

FIG. 3

"I'm switching one and two." This switching continues as long as the spectator wishes, but the spectator tells the magician what he is doing each time. The magician then turns around and quickly lifts the cup that was placed over the ball.

How It Works: Two keys are used: one of the cups, whose position is noted at the outset; and the beginning position itself. The combination of the two graphically tells the conjurer where the ball must be.

What You Need: Three playing cards. A small ball. (A coin will also do.) Three cups (these should be in different colors or patterns for ease of working).

Preparation: Set the tableau of objects as described.

How to Do It: The subject must follow the magician's instructions explicitly, so it is wise to "talk him through the trick." It is important to decide on one of the cups as your key. It doesn't matter which one or where it is at the beginning of the trick, provided that you remember which cup was chosen and which card it is over. For example, let's imagine that the three cups being used are red, green, and yellow. (I use three metal ones. Their outlines are shown in Fig. 3.)

Suppose the magician has picked the red cup as his key, and he notes that it is above the three spot before he begins. He now turns his back and asks the spectator to put the ball under one of the three cups, then switch the position of the other two without revealing any of his moves. When the magician is told the instructions have been carried out, he invites the spectator to switch the cups two at a time as much as he likes, provided that he calls out which two positions are being switched each time. While this is being done, the magician carefully listens for the number to be named where his key cup first stood. When he hears the number named, he immediately substitutes the new one in that position for the original.

Let's say the magician knows the red cup started over the three spot, so he waits to hear the spectator say he is switching number three. First he hears, "I am switching the cups at positions one and two." Neither of these is the red cup, his key, so the magician does nothing. Next he hears the spectator say, "I am switching the cups at positions two and three." The magician now *forgets* about position three and remembers *position two*, because that's where his key has moved. If the spectator switches the cups some more and the magician hears him say, "Switching one and two," the conjurer immediately forgets position two and adopts position one as his key. Thus he proceeds, ignoring the switch if it does not include whatever key number he is thinking of, or changing key numbers if the one he had in mind is called.

Once the spectator says he's finished, the magician turns around and looks at the layout. *If his key cup is above his latest key number, then the ball is under it.* Thus, if the last number he switched to is the one and he turns to find the red cup over the ace, he will find the ball beneath the red cup.

The only other possibility is that the key cup will not be above the last number he is remembering. If this happens, the ball will not be under the key cup *or* the cup that's over the latest key number. It will be under the third cup. For example, if the magician has the number three in mind and he turns to find the green cup over the three spot, then the ball is not under it. It is not under the key cup—the red one—either. It is under the yellow cup.

Tips for Presentation: 1. Give this trick only two or three showings, then challenge the spectator to spend an evening solving it. Some performers have used Find the Ball as a mental effect, but this seems silly since calling out all the moves certainly makes any kind of telepathy suspect. If you *could* read minds, why would you have to resort to such convoluted foolery? Better to treat it as a superpuzzle; it will still prove quite entertaining.

2. Remembering the shifting key numbers can be difficult if the performer is the least bit tense. An easy way to keep track of the shifts is to hold the key number of fingers on one hand inside the clasp of the other hand, and add or subtract fingers as necessary. For example, if you start with the red cup at three stick your index, middle, and ring fingers of one hand into the clutch of your other hand. If the spectator says, "Switching two and three," fold one of the fingers back, making your new key two. And so on.

3. Once you have become adept at this system, it is possible to further mystify the viewer by using cups *all of one color.* All you have to do is be sure that one of the three can be recognized—perhaps by a chip or crack.

4. An even odder way of performing the trick is to put three coins of the same denomination down uncovered, all heads up. You tell the spectator to mentally choose one, then turn it tails up, switch the other two, and proceed as usual. When he has finished switching coins, tell him to turn the chosen coin heads up again. Still you are able to tell which one was picked. In this case, it is only necessary to be sure one coin is either more or less shiny than the other two. Or perhaps you can simply get two with the same date and use the coin with the odd date as the key.

Some tricks are called "flash" effects because of their sudden, dramatic conclusions, sometimes taking place "visibly"—that is, without a cover. The Penetrating Cup had a "flash" conclusion, even though the napkin shell prevented the spectator's eyes from seeing the penetration.

The next effect is a pretty piece of "flash" magic.

THE COLOR-CHANGING PENCIL

Basic Illusion: A bright-colored wooden pencil changes color in a split second.

How It Looks: The magician takes a colored handkerchief from his breast pocket and wipes the pencil with it lightly, as if stroking it. On the third stroke, the pencil takes the color of the handkerchief—as if the cloth painted its hue on the wood.

How It Works: The pencil is disguised with a paper shell.

What You Need: A large pencil the same color as a pocket handkerchief. A sheet of construction paper the same color as another pencil.

Preparation: Cut a tube of construction paper to fit smoothly and snugly around the pencil from the eraser to the point. Place hanky in pocket.

How to Do It: Take the pencil out of a pocket or off a table. Remove the hanky from its pocket and wipe the pencil casually a few times, making sure the cloth covers the palm of the hand and that the palm covers the pencil. This way it is simple to wipe the tube right off the pencil point into the clutched hand. The hand then crumples the cloth and the construction-paper tube and sticks them back into the pocket.

Tips for Presentation: 1. It is not essential to show the pencil beforehand, but the magician could pass out a pencil of the same color as the construction paper, then switch it for the gimmicked pencil. To make the switch smoothly, have a cup of pencils on the table; put the demonstration pencil back in while you get out your hanky, then take out the disguised pencil.

2. This trick should not be performed with any buildup, but casually, offhandedly. One might begin wiping the pencil and ask the audience what color the pencil is. Just as the color is being called, wipe off the tube.

3. As soon as the tube is wiped off, toss the pencil onto the table. The movement and sound will attract the spectator's attention, and most likely he will pick up the pencil to examine it. This provides ample time to dispose of the cloth and tube.

In order to see magic through the audience's eyes, the magician must reexamine the objects he employs. We have used cups several times because of their basic properties: they are solid, so we make them penetrate other objects; they are opaque, so we look through them. Examining pencils, we find they have hue, so we change it. In the following trick we contradict a pencil's susceptibility to gravity; further on, we will take advantage of the pencil's prime function, writing.

This classification of props by function is useful in thinking up new magic routines or in finding a theme of presenting a trick—as in the Floating Pencil.

THE FLOATING PENCIL

Basic Illusion: A pencil, apparently endowed with a life of its own, defies gravity.

How It Looks: The magician shows a pencil to his spectators and allows them to examine it. He then drops the pencil into a Coca-Cola or wine bottle and makes a few cabalistic passes over it. On command, the pencil begins to rise slowly in the bottle. It descends and rises, at last floats almost to the top—and then falls back inside. The magician shows it to the audience again. It is just an ordinary pencil.

How It Works: A thread is temporarily attached to the pencil.

What You Need: A dark suit. Some strong dark thread. Some wax (Magician's Wax, the preparation sold by dealers, is particularly fine). A bottle.

Preparation: Pin the thread inside your jacket near an inner pocket, or on your pants just below the belt, whichever is better for your height and figure. Dab a small bit of wax at the end of the thread and be sure that when the thread hangs down you can easily procure the wax with your fingers.

How to Do It: While the audience examines the pencil, get the waxy end of the thread in one hand. Take the pencil back with this hand, and at the same time pass around the bottle for inspection.

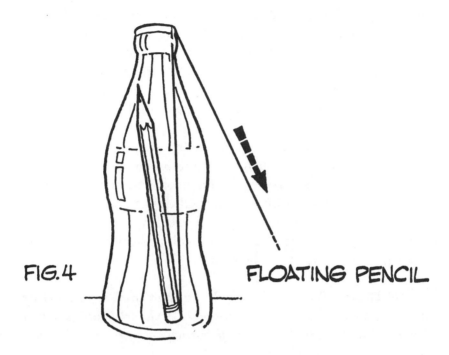

FIG. 4   FLOATING PENCIL

While the audience's attention is thus diverted, firmly press the wax to the eraser end of the pencil so that it sticks the thread to the pencil. Get the bottle back and drop the pencil, *eraser down,* in the bottle so the thread travels up the pencil's side. *(Fig. 4)* It will now be an easy matter to make the pencil perform by moving the thread in the crotch of index finger and thumb, or simply by moving the bottle away from the body. Practice in front of a mirror until the moves look smooth. At the end of the routine, drop the pencil back in the bottle and pour it into the hand, breaking the thread and wax off with the fingers. Pass the bottle out right away for inspection and follow with the pencil, when ready.

Tips for Presentation: 1. Other objects can be substituted for a pencil to good effect. In one of his books, Tony Shiels suggests an eerie routine using a pared root. Others have employed a penny and, instead of a bottle, a wide-mouthed jar.

2. If you are at all handy, find a cork the size of the bottle you intend to use. Cut a notch along the length of the cork, and test to make sure the string will run smoothly through the notch. Now you can make the trick even more startling by apparently stoppering the bottle with the pencil inside. With a little practice, you can separate thread and pencil by tugging the pencil up to the cork. Using this method, of course, the magician must himself unstopper the bottle and pocket the cork.

3. The pencil can answer questions by rising once for no, twice for yes. It can also, in this manner, count to a number named.

4. The effect may be passed off as a proof of mediumship, as long as it is done in a light fashion. Music will aid the illusion.

5. A theme that recognizes the basic physical nature of the pencil might be to suggest that trees seek sunlight; pencils, being made from living wood, do the same.

The Floating Pencil could be called a "plot" trick, in as much as a story can easily be concocted around it. A plot trick differs from a "process" trick, in which the very business of executing the trick must take priority in presentation.

Here is a pair of process tricks.

A RELIABLE PREDICTION

Basic Illusion: The magician predicts the answer to what seems to be a random arithmetic problem.

How It Looks: The magician asks the audience to call out any three digits, from zero up to nine. A spectator writes them down, then reverses them and subtracts the smaller amount from the larger. He reverses the answer he gets and adds the last two figures together. The magician then reveals the final answer before the spectator tells what it is.

How It Works: This is an automatic trick that always comes to the same total as long as the magician's instructions are properly followed.

What You Need: A pencil and paper. Or, in larger rooms, chalk and slates.

How to Do It: The magician claims that he can predict the result of a complex arithmetical process. He writes down the number 1089 on a piece of paper or slate and sets it aside without showing it. He then asks a spectator to write down any three numbers called out. Suppose 457 is selected. The spectator writes it down on a piece of paper, then, reversing it, writes 754 above. He subtracts the smaller number from the larger:

$$\begin{array}{r} 754 \\ -457 \\ \hline 297 \end{array}$$

He now reverses the answer, 297, and gets 792. He adds these two figures together.

$$\begin{array}{r} 297 \\ +792 \\ \hline 1089 \end{array}$$

The answer will always be the same: 1089.

Tips for Presentation: 1. Naturally, this trick is *not* a repeater. It should be done once only and with considerable buildup. Point out the random selection of numbers, and present the arithmetical work as means to further involve pure chance. Before revealing the "prediction," remind the audience that the final sum has been yielded by a difficult process.

2. This trick can also be used as a mind-reading test. The magician leaves the room, and the assistant sets up several problems for the performer to overcome. (Hidden Treasure, as was noted, may be similarly used.)

A CHRONOLOGICAL PREDICTION

Basic Illusion: The magician seems to know in advance the answer to a random addition problem.

How It Looks: The magician asks someone to assist by writing down any number that the audience calls out. (For ease of execution, it had better be restricted to two digits.) The spectator is now told to write the year of his birth beneath it. He is then instructed to write down the year of some important public event. Next he puts down his present age. Finally he adds the number of years that have elapsed since the important happening took place. He then adds them all together and finds that the magician has already written down the answer.

How It Works: This really audacious trick is an old one, and is founded on the simple fact that the addition of one's birth date and age equals the present year—as does the addition of the year of an event and the number of years ago it took place. The only variable is the number called out by the audience, and the magician knows what that is.

What You Need: Pencil and paper, or chalk and slates.

How to Do It: The magician multiplies the current year by two and secretly writes the answer on the piece of paper or slate. He then asks a spectator to add the various numbers. While he does, the magician adds the called number to the figure on his slate, crosses out or erases his figuring and shows the result at the proper time. Here is a detailed example:

The year is 1973, the magician writes down 1973 × 2, or 3946. The audience calls out the number 37. The magician adds this to 3946 and gets 3983. Meanwhile, here is the spectator's addition problem:

Number called	37
His birth year	1941
Year of Orson Welles' *Invasion from Mars*	1938
His age	32
Years ago Welles did show	+35
Total	3983

Important: When the spectator adds his age, he must figure it as of the current year. If his birthday is July 4 and you are doing the show in February, tell him to count his age as of December 31 of the current year. If, on the other hand, you know what his birthday is, then tell him to add his age as of the moment, then, if necessary, subtract 1 from your result.

Tips for Presentation: As in the previous effect, be careful to present the various numbers added together as the result of random choice. When telling the spectator to add the various years and ages together, do it in an offhand fashion as if the particular notion just crossed your mind.

Fail-safe magic is as much at home on stage as in the living room. In fact, many professional magicians welcome easy-to-do effects in their acts because these tricks frequently lend themselves to highly individual interpretation. The following two belong in a platform or stage show rather than at an informal gathering, yet they are simple to work.

INVISIBLE FLIGHT

Basic Illusion: Two handkerchiefs change places invisibly.

How It Looks: The magician displays two silk handkerchiefs of contrasting colors. He wraps each in a square of newspaper and places them far apart. After some magic words or gestures, he tears the papers open to show that the handkerchiefs have changed places.

How It Works: Duplicate handkerchiefs and newspaper squares with secret pockets.

What You Need: Some newspaper. Glue or paste. Scissors. Tape. Four silks (this is the technical name for the extremely sheer handkerchiefs used by magicians; they are available in various sizes and colors from most magic dealers). The silks for this trick are two-color sets. For instance, let us assume we are working with two green and two red ones. All, of course, are the same size.

Preparation: Cut a corner of newspaper as big as one quarter of the total sheet. Paste it in the center of a second full sheet of newspaper, and open at the top, so a pocket is formed. Place one green silk within it and seal up the top of the pocket. You now have a sheet of newspaper with a large blister of paper in the middle scaled on all its sides, with a green silk within. Repeat the procedure with a second sheet of newspaper and put a red silk in the pocket formed. Lay the two "silk sandwiches" on opposite ends of the table, or on two separate tables. Be sure each pocket is underneath, resting on the table surface.

How to Do It: Show the two silks and call attention to their colors. Put one down and walk with the other to one of the pieces of newspaper. Put the displayed silk in the center and fold the paper around it. Tape the packet together and, in the process, turn it over. Do the same with the second display silk and the other newspaper. It is now a simple matter to tear into each pocket formed by the squares of paper and reveal the duplicate silks.

Tips for Presentation: 1. Handle the silks gracefully, making sure their colors can be seen. Take the silk by one corner, pull the other corner out so the silk is viewed flat, and then hold it by one corner again. When folding the newspaper, work deliberately and slowly so the audience can see the silk still inside the paper when the fold is made.

2. There is a "dead spot" in this trick after the silks are wrapped and before they are revealed. The magician should not simply tear the papers open immediately. Allow the audience to believe the transposition has not yet taken place. Gestures with a magic wand, an incantation, or dramatically counting to three might fill the time. Personally, I would have a volunteer come onstage at this point and give him a Breakaway Fan. This well-known comedy device—obtainable from most magic dealers—opens into a fan for the magician but becomes separate pieces of cloth and wood when the spectator handles it. One might show the volunteer what to do and ask him to pronounce some difficult word such as "aldiboron-tiphosky." Not only does he get the word wrong, but the fan breaks on him. This can be repeated once or twice, after which you open the packets and reveal that the magic worked anyway. Send the volunteer back to his seat while asking the group to give him a hand for his help. The applause helps fill the time till he sits and you are ready for the next effect.

A RING ON A ROPE

Basic Illusion: A bracelet seems to penetrate a rope tied around the magician's hands.

How It Looks: The magician has a piece of soft cotton rope tied to one wrist by a spectator. A length of it is stretched between his hands, and the other end is tied to his other wrist. He then displays a ring about the size of a large bracelet; the audience may verify that it is solid. Holding it in both hands, the magician swings his arms to one side and back again. He shows his hands: the ring is now threaded on the rope.

How It Works: A duplicate ring is up the magician's sleeve.

What You Need: Two identical rings. Some rope.

Preparation: Put one ring on the arm and let it drop back to the elbow. Be sure it is covered with the sleeve of the jacket.

How to Do It: With elbow bent, the magician enters, rope in hand. He has the arm with the ring on it tied up first. When both wrists are secured, he shows the free ring and, holding it with both hands, swings aside. When his body is interposed between the audience and his arms, he quickly sticks the free ring in a convenient pocket, then swings back with a very broad gesture, throwing both arms out straight. The force of the movement will toss the ring onto the middle of the rope. With rope stretched taut, the magician shows the ring suspended in the middle. Practice the swings so the ring exchange happens smoothly with no time lost in changing directions. It is not hard, and can be done slowly, as long as the gesture is a *big* one.

Tips for Presentation: 1. It will be impossible to do any tricks before this one, because the ring up the sleeve will hamper movement. Therefore, this is an opening trick. Enter with the free ring in one hand and the rope in the other. This provides an excuse to naturally bend the elbow, as if gracefully trying to show the props. Immediately ask a spectator to tie the rope around the wrist of the arm with the ring on it. Stretch that arm forward. Do not bring the volunteer onstage if it can be avoided, but have him stand and reach up at the edge of the stage. Bend down slightly to help him if necessary, but don't let the hidden ring drop.

2. The magician might enter with the rope already tied around the wrists and merely ask a spectator to pull lightly on the center of the rope to see that it is solidly tied. This way, the magician can do the ring exchange very soon after his entrance, which gets the act off to a fast magical start.

The rest of the tricks in this chapter involve a deck of cards, one of the most common pieces of equipment a magician can use. The basic nature of cards is rarely considered. For instance, a card manipulator who likes to make many cards appear magically might remark that a deck consists of fifty-two cards, but he can make it yield an unlimited number. Though most card tricks are identity-revelation effects, our next trick depends on another characteristic of the cards: color. It is a repeater that may be performed several times with different results.

TWO-TONE PREDICTION

Basic Illusion: The cards are dealt in piles according to color and the magician predicts the ratio of red and black in two of the piles.

How It Looks: Seated at a table, the magician takes out a deck of cards and has it thoroughly shuffled and cut by a volunteer. Then he asks the volunteer to deal two cards at a time face up onto the table, running through the entire deck. If the volunteer turns up two black cards, he puts them in one pile; if he turns up two red cards, he puts them in a separate pile. If he turns up a red and a black together, he drops them in a heap between the red and black piles. When the pack is exhausted, the magician scoops up the middle pile of red and black cards, riffles it, and predicts that there will be, for example, "two more cards in the black pile than there are in the red pile." Or he may predict "four more red cards than there are black," or "an equal number of red and black cards in the two piles." The volunteer counts up each pile and finds the magician is right.

How It Works: No matter how many red and black cards one sets aside, there will always be an equal number of each color left. So to change the number in the predictions, the magician secretly steals a certain number of cards from the pack, before the trick begins.

What You Need: A deck of cards.* A table.

Preparation: Sit at the table and, while shuffling, remove two cards of one color and hold them on your lap under the table, while handing the deck to the volunteer.

How to Do It: Tell the volunteer to shuffle the cards, then deal them out as described. When this is done, gather up the mixed heap and riffle them, pretending to divine the answer. Actually, there will simply be two fewer cards of the color that was stolen. Thus, if you took away two black cards, there will automatically be two more cards in the all-red pile than there are in the all-black pile. While the volunteer is counting up the heaps, there will be plenty of time to lower the mixed heap below the table edge and put back the stolen cards. Then steal instead four red cards. This will cause four more blacks than reds to show up on the next deal. Finally, add the reds, give the whole deck to the volunteer, and predict that on the third deal the colors will come out evenly.

Tips for Presentation: Though this trick can be repeated many times, three deals as explained above are quite enough at one sitting. The alternate results build the mystery to the climax when the colors come out equal. This also leaves the whole deck in the magician's hands for the next trick.

Most tricks have at least one weak spot where the handling must be unnatural or the method might show. In the previous trick, this spot is the stealing of cards below the table, but the spectator's counting of the heaps covers this action nicely. In the next effect, the identity of the card could be ascertained by a more elaborate control or by forcing a card (techniques covered in a later chapter). But since we are dealing with fail-safe magic, we employ the "one-way back" principle. This method has one weak spot, but it is naturally covered with the fanning move described.

---

* In all tricks in this book, it is assumed that the jokers have been removed. If they are needed, they will be called for specifically.

THE WISE-GUY TURNOVER

Basic Illusion: The spectator picks a card and the magician reveals its identity.

How It Looks: The volunteer selects a card and returns it to the deck, which is then shuffled. The magician turns over one card at a time, eventually passing the chosen one without showing any recognition. Several cards later, the magician holds up a card face down and triumphantly says that the next card he turns over will be the chosen card. The spectator shows some skepticism—even sarcasm. The magician challenges him, perhaps even wagering a nickel (or a kick) that he will fulfill his promise. The magician gestures with the concealed card, evidently ready to slap it down face up. But when the spectator finally dares him, the magician drops it face down, reaches into the heap on the table, finds the card that was actually picked, *and turns it face down*—thus fulfilling his promise to "turn over" the right card.

How It Works: The magician uses a deck with a one-way pattern (one whose design has an "upside down" and a "right side up," as opposed to decks with symmetrical designs that look the same either way).

Preparation: Turn all cards so the pattern is in the same direction. Fan the cards and have the spectator pick one. Turning the deck the other way, have him replace the card. Now, as long as the cards are not riffle-shuffled, the chosen card will have its back facing the other way from the rest of the deck. When turning cards face up, it will be simple to spot the proper card.

Tips for Presentation: 1. Each person will react to the bluff differently. There will be wiseacres, of course, who can be strung along for great humorous effect. Then—though this trick is technically called a "sucker effect"—there will be people who will be very polite about the mistake they think you're about to make. These people must be drawn out as much as possible; try to get them to express doubt that you will succeed. In either case, do not really try to embarrass the volunteer. Play things for fun, and when the assistant gets stung, laugh with him and not at him.

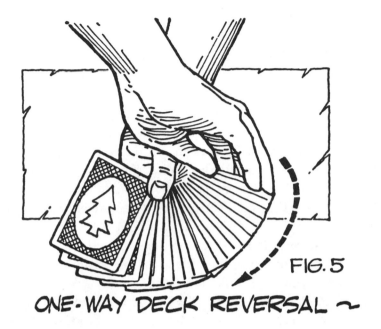

FIG. 5

ONE-WAY DECK REVERSAL ~

2. There is an easy, smooth way to turn the deck around without the volunteer noticing. Fan the cards out in one hand, have the card selected, and reach the other hand to the far side of the spread deck. Push the cards closed and in the process, rotate them in the direction of the heel of the hand that holds them. *(Fig. 5)* This pushes them into the hand in the proper direction and turns them end for end.

3. Once in ten thousand times, a volunteer may reverse *his* card. I have never seen it happen, but if it did, I would simply have him replace the card on top of the deck, riffle the deck upward as if out of habit—but in the process, bend the corner of his card back against itself, then downward. Cut the cards, and have him cut them again. The card would then be identifiable because of the slightly bent corner.

TELEPATHIC TONE

Basic Illusion: By listening to the spectator call out the names of cards, the magician is able to tell the identity of a noted card.

How It Looks: A deck of cards is shuffled by a spectator, and the magician turns away for the duration of the trick. He tells the volunteer to put the pack on the table and take away about half—"just so you have at least twenty and fewer than thirty cards in your hand, it doesn't have to be exact." Next the volunteer is told to count the number of cards he holds, then add together the two digits. (Example: the volunteer cuts off twenty-eight cards, so he adds together two and eight and gets ten.) Now the volunteer squares up the cards in his hand, the faces toward him. He counts down the same number as he added. (In our example, he would count down ten cards.) He remembers the tenth card. Now he puts the deck back together, placing the half that includes his card on top. One at a time, he turns the cards over and names them, starting at the top of the pack. When the magician hears the chosen card, he declares it.

How It Works: This is an application of Alwyn Stevenson's No-name Card Trick. It is an automatic way of finding out the name of the nineteenth card from the top of the deck.

What You Need: A deck of cards.

How to Do It: Follow the working described above. When the volunteer calls the cards, mentally count them. The nineteenth one named will be the chosen one.

Tips for Presentation: There must always be between twenty and twenty-nine cards in the pack the volunteer holds. Do not copy the wording suggested above, but find an apparently offhand way to get the deck cut between these critical numbers.

2. The trick can be performed over the telephone with great effect.

The following process trick, though amazing, is totally automatic. It is based on an old effect by John P. Hamilton, Eyes of the Gods. I have a prejudice against tricks that require counting cards into heaps; the process is time-consuming and not interesting to watch. In this effect, however, the climax is so impressive that it is worth tolerating the potentially dead space while the cards are counted. Hamilton's original effect had a "spelling" climax, one in which the spectator or magician turns over one card at a time in cadence to the spelling of some word or words (often the name of the chosen card); as the word is completed, the last card turned over is the selected one. I have always considered spelling dull to watch, so I have altered the ending of this effect accordingly.

OLYMPIAN VISION

Basic Illusion: Two spectators each select cards. The magician reveals their identities.

How It Looks: The magician calls two volunteers to assist and has them stand side by side at a table, or possibly at separate tables. (For the sake of clarity, let's assume we're using separate tables, and that the person standing to the magician's left is named Laura; the one on his right, Bob.) The magician hands the volunteers a deck of cards, and tells them to shuffle it, then divide it up equally. (Laura and Bob each now have a packet of twenty-six cards.) They shuffle these, while the magician dons a blindfold. He asks them both to look at the bottom card of their packets, but to disregard the suit. "I only want you to note the *number* of the card. Ace equals one, jack is eleven, queen is twelve, king is thirteen. Got that? Now turn the deck over again so it is face down and deal the same number of cards from the top of the deck face down onto the table." (Example: Laura turns over her twenty-six-card packet and sees a seven of hearts. She ignores the suit, remembers "seven," and turns the cards back down in her hand. She deals seven cards from the top of her packet onto the table. Bob proceeds similarly.)

"Now," says the magician, "I want you to look at and remember the last card you dealt onto the table. Don't get it confused with the first one you saw. Look at it long and hard and fix it firmly in your memory." (Laura picks up the top card of the heap of seven she has dealt and remembers it. If there is an audience, she may even hold it up for all to see. Bob proceeds similarly.)

"Have you remembered the card?" the magician asks. "You have? Then put it back on top of the heap you dealt on your table. Now I'm sure you'll agree I have no way of knowing how many cards either of you dealt onto your tables. The only thing I know is that Laura is holding one group of cards in her hand and has another group of cards in front of her on her table. The same goes for Bob. Now, to mix me up completely, I'm going to ask Bob to walk over to Laura's table with the cards he has in his hand and drop them on top of the cards Laura dealt on the table. At the same time, I want Laura to walk over to Bob's table and do the same thing." When they are done, the magician removes the blindfold and turns around. He reminds the volunteers of the fairy way in which both of their cards have been buried in the deck. Now he asks Bob to pick up the heap of cards on the left-hand table, take it back to his original table, and drop it on the heap sitting there. The magician now picks up the deck and deals out cards one at a time from the top. He has a little trouble finding one of the cards, although he finally succeeds. But then, spreading the rest of the deck on the table *face down,* he immediately pushes the second card out with the first!

How It Works: This trick actually works itself, because of the way the heaps are combined. One of the original *number* cards winds up in a key position that reveals where both selected cards are.

What You Need: A deck of cards. Volunteers. A blindfold (optional—it's only for effect).

How to Do It: The main thing the magician must do is locate the key card. When he gets the reassembled cards in his hands, he begins to deal them face up onto the table. As he does, he counts to himself the number he deals. Once he has twelve cards on the table, he is ready to find the key card. *The key card will show up somewhere in the next thirteen cards—and one of the selected cards will be right beneath it.* When the magician lays down the thirteenth card, he thinks "King." If he turns over a king, it *may* be the key card. If he does *not* turn over a king, he lays down another card and thinks "Queen." If he gets a queen, *that* may be the key card. *The key card will correspond to the denomination the magician thinks as he mentally proceeds from "King" down to "Ace."* The only problem is that a stray card or two might accidentally appear in the position the magician is thinking of. To safeguard against this, when the magician gets a "hit" (the card corresponding with the position) he does not stop but keeps dealing cards until he either gets a second hit or makes it safely all the way down to mental "Ace." If he does get all the way, he knows the key card is the sole hit he got. However, if he *should* get a second hit, he stops and asks Laura and Bob whether either of their cards has turned up yet. If one of them says "Yes," then it is the card that was dealt right *after* the first hit. If they both say no, then it is probably going to be the very next one to be dealt. But to be entirely safe, deal that card anyway, and keep going till you either get another hit or until you have safely reached mental "Ace." If you do get a third hit, ask them once more if either card has turned up and proceed as above according to their answers. (Example: The thirteenth card you turn over is the king of clubs. This could be the key card. But you turn over the next card and think "Queen" and it turns out to be a four of hearts. You think "Jack" and get the jack of spades. This could also be the key card, so you ask if Bob or Laura's card has turned up yet. They say no. You then keep turning over cards till you get to mental "Ace" and have no more "hits." You therefore know the first selected card is the one you dealt just *after* the jack of spades. You pull it out of the pack. You have now located the first card!) The second card is much easier. Take another look at the key card (in our example, the jack of spades). *The second card will be the same number up from the bottom of the deck as the number of the key card.* (The jack of spades is equal to the number eleven, so the second selected card will be the eleventh from the bottom.) Spread the deck out face down and count over the proper number of cards from the bottom. Push this card out with the first one you found. Finding it without even seeing its face will seem a real miracle.

Tips for Presentation: 1. Do not disregard this trick because the instructions are long. It plays *much faster* than it reads. Follow the moves exactly and there will be no difficulty in finding both cards.

However, do *not* copy the dialogue given the magician in the above description. It was only used to make the process clear to the reader. Find your own way to play the trick.

2. The identity of each card can be revealed in a variety of manners. Some of the sleights described in a later chapter will prove helpful. For instance, by using the "glide" the way it is used in an upcoming trick called Eliminating Cards, the revelation of the second card in *this* trick can appear even more uncanny.

Now that we have looked at some samples of magic tricks, it should be apparent that there are really a limited number of effects that one can do. Dariel Fitzkee once broke down all magic into about nineteen varieties of climax: appearances, disappearances, transpositions, revelation of identity, mind reading, prediction, levitation, suspension, etc.

Though the basic types of trickery are few, there are no limits to the style of performance in which an illusion can be set. The magician who rehearses sufficiently, avoids "canned" presentations—including those in this book—and concentrates on finding his own style will succeed as an entertainer.

Rehearsal is a vital part of performing magic of every kind. No matter how simple a secret seems, it may fall flat unless the performer repeats it privately to the point of total facility (and, if necessary, boredom).

Rehearse for weeks if necessary and watch all moves in front of a mirror—*at first*. But get away from the glass once the moves are down pat, and start playing the trick to furniture or whatever invisible spectators you can address. When you make mistakes, correct them right away. Be ruthless in appraising yourself. When the routine starts to become second nature, you are probably ready to show it for the first time.

It should be noted that in the preceding tricks no clear line was drawn between stage, or platform, tricks and close-up, or parlor, tricks. Some fail-safe magic works in either or both kinds of show situation, though the magician must learn to tone down his delivery and movements in the case of the small-room show.

This book does not delineate the two kinds of show, parlor and platform, because there is *no essential difference.* The same principles of showmanshrp apply in each case, except that they must be modified for the smaller room. In a theater, one might rely on a master of ceremonies to polarize the audience for your act. But even in a living room, it will be necessary to turn the talk to magic or at least find out whether the people assembled want to see a few tricks before one can proceed. This is still a version of the polarization process.

It is also important to construct a *routine* of tricks for both sizes of rooms. At a formal show, it is expected that the entertainer will have a carefully chosen act. The same should be true of the parlor. Even when called upon for an "impromptu" and the only available equipment is a deck of cards, the conjurer should have a short series of tricks at his fingertips so he can give a unified, *brief* show.

Living-room shows generally should be brief. Chances are the people assembled there want to talk more than they want to watch magic. Even when the audience is eager, leave them wanting more. It is good showmanship not to wear out one's welcome.

There is one essential difference between the parlor and platform show. Parlor audiences tend to be composed of friends and relatives, most of whom are not easily convinced of a magician's prowess. The trouble is that they know the performer too well, and have seen him being less than omniscient. This fact makes it doubly advisable to be well prepared. And since parlor audiences tend to be right on top of the magician—and often demand to examine the props—it is triply advisable to restrict such shows to fail-safe magic.

MORE TRICKS

Here is a short list of additional fail-safe magic tricks recommended for the beginner. Prices and availability vary greatly, but information on most of them can be obtained from any major dealer (see appendix).

Acrobatic Silks: Three silks are threaded through a wooden post and twisted so it seems as if two yellow ones are in the middle and end holes, with a blue silk in the other end hole. After some by-play, the silks are yanked and the blue one seems to jump into the middle while a yellow one leaps to the end hole. This is a pretty flash effect, suitable for small or large rooms; especially good for children.

Blasted Jr.: The smaller and better of two tricks with a similar name. A metal tray is covered with a plastic Petri dish, and a coin is put beneath the cover. A second coin is tapped on the cover, and it suddenly seems to penetrate inside—for it is seen resting next to the other coin. An ingenious hollow coin covers a duplicate of the second. The tray itself helps propel the duplicate into place.

Color Vision Box: This award-winning "pocket" trick involves a block with several color faces. When it is enclosed in an opaque box, the color of the top face of the box can still be divined. The very shape of the block makes it possible for the performer to get a peek.

Deceptive Transparent Change Bag: There is no sneakier way to force a card and other objects than this clear-plastic bag into which everyone sees.

The Haunted House: By using double-sided cards and then switching them for a set of blank cards, the magician changes the word "house" on the face of the cards for "ghost." Finally, the ghost "vanishes," leaving the card faces white as a sheet.

Invisible Bovine: This comedy equipment can be used as the basis of an extended humorous routine. It consists chiefly of a "foo can," a can that has a partition running down it. When tipped one way, it looks as if the can were empty, because the partition holds the liquid. Tipped the other way, it allows the contents to run out. The can is made to look like a can of condensed milk. After showing it empty, the magician "milks" a rubber glove into it, and the can becomes "full of milk."

Key-R-Rect: This is one of the finest sets of mental equipment available. It sells for at least ten dollars, if not more, but is well worth the cost. It is a completely mechanical version of an old trick called Seven Keys to Baldpate, in which the magician finds the key to open a padlock from a group of keys mixed together in a container. Key-R-Rect has a lock so ingeniously rigged that only one key will open it *at first.* But once it has been sprung, it will respond to any key picked. *A must.*

Mirror Glass: This is a basic utility device for platform and stage work. It is excellent for vanishing and producing silks with little effort or skill.

Phantom Pencil: A small but clever way of making a pencil vanish. After examining a solid pencil, the spectator returns it to the performer who substitutes an identical-looking implement made chiefly of a collapsible material. When wrapped in newspaper, it can be crumpled along with the paper and "thrown away."

Squircle: A diverting opening trick involving a square of newspaper—really a doctored double square. A circle is apparently cut in the paper, but when it is opened, the hole seems to have become a square.

Supersonic Card Prediction: Originated by Dr. Jaks, this great mental trick involves the apparently free selection of a card by a spectator. The card is placed in a frame with nine other cards; the chosen card is reversed and the others are turned around to show they are all the same. The conjurer's prediction is read, and when the cards are swung around again, the face of the chosen card corresponds to the prediction. Essentially a "force" (see glossary) of any kind of several dual-printed cards, the effect is memorable because of the swinging stand which allows all of the cards to be dramatically pivoted at the climax. A newer version using only five cards has been marketed, but is less dramatic.

Tel-A-Color: In this pseudo-telepathic trick the spectator deals out several pieces of posterboard of different colors, one of which he turns over. He then mixes them and hands them over to the magician, who redeals the cards and turns the chosen color back over. The principle is clever, hinging on alternate corner textures on the two different sides of each card; the turnover makes that card feel different from the other.

Wizard Deck: This is the trade name for the stripper deck, a standard set of magic cards that can be used in both simple and complicated tricks. The edges of the deck are tapered, making it easy to find reversed cards by feel. (Uses the one-way card-reversal technique described in this chapter.) An essential piece of equipment.

REFERENCES

Al Stevenson's *75 Tricks with a Stripper Deck* has many effortless bits of magic in it.

Scarne on Card Tricks is chock full of fail-safe magic, as is his companion volume on magic tricks.

Practical Magic by David Robbins and *131 Magic Tricks for Amateurs* by Will Dexter both have plenty of easy tricks in them.

Math and Magic by Royal Vale Heath and *Mathematics Magic and Mystery* by Martin Gardner are both treasuries of fascinating mathematical principles and automatic "number" tricks.

4

What Do You Say and How Do You Say It?

The answer is to use outlined patter . . .

Ken and Roberta Griffin, in
Illusion Show Know-how

In the course of performing tricks, most magicians talk to the audience. But instead of calling this process "speaking," conjurers have labeled it with the peculiar term "patter."

According to the Funk & Wagnalls dictionary, patter is "glib and rapid talk; idle chatter or gossip." This is an unfortunate connotation, but usage has fixed the word permanently in the magician's vocabulary. Despite this, experienced performers try to avoid the steady stream of verbalization that some amateurs think is necessary in a magic show.

There are many ways of speaking to the audience—humorous, serious, florid, casual—and each has its merits, provided the magician is at ease with that style. The trouble arises when a performer gets the notion that he must conform to some established type of patter.

One way of talking generally avoided today is the ultramysterious style, in which the magician acts as if he were a veritable Merlin. He speaks in tones and phrases meant to awe the spectator. I suppose a first-rate entertainer still could bring this off, but it looks pretty silly when the amateur tries it.

The patter style that is presently and painfully prevalent is the joking type. Puns and inane jests are larded on with a trowel. Most of them are the products of Robert Orben, who has written a number of joke books, one-liners, and canned routines for standard magic tricks. Every time I have heard a magician employ such material, it has fallen so flat that the thud resounds for blocks. I do not know whether a skillful performer would make these extraneous jokes and gags entertaining. I know I have always avoided them.

There is, of course, nothing wrong with humor in a magic performance, but it must be unforced and relevant. The key to achieving this seems to be to shape the dialogue of a magic act improvisationally.

But many magic texts advise that all patter be written beforehand and memorized by the performer like a part in a play.

This approach is disastrous to spontaneous delivery; it yields wooden results. Resorting to canned patter—that is, someone else's dialogue—seriously hinders the development of personal style. Likewise, writing out one's own patter beforehand and memorizing it turns the performer into an automaton. That method may provide a degree of confidence, but the benefit is more than offset by the loss of naturalness.

A good magic performance is like a jazz session: it should be fluid, free-form, adaptive to the exigencies of the moment. No show or audience is alike, and unexpected things will happen. The magician who performs by rote will not be able to adapt to the unexpected; he will either be thrown off the track entirely, or else will proceed as if nothing had happened. Say, for example, that an audience member complains that he cannot see the card that a volunteer holds up. The thing to do, obviously, is to ask the volunteer to hold the card up higher or even have him walk forward to a point where it can be seen. A "rote" performer might ignore the remark, as if he were playing in a soundless vacuum.

Henning Nelms makes a valid suggestion concerning patter; he urges magicians to use "subtext" just as a professional actor would. Subtext is the mental script which runs through the mind of a character between spoken lines. An actor playing Hamlet might think the following subtext:

> *(Should I kill myself?)*
> To be, or not to be—that is the question:
> *(Should I accept what fate allots)*

Whether 'tis nobler in the mind to suffer
The slings and arrows of outrageous fortune
(or should I take my life into my own hands?)
Or take arms against a sea of troubles . . .

By employing a subtext while performing magic, the magician will find his dialogue flowing smoothly from point to point. However, Nelms also suggests that the magician write out his subtext and memorize it the way an actor would. I cannot endorse this advice, either as a magician or as an actor. Subtext should be *discovered* during the course of rehearsals. Gradually, subtext *and* text will set themselves when they feel natural and have the proper flow and tempo.

Nelms suggests composing patter while in character—that is, while playing the part of a magician. Ken Griffin works improvisationally and picks out the important points when he discovers them in rehearsal. He uses these regularly in performance, and extemporizes in between.

The way to proceed, then, is to experiment with the theme of what you say. When a theme seems to fit your personal style, adopt it and rehearse the trick, speaking improvisationally. After several rehearsals, some sections of the trick will start to fall into place, and the uncertain spots will begin to disappear. Work for economy of expression and tighten up the tempo to the bare essentials. If there is a weak spot in the physical handling of the trick, see whether a humorous or dramatic remark will help cover it. When the spoken presentation begins to turn out pretty much the same each time, your patter is ready to use before an audience. However, be alert in performance to unexpected occurrences, and if an opportunity arises to crack a pertinent joke, or if the situation simply requires making a parenthetical remark, *do so*. The accomplished showman is the one who has his performance so much under control that he can adapt to the surprises of the occasion.

Let's examine a magic trick to see how this process might work. In the preceding chapter, the Color-changing Pencil provides a simple example. It is a trick that can be done with either process (you simply talk about what you're doing) or plot (you make up a little story) patter. Let's start with an example of process patter.

FIRST REHEARSAL

MOVES	PATTER
The magician picks up the pencil.	"Here is a pencil."
He raps it on the table.	"It is solid."
He points to it.	"It is colored orange."
Removes hanky from pocket.	"Here is my pocket handkerchief. It is blue."
Wipes the pencil.	"Now I wipe the pencil once . . ."
Repeats.	". . . twice . . ."
Repeats, peeling off paper shell.	". . . and a third time . . . and now the pair match."
Holds up pencil and puts hanky back in pocket.	"Thank you very much."

A quick analysis by memory (or tape recorder, if available) will show the performer that he has said several unnecessary things. "Here is a pencil" calls attention to an obvious fact. "It is solid" is unnecessary, for the tap on the table provides this information. "Thank you very much" is a cliché, overused at the end of tricks.

SECOND REHEARSAL

MOVES	PATTER
The magician picks up the pencil, shows it, and raps it on the table.	
He holds it up again.	"Here is an orange pencil."
Removes hanky from pocket.	". . . and my handkerchief is blue . . ."
Wipes the pencil.	"Now I wipe the pencil once . . ."

Repeats.	"... twice ..."
Repeats, peeling off paper shell.	"... and a third time ... and now the pair match."
Holds up pencil, puts hanky in pocket, and bows.	

Though this approach is better, naming the colors still insults the audience's eyesight. Perhaps it would be better to disguise the technique by checking to see whether the audience can see properly. Also, counting the three pencil wipes is self-evident. The words "once" and "twice" are useful in that they prepare the audience for the magic to come, since people are used to things happening in threes. But "the third time" is already after the fact and is unnecessary.

THIRD REHEARSAL

MOVES	PATTER
The magician picks up the pencil, shows it, and raps it on the table. He holds it up again.	*(To audience)* "What color is this pencil?"
Removes hanky.	"And my handkerchief?"
Wipes the pencil.	"Now I wipe the pencil once ..."
Repeats.	"... twice ..."
Repeats, peeling off shell.	"... and now the pair match."
Holds up pencil, puts away cloth, bows.	

By asking the audience a question, the magician involves it directly. This terse dialogue will carry the trick as a flash effect.

Suppose, however, that you were doing the trick in a living

room and someone wanted to examine the pencil. It might be necessary to instantly revise the routine to meet the situation:

UNCLE LOU: I want to see the pencil!

MAGICIAN *(holding it up):* Sure. What color is it?

UNCLE LOU: Orange. Let me—

MAGICIAN *(interrupting):* And what color is my handkerchief?

UNCLE LOU: Blue.

MAGICIAN *(immediately wiping the pencil):* Are you sure?

UNCLE LOU: Yeah.

MAGICIAN *(holding up pencil again):* You're wrong. They match.

The above routine employs "process patter," since it only serves to call attention to the props and the movements. If the effect were played as a plot trick, the routine might end up like this:

MOVES	PATTER
The magician picks up pencil shows it, and raps it on table. He holds it up again.	*(To audience)* "What color is this pencil?"
	AUDIENCE: "Orange."
Removes hanky.	"And what's this?"
	AUDIENCE: "Blue." "A blue handkerchief." Etc.
	"Did someone call it a blue handkerchief? . . . Well, it's actually a blue paint brush."
Wipes the pencil.	"You see, if I just give the pencil a base coat . . ."
Repeats.	". . . and a second one . . ."
Repeats, peeling away shell.	". . . the color comes off the cloth."
Looks at pencil.	"No wonder it's blue—it just got the brushoff."
Puts it down.	

The pun can be improved, but it does provide a cadence which clearly says, "The trick is done."

These examples are, of course, oversimplified, and I doubt that Uncle Lou would be quite so easy to mollify. But the sole purpose of the above is to demonstrate the script-forming process. The reader must not copy these routines, or any others in this book. He should instead tailor his patter to his own talents.

There are several classic do's and don'ts associated with patter. One of them is, "Never tell the audience beforehand what you are going to do." Generally, this is a good rule, because an audience that knows what to expect will be harder to distract at the time of the crucial secret move. Also, some of the surprise will be sacrificed if the climax is too clearly foreshadowed in the conjurer's patter.

On the other hand, there are occasions when it is virtually impossible to avoid letting people know what is coming. Mind-reading experiments generally set up the expected results at the outset of each trick. Even in the Color-changing Pencil, the necessary noting of color and the two anterior wiping motions lead the audience to expect some kind of transformation of hue, even though the expectation may not be completely spelled out. I would say that a magician may reasonably tell what is coming when 1) it is unavoidable, anyway, by the very nature of the trick; or 2) when the foreshadowing clearly adds some entertainment value to the presentation. What would a guillotine trick be unless the audience were told beforehand that the volunteer's hand was about to be chopped off? The fun is in the buildup.

Another patter don't suggests avoiding "thank you" at the end of tricks and "Ladies and Gentlemen" at the outset. This is a flexible rule. If it is natural and unobtrusive to employ either or both, do so—but not before and after *each* effect unless there is some real reason to do so. (Perhaps if you are playing the part of a sideshow magician these phrases would fit the style.)

If there is any word that I would agree should be struck from the magician's vocabulary, it is "ordinary." As soon as you call something "ordinary," the audience will immediately become suspicious of that prop. Don't hold up "an ordinary blackboard." The audience will *assume* it is ordinary unless you call attention to it.

Many words simply would not be used by a true occult magician. He would not talk about "silks" or "patter" or his "act." None of these technical words should be used in a routine, unless the circumstances are very special. (If you are pretending to be a sorcerer instructing his pupils, *maybe* they would fit.)

There is an alternative to composing patter for the presentation of magic—the "silent" act. One writer recommends doing magic to pantomime and music if the magician does not have a pleasing speaking voice. *This is dreadful advice.* There is no tougher act than a silent one. Every gesture must have a purpose; all movements must have the poetry of ballet. Even a humorous silent act requires a fine sense of rhythmic movement and gestures. Any professional actor will tell you that pantomime is one of the hardest of theatrical arts; it requires the training of a dancer plus the ability to fill empty space with movement and form.

James Reneaux veers to the other extreme when, in *The Professional Technique for Magicians,* he says that one of four things should be happening every minute of one's act: the magician should be talking; music should be playing; or the audience should be either laughing or applauding. There are legitimate reasons for an occasional silent spot in an act, provided the silence is brief and contributes to the overall effect. There might well be a pause of a few seconds just before the blade comes down in the guillotine trick in order to heighten the tension.

The remedy for a less than pleasing voice should not be pantomime but vocal practice and instruction. There are various inflectional and rhythmic devices that can aid a performance, but by and large, the beginner should concentrate primarily on achieving good breath control, precision of elocution, and vocal projection of the voice.

Breath control is a matter of proper breathing and good vocal placement. Breathing should occur from the diaphragm rather than from the chest. Practice by pushing the stomach out with each breath and contracting it during exhalation. The posture should be good—shoulders back naturally, head up. Imagine a rod proceeding diagonally through the body from the center of the breastbone down to a point just above the buttocks. Also imagine an imaginary string running from the center of the breastbone outward in the direction you walk. These devices should help the body attain a pleasing posture; at the same time, the potential air space in the lungs is maximized. When you breathe in, the whole chest cavity fills up like a bag.

Care must be taken not to strain this posture or exaggerate it. It should be pleasing and comfortable. The minute any muscles begin to get stiff or tense, the posture is wrong. Further, if the chest and throat become tense, the sound will come out strained and the larynx will suffer.

Work to expand the capacity of your lungs by diaphragm breathing. Get a long selection of poetry and see how much you can speak at one time without taking a breath—*but without straining.*

Increased breath capacity will enable one to project, to be heard well at the back of any room or stage. Houdini used to speak to the back of the house, figuring that the nearer rows of people would easily hear if those in the back could. He was right.

But what about microphones? There seems to be a conspiracy nowadays to hang one, with or without cord, around everyone's neck, and I know one singer who, though he hates it, will use a mike if everyone else on the program does (so the difference in sound between his voice and everyone else's will not jar the audience). A magician has a hard time using a mike since he must move around and handle props, direct volunteers, and so on. But a proper mastery of projection makes a mike unnecessary. Use of one simply indicates that the performer is not skilled enough to make himself properly heard.

Together with good lung capacity and placement, articulation is necessary to good theatrical speech. Articulation is concerned with the tongue, lips, and teeth and the careful enunciation of each word and syllable. Before going onstage, I often repeat the following verse from a Gilbert and Sullivan operetta:

My eyes are fully open to my awful situation,
I shall go at once to Roderic and make him an oration.
I shall tell him I've recovered my forgotten moral senses,

And I don't care twopence-half-penny for any consequences.
Now I do not want to perish by the sword or by the dagger,
But a martyr may indulge a little pardonable swagger,
And a word or two of compliment my vanity would flatter,
But I've got to die tomorrow, so it really doesn't matter!

Martyn Green used to sing this entire verse rapidly in one breath, and every syllable was as clear as could be. This is a goal to work for: if you can "bite off" all those words cleanly and later work on the breath control, it will prove a most helpful exercise. (Incidentally, it's pronounced "tuppence-haypenny.")

The subject of proper speech is an important one and would require a book of its own for thorough coverage. The suggestions in this chapter should be taken solely as beginning aids to good speech. Such problems as regionalisms, slurring of endings, odd inflections, and so on should be handled in association with a qualified speech teacher. It is often beneficial, too, to work with a community theater group in whatever parts you can get; however, if you do, thoroughly investigate the director's credentials, since improper training can cause more problems than it is worth.

If no qualified assistance is obtainable, at least go to the library and read up on public speaking and theatrical speech. Listen to "spoken word" records of able speakers—John Gielgud, Emlyn Williams, Basil Rathbone, Paul Scofield, Anthony Quayle. Keep in mind, though, that many have British accents, tempered by training in the classics (Shakespeare, Congreve, Molière, etc.). It might be going to extremes to adopt "international theater diction" such as some of these actors use. But that is the general direction you should be leaning toward.

FURTHER EXERCISES

Articulation: Prepare for performance by putting the upper teeth against the lower lip and violently produce a prolonged *v* sound. Change, by pursing the lips, to a prolonged *w*. This helps get the mouth equipment tingling and alive.

Breath Control: Take a deep breath and, with lips closed, produce a musical *m* sound in a comfortable register. Continue it, but feed less air from the lungs until you can slowly fade the sound into silence with no appreciable change in the timbre or quality of the tone.

Projection: Produce the same *m* sound as above, then open the lips and change to an *n*. Take the tongue away from the teeth and, with mouth open slightly, change the sound to a glottal *ng*. Finally, open up the mouth and throat and—still on the same tone—change the sound to *aah*. The resonance should fill the room you are in.

REFERENCES

There are myriads of worthwhile books on speech and vocal development in every library; among them are *Drama* by Andrew Brown, *On Stage* by Muriel Steinbeck, and *The Art of Public Speaking* by John Dolman, Jr.

5

When Do You Move and Why Do You Do It?

The first and most important principle in the design of
stage movement is to avoid all purposeless movement.

John Dolman, Jr., in

The Art of Play Production

There are several reasons why an actor moves onstage, and most of
them are applicable to magicians. A movement may simply be a
part of what the magician is doing, or it may help to define the
character or state of mind he is trying to portray. Movements help
emphasize important points, and can build a feeling of suspense.
They help change the tempo, keep the eyes of the audience from
looking at one thing too long, and help the performer get ready for
the execution of essential upcoming action.

Movement helps the magician control the attention of the
spectators, which is another way of saying it is used in "misdirection," a term which will be discussed in great detail in Chapter 9.
Movement also contributes to the visual beauty and balance of the
stage scene.*

A magician must learn to make bodily movement work for him.
Movement attracts the eye, so it follows that only purposeful
movement should be utilized in a magic routine. Random
movement may call attention to some maneuver which the
magician does not want the audience to see—or distract the
audience from something it was supposed to look at.

---

* Though the present chapter will discuss movement in terms of stage and platform shows,
the principles involved apply in modified form to intimate shows as well.

There are many kinds of movement in a magic act. There are bodily movements in place, including bows, turns, and sitting; there are hand gestures; and there are the processes of walking on, off, and across the stage. (A magician also has to contend with secret moves that make his tricks work; in this book these are either covered in the individual instructions for tricks or treated in Chapter 9.)

The ultimate quality for which the magician strives is stage presence—and it should be evident whether he is walking or standing still. Stage presence is the ability to look and feel comfortable on stage. A person with stage presence exhibits confidence and is in total control.

Stage presence involves extreme economy of movement and gracefulness. One strives for naturalness, so that the movements and speech employed fit the circumstances without appearing strained. In a magic act, this naturalness is all-important. The magician must establish a norm in his speech and movement pattern—partly because he must be poised, but also because any departure from the norm may attract audience attention at the wrong time. For instance, if the conjurer uses a piece of elastic hidden under his coat to make an object disappear, but involuntarily jerks when the elastic snaps back, the movement will prove an unfortunate telltale. The spectators may not know exactly *what* occurred, but they will know that *something* happened—and that will destroy the illusion.

The ability to control one's movements onstage requires both physical and mental coordination. It is necessary to be in charge of everything the body does. Anyone who has ever watched a novice actor walk across stage will know just how difficult bodily control can be. Every separate part—arms, torso, feet, head—seems to take on its own gangly life. The serious performer must train himself to be self-aware at all times. Such self-consciousness is difficult to achieve, and often takes years to master. Personal maturity, and its attendant reduction of self-consciousness, helps immensely. The adolescent has the worst time of all controlling his body, since it is his very lack of personal ease that contributes to his awkwardness, which, in turn, adds to the lack of ease—and the two feed one another.

Being aware of the problem is a big step in the right direction. The bulk of this chapter will be devoted to some of the traditional methods of moving upon the stage. If the novice appreciates these techniques in theory, practicing them will become that much easier.

We will consider the various areas of the stage, their strengths and weaknesses, in greater detail in Chapter 13. For now, we will simply note that the part of the stage closest to the audience is "downstage," while the part farthest away is "upstage." Even a step away from the audience is considered going upstage (or just "up"). In addition to up and down, we should also note the terms "stage left" and "stage right," which are the *performer's* left and right as he is looking out at the audience. Thus, when we say an actor is standing "up left" it simply means he is on his left side of the stage and away from the audience. We can also have positions "down left," "up right," and "down right."

There are eight basic positions the performer can adopt in relationship to the audience. He can stand full front, looking at the audience with his face and body straight ahead. He can stand with his back to the audience (full back), or in profile (half turn). In addition, he can turn his body and face so they are halfway between the full front and profile positions; this is called standing quarter left or right, depending on which way the actor is facing. Similarly, the magician can stand in a position halfway between profile and full back; this is known as three quarters left or right.

The important thing to know about these basic positions is that they have unequal weight in commanding the audience's attention. A person standing full front to the audience tends to compel more attention than someone standing in a one-quarter position. A person in a three-quarter position will probably lose attention, or at least command a lower level of interest. Practically speaking, most solo magic will be performed in the full front position, mixed with some one-quarter positions. When the audience is spread out over a wide area, the magician must alternate, or work to each side of the audience in one-quarter position in order to maintain personal contact with the whole group.

A profile position may be adopted on occasion if the magician is

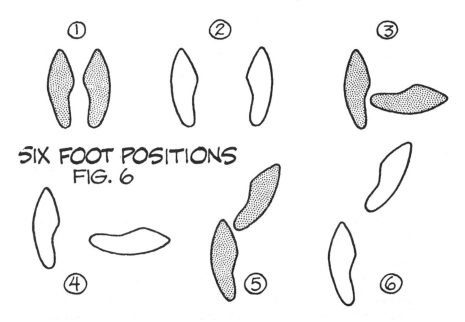

SIX FOOT POSITIONS
FIG. 6

addressing a volunteer onstage—especially if the magician wants to conceal his upstage hand for some secret move. A profile or quarter position divides attention equally between two people, provided they are both standing the same way. A magician may be standing at stage left turned one quarter right, while his assistant may be stage right turned one quarter left. All this means is that both are on opposite sides of the stage looking at one another, each with his face and body turned slightly toward the other. This is a common position in a magic act (or in any two-character play where both people are of similar importance). When the two speak back and forth, the audience will alternately give its attention from one side to the other like spectators at a tennis match. If both people onstage are temporarily silent, both will receive an equal share of attention.

The positions from full front through profile are known as "strong" positions because they are capable of commanding considerable attention. The three-quarter turned and full back stances are usually considered "given," since they tend to diminish attention for the performer. However, a full back position can sometimes be very strong. If a magician turns his back to the audience to get out of a pair of handcuffs, he will certainly hold every eye. The three-quarter stance would rarely command much strength, but could be useful in card tricks and mental routines where the performer must face away from the action. In such cases, the three-quarter mode will allow the audience to see just enough of the performer's head to eliminate suspicion that he may be peeking.

The magician's feet are also capable of a variety of postures in relation to each other. There are six basic positions that they may take—the same stances learned by ballet dancers and professional actors.

The first position is with the feet together, side by side, toes pointing forward. Second position is achieved by moving either foot one step sideways, so the feet are about twelve to twenty-four inches apart. In third position one foot is placed perpendicular to the other, with the heel of the perpendicular foot touching the arch of the foot that points forward. Fourth position is the same as third, except that the perpendicular foot takes a step in the direction it is pointing. Fifth position consists of one foot pointing forward, while the other makes a forty-five-degree angle with the straight line of the first foot. The heel of the angled foot touches the toe of the other. Sixth position is the same as fifth, except the angled foot takes a step in the direction it is pointing. The third through sixth positions may be performed with either the left or right foot held perpendicular or angled. *(Fig. 6)*

Even though some of these foot positions would rarely occur in a magic act, the magician should familiarize himself with all of them. The ability to stand *comfortably* in all six postures will contribute to the performer's stage presence.

When first entering the stage, the performer should proceed from a point just out of sight of the audience and enter briskly. The first step should be taken with the upstage foot. In exiting, it is again the upstage foot that leads off (or, if starting from a full front position, the foot that is upstage after the performer turns in the direction he is going). So if the magician is going to exit left, his left foot takes the first step; if he exits right, his right foot leads. In general, when moving onstage, the foot nearest the goal takes the first step.

A brisk walk helps establish a good tempo for the show. When entering, it is important to prepare oneself mentally. Actors call this technique the *offstage beat;* it means that the entertainer gets himself ready physically, mentally, and emotionally for his entrance. A man who is supposed to walk onstage "drunk" may take a few seconds before his entrance to remember what it feels like to be tipsy. He may even go through the pantomime of swilling down several shots. Then, when he starts to walk on, his body will immediately tell the audience what condition he is in. A magician's offstage beat might be: "I'm going to go out there and have *fun!*" followed by a brisk, lively walk onstage. Other rhythms are possible, of course, for an entrance. If the magician is playing the part of a humorously decrepit old man, he will enter as if all the aches and pains of senility were oppressing him.

Once onstage, the magician will have several occasions to move from one spot to another. If the distance is short, he should cross it in a straight line. However, if it is long, the magician should get used to walking in a slightly curved line. This curve will generally start downstage, go upstage, and end up downstage on the opposite side. Watch actors in a live play execute this kind of cross; it will be perfectly natural and hardly noticeable. However, a curved cross adds grace to the walking movement and, more important, keeps more of the face of the performer turned to the audience than is possible in a straight-line crossing.

There is one other basic kind of foot movement onstage, known as *dressing.* To maintain a pleasing stage picture, an actor will move slightly right or left whenever another person crosses in front of him to go to another side of the stage. Watch these subtle balances and counterbalances in a professional or good local theater production. Better yet, see if you can get permission to observe a rehearsal when the cast is learning its *blocking*—its patterns of stage movement. Dressing is of primary concern to a magician who uses several volunteers and assistants. If he plans a large-scale show, with several people moving back and forth onstage at once, he will need to study theatrical blocking in all its forms.

Stage movement also involves the hands, especially as they are

used for gesturing. The overall principles of economy and naturalness apply very strongly to the hands, since they are the parts of the
body most likely to appear awkward if the performer is not sure of
himself. Some magicians make it a point to enter with a magic
wand or other prop held in one hand. Holding the object gives the
performer confidence and keeps at least one hand from fidgeting.

There are two prime gesturing errors that afflict many magicians: smallness of gesticulation, and failure to hold props so
they can be seen. The latter is easily corrected once the performer
is aware of the problem, but inadequacy of gesture requires some
practice to correct. One should strive for larger-than-life movements, graceful and not too fast. The hands should not bend, but
follow the line of the arm, when gesturing. Imagine you are performing under water; the liquid would offer considerable resistance. Take care to extend each gesture a little farther than one
would in normal conversation. Strive for "sweep"—follow through
a gesture like a golfer driving a ball. If there is a first-rate children's
theater in your vicinity, observe some of its work and notice how
the hand movements of the actors help tell the story. (Better yet,
audition for the group and become an actor in it.)

Your body should generally face the audience when you are
talking. If you have to make a turn, do it so your face stays outward
(unless you are in a three-quarter position and a turn in the opposite
direction would mean going all the way around the clock). If you
have to kneel, do so on the downstage knee. Should there be a
reason to sit, learn to do so gracefully without fumbling for the seat.
An actor will spot the chair, walk to it, then turn around, feel it with
the back of his leg, and lower himself into it. Observe this technique
at a live play or on TV and practice it. If you can meet a competent
actor, ask him to show you how he sits onstage.

The most unusual movement the body must execute onstage is
the bow. There are all sorts of styles of bowing, but some magic
books recommend individual methods as if there were only one
physique in the world. Some people will find it comfortable to bow
from the waist; others will find it less pretentious merely to nod
with the head. No bow is wrong if it looks graceful and the performer is comfortable doing it.

Naturally, there is a lot of standing in one place during any magic act, even though something—hands, body, mouth—is usually moving. Nevertheless, the performer must learn to stand without moving a muscle; ability to do so will contribute to his total mastery over himself.

When standing still, learn to adopt a pleasing stance—head up, shoulders back, stomach in, feet in the number two position (or number three or four, whichever provides the greatest feeling of poise). Do not make good posture look like labor; seek to make a pleasing stance the natural one *at all times.* When walking, imagine that a string attached to the midpoint of your breastbone is pulling you along—this is the way an athlete might walk.

Standing still requires the ability to suppress foot shuffling and weight shifting. Not only are these movements distracting, but shifting weight can weaken one's stage presence in a purely mechanical sense. A person standing with his weight either evenly distributed or slightly forward will appear much more assured than an individual standing in number one position, with his weight on his heels (the stance an actor uses to play an old, weak person).

There is a simple technique some performers use for keeping the hands still when they're not moving: let them hang by your sides and lightly press each thumbtip to the ball of each middle finger. This indetectable device provides a certain "rooted" feeling and helps put the hands at ease.

There are a few classic do's and don'ts connected with stage movement, but most of them are subject to qualification. For instance, it is a cliché that a magician should never turn his back on his audience, but we have already noted the necessity of doing so in a mental act. Then we are told that the magician must never leave the audience's sight. In my own act, I break this rule in two different tricks to good effect. For instance, when performing the well-known guillotine trick, I keep the blade offstage and the base onstage, covered with a black velvet cloth. After inserting the victim's hand in the chopper hole, I go off to get the blade, whipping the cloth away and taking it with me. The sudden appearance of the chopper base with the familiar sack—together with the look on the volunteer's face—is ample spectacle to amuse the audience till I return. Then, when I do so, bearing the blade, the excitement grows. In another trick, I go off to get a chair (and to load a rubber chicken in my jacket). Meanwhile, onstage, a volunteer is busy taking off his jacket and emptying his pockets. It is perfectly legitimate for the magician to exit briefly, provided there is something else for the audience to watch in his absence.

The only classic "do" of stage movement I would accept is, *Look where you're going*—which is a variation on the basic principle that the performer must always be in control of his body. To master this, he must work at it all the time, not just when he is performing. A man who sings well but talks with a squeaky voice is abusing his vocal mechanism, and may find that his singing begins to suffer. The same goes for movement and posture: if they are good in everyday life, they will be acceptable onstage. Make them second nature!

EXERCISES

Good stage movement is best achieved through constant exercise. If there is a good theater dance class available in your town, enroll in it. Or join a competent theater group. Remember that actors often make better magicians than vice versa.

Here are a few exercises which will help develop poise in movement and body control:

1. Adopt each of the six ballet positions in turn and walk back and forth in each, keeping the feet in the same relative positions. (Example: In position three, walk so that the perpendicular foot stays perpendicular and the heel touches the arch with each step. Alternate feet in positions three through six. Keep doing this exercise till you can cross a room in each position without feeling uncomfortable.)

2. Imagine that you are walking a tightrope from one end of the room to the other. *See* the rope and keep shifting your weight to stay on it. This is a very difficult exercise, but it will help enormously in achieving bodily control.

3. Pretend you have a ball of mercury in your hand. Imagine

that you can roll it up one arm, down the other, over the neck, down the body. Kick it from your foot up to your hand. Feel the heaviness of the "spot," and work to move *only* the portion of the body where it is.

4. Imagine that your forehead is tense, but no other part of your body. Then extend the tightness to your eyes, then your neck, and so on till your whole body, one part at a time, joins the tension. Maintain the feeling for a few seconds, then, working backward, relax the whole body, one part at a time. Do not hurry this exercise; it should take several minutes.

REFERENCES

There are many worthwhile books concerned in whole or in part with stage movement. They include John Dolman's *The Art of Play Production,* John Gassner's *Producing the Play,* Alexander Dean's *Fundamentals of Play Directing,* and Muriel Steinbeck's *On Stage.* Consult your library for additional sources.

6

Essential Fingerwork

[Amateurs] spend hours working on elaborate sleights and methods that would have no meaning except to another magician who already knows the secret of some old trick ... Both versions would look the same to an audience.

Bill Severn, in
Magic and Magicians

Many magicians are sleight-of-hand snobs. Encouraged by the attitudes of many dealers, they think a conjurer can't be good unless he devotes hours every day to the mastery of complicated hand and finger manipulations. Sleight-of-hand snobbism is unfortunate, because it undoubtedly discourages many amateurs needlessly. The unsuspecting beginner who reads magic periodicals probably gets the impression that he'd have to spend years learning the moves described there.

Sleight of hand, or fingerwork, need not be hard to master, nor is it necessary to learn in order to become a good entertainer. There are only two essential skills needed by the magician: showmanship and misdirection. Without the showmanship, the world's most skillful manipulator would bore an audience to death. Misdirections, which will be discussed more fully in Chapter 9, can serve as a viable substitute for fancy fingerwork.

The pride that some amateurs show in their sleight-of-hand proficiency is really rather pitiful. Even the magician's toughest manipulations are simple in comparison with the manual skills required in other entertainment arts. In *Magic by Misdirection*, Dariel Fitzkee puts it succinctly: "Such moves are puerile compared to the dexterity necessary in becoming a good pianist or, particularly, a good violinist."

Sleight-of-hand snobs are bad enough, but some of the books and people that profess to teach manipulation are worse. Far too many reinforce the idea that each sleight can be executed only one way. No less an authority than John Scarne has declared that most magicians are greatly mistaken in trying to do secret moves in the exact same manner as one another. All hands, says Scarne, are different. Some are too small or unsupple to accomplish certain moves gracefully.

Each sleight should be adapted to the needs and limitations of the individual performer. The reader may already have noticed that trick descriptions in this book do not specify which hand should hold an object. Since some readers are left-handed, instructions to, say, "grasp a coin in the right hand" might set up unnecessary obstacles for them. Similarly, the following descriptions of sleights ought to be modified to suit the style and manual dexterity of every reader.

Sleights are simply tools for achieving effects. Moreover, they are *secret* tools, of no significance to the audience. Magicians who indulge in fancy flourishes and strange-looking moves are asking the audience to applaud their dexterity—like jugglers—but are throwing away their capacity to surprise. Magic is mystery, not manipulative exhibition, and should appear effortless, artless.

Sleights are necessary mechanical evils. If they are too hard to perform, they should be eliminated. Only if a sleight accomplishes some goal that cannot be achieved otherwise should it be considered essential. If there is another, easier way to do the same thing, it is to be preferred. For example, I have never found any kind of "glimpse" (a method for secretly peeking at a chosen card) natural to perform. I never use the move; instead I simply use one of two equally useful alternatives, to either "control" the card or "force" it. (These terms will be discussed later.) Similarly, I avoid the double lift, in which more than one card is taken from the top of the deck as if they were one. I find this move undependable; it sometimes gives you more cards in the hand than you want. When a double lift effect is unavoidable, I simply use a "stripper" deck

—one whose edges are tapered. By turning the required cards around on top of the deck, it is then easy to pick up just as many as are needed, and no more.

Even when a sleight performs some service that cannot otherwise be accomplished, it should be avoided—along with any tricks employing it—if the individual magician cannot be sure of executing it in fail-safe fashion.

Sleights that do not look absolutely natural should also be given up. "Mexican turnovers," "slop shuffles," the old-fashioned "pass," can be found in many conjuring texts; each requires cards to be handled in ways that one would almost never see in a regular card game. These moves are, to my mind, suspicious-looking and absolutely without value.

At the same time, it should be noted that some sleights that seem unnatural at first can, with a little effort, be made to appear perfectly natural. One "force" explained later requires that the cards be cut behind the back. However, the magician makes an excuse for the odd method by explaining that it prevents him from manipulating the cards.

The moves described in the following pages are those I consider practically indispensable. Many of their principles will be employed in later chapters.

CARD SLEIGHTS

The first move is not so much a sleight as a convenient method of showing all the card backs or faces at the same time.

CARD SPREAD

How It Looks: The cards are spread across the table like a long bridge hand with the tops and bottoms evened up, making a horizontal ribbon of cards.

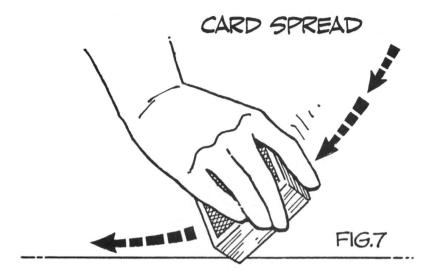

CARD SPREAD

FIG.7

How to Do It: Hold the cards with the thumb on one narrow edge and the fingers on the other—except for the index finger, which should rest on the long edge. Bring the cards smartly down onto the table and spread them out in the same movement. *(Fig. 7)* The bottom cards strike the table first and the index finger starts to push them apart. The other fingers let go, and the palm of the hand keeps pushing the cards in the same direction so that each one overlaps the last slightly. (Some table surfaces, especially glass, will be too slippery to work well.)

There are two shuffles used commonly in America, dovetail and overhand. The magician must be able to fake both.

FALSE OVERHAND

Basic Use: To keep the deck, or some portion of it, in the same order after the shuffle is completed.

How It Looks: This is the most familiar shuffle, in which one hand "chops" the deck down at the other hand's upturned palm. The upturned hand peels off a few cards with the thumb, lets them fall against the curve of the fingers, then peels off more and lets them drop against the first peeled-off cards. The action is repeated rapidly until the deck has more or less been reversed.

How to Do It: False overhand shuffling differs from the genuine version in only one way: the magician alters the manner in which he stops and starts.

To Keep the Top Cards of the Deck in the Same Order: The magician shuffles in the normal overhand manner. But when he gets near the top of the deck, he just lets the already shuffled cards fall back on the palm of his hand. He then puts the top of the deck upon the rest of the cards and squares the whole deck. To the audience, it looks as if the last cards have been casually added to the rest.

To Keep the Bottom Cards in the Same Order: On the first chop, peel off all the bottom cards and let them rest against the heel of the hand and base of the thumb. Shuffle the rest of the cards in the usual overhand manner. The bottom cards will form a V with the other cards resting against the fingertips. When the deck has been exhausted, the hand simply snaps the two heaps together.

To Keep Both Top and Bottom Cards the Same: Combine the first two methods. In other words, peel off the bottom cards and keep them separated. Then, when the top has nearly been reached, snap the peeled cards together and drop the top cards onto the remainder.

To Keep the Deck in the Same Order Throughout: Note the bottom card of the deck. Now rapidly shuffle in normal overhand fashion *but only one card at a time.* When the selected card appears on the bottom, the deck is once again in order. Practice for a speedy execution.

FALSE DOVETAIL SHUFFLE

Basic Use: To keep the top and/or bottom cards in order. (It is possible to keep the whole deck in order using the dovetail, but I regard it as a most unnatural move for this purpose, and will not endorse it.)

How It Looks: The hands divide the deck into two heaps and flip the corners so they fall together interwoven. The cards are then pushed together.

How to Do It: The magician decides which cards will be flipped first and/or last.

To Keep the Top Cards in Place: When dividing the deck, remember which hand holds the top cards. Let these fall last when riffling the two heaps.

To Keep the Bottom Cards in Place: Let the bottom cards fall first during the shuffle.

To Keep Both Top and Bottom Cards the Same: Let the bottom cards fall first, and retain the top cards till last.

Cutting the cards is also a popular way of mixing the order. Here are two methods that leave the deck undisturbed.

THREE-PILE FALSE CUT

How to Do It: Put the deck on the table. Cut off about two thirds and drop this portion to the right of the remainder. (For clarity, let us call the right-hand, bigger pile A and the left-hand, smaller pile B.) The same hand immediately cuts off the top third of A and drops this new heap (pile C) *between* A and B. In the same move, the hand returns to A and drops it on B, then goes to C and puts it on top of the combined AB. The deck is now back the way it started.

Note: During false cutting, the magician must speak and otherwise draw attention away from his action. The three-pile cut should be executed smoothly, as if it were one flowing movement.

FALSE OVERHAND CUT

Basic Use: To control the deck and keep it in order.

How It Looks: This is a variation on the common two-pile cut, in which the deck is divided into two piles and the bottom half is replaced over the original top. In the false-cut version, the division takes place in the conjurer's hands. One hand holds the pack above its upturned palm and grasps it between fingers and thumb. The other hand seems to cut the top half of the deck and drop it on a table, then comes back to put the rest of the cards on top of the tabled portion.

How to Do It: The trick is to really take the *bottom* half when the audience thinks the top half is being removed and put on the table. The moving hand, with palm down, is brought to a position above the deck. It seems to pull the top portion off, sliding it over the bottom cards. But the uppermost hand really grasps the *lower* portion of the deck with fingers on one side and thumb on the other.

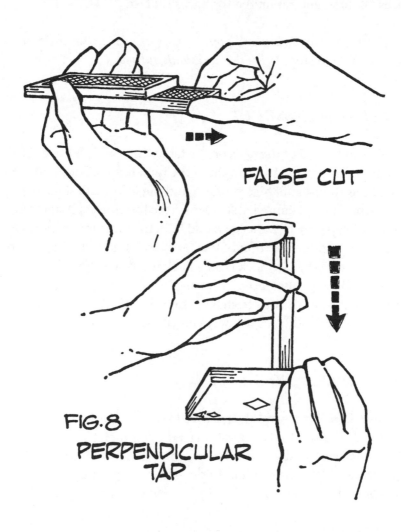

FALSE CUT

FIG. 8
PERPENDICULAR
TAP

It pulls this portion off with the sliding motion described and immediately swings it upward a quarter turn so it is perpendicular to the rest of the pack. This perpendicular half is now tapped against the horizontal half to square it. *(Fig. 8)* The tapping reinforces the idea that the magician has cut off the top of the pack. The cut portion is now put on the table and the hand comes back and grabs the remainder of the deck and drops it on the tabled heap.

The Palm is one of the most basic card sleights. There are several ways of doing it. Here is the easiest.

THE PALM

Basic Use: Control of the top of the deck so a card can be removed or added.

How It Looks: It is invisible. The only thing the audience sees is the magician's hands squaring up the cards.

How to Do It: When palmed, the card conforms to the inner curve of the hand. The heel of the hand and the fingertips press the narrow ends of the card gently and hold it in place against the palm's arch. Observe how the hand hangs naturally at the side of the body when at rest, and strive to hold a palmed card in this fashion.

To Get the Top Card in Palmed Position: Hold the deck on the palm of the hand, fingers and thumb on opposite long sides. The other hand, with palm down, reaches above the deck. The fingertips slide the top card forward slightly. Now the upper hand leans the fingertips on this jutting edge: the first crease of the index finger nearest the nail touches the left-hand corner of the card. A slight pressure will cause the card to rise into the hand. Use the deck itself to "wipe" the card into the palm. *(Fig. 9)*

The following sleight is very simple to master, but it has many uses. It can be used to magically change the bottom card or even to deal "seconds" (see glossary) in order to retain the top card on the deck.

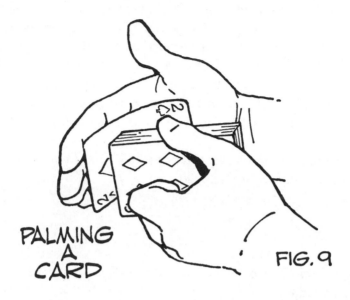

PALMING
A
CARD   FIG. 9

THE GLIDE

Basic Use: To control the deck so the top or bottom card may be retained during a deal.

How It Looks: The glide is invisible.

How to Do It: To retain the bottom card: Hold the deck in the palm of one hand, fingers curled over one long edge and all the way around to the bottom. The thumb rests along the other long side. Show the bottom card to the audience. (See Fig. 10 for finger position. At this point, the six is completely covered by the ace.) The other hand reaches with its fingertips to pull out the bottom card. As it does, the deck is turned parallel to the floor, so the audience cannot see the bottom card. Now, the ring finger of the hand holding the cards slides the bottom card back so the other hand can grab the edge of the second card, which it then pulls out. The ring finger slides the bottom card back in place. *(Fig. 10)* The X shows the finger that pulls the ace. The six is then removed. *To retain the top card,* hold the deck in dealing position. As the other hand covers the cards momentarily to deal off the top card, the opposite thumb pulls this card back slightly so the second card can be taken. The top card is immediately shoved back in place.

FIG. 10

THE GLIDE

It is sometimes necessary to secretly reverse (turn over) a card in the deck, or at least to shift a card from bottom to top. Here is a sleight that accomplishes both in one natural maneuver.

REVERSE SLIPAROUND

Basic Use: To move the top card secretly to the bottom and reverse it at the same time.

How It Looks: Invisible.

How to Do It: Hold the deck face down on the palm of the hand with the thumb at one long edge, fingers around the other. The other hand covers the top card and slides it off the far side. The lower fingers push up on the deck, and at the same time the top hand slides the card around the edge and under to the bottom of the deck. *(Fig. 11)* It seems as if the deck is only being squared up.

Sometimes the magician wants to make it seem as if he were holding more cards in his hands than he actually does.

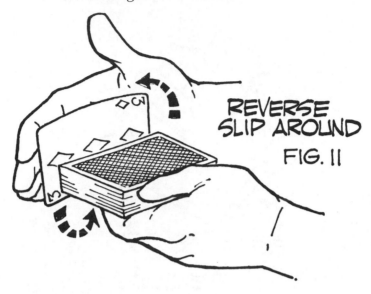

FALSE CARD COUNT

Basic Use: To disguise the number of cards the magician is holding.

How It Looks: It appears as if the magician were fairly counting the cards by sliding them from left to right.

How to Do It: The method is simplicity itself. The hands hold the cards between them, and run them off sideways, one at a time. As each card is pushed to the side, the magician counts it aloud. But whenever a false count is desired, the thumb simply pulls the card back to the left and pushes it forward a second time.

Another Method: Hold the deck in one hand. With the other hand, take cards from the top of the deck, wiping them off with the thumb and grasping them with fingers beneath. When a false count is desired, the hand just wipes the edge of the already counted cards smartly on the top card of the remainder of the deck. This sound imitates that of a card being counted off.

The above sleights are all concerned with various kinds of card control. The next two are involved primarily with the location of a freely selected card once it has been replaced in the deck.

The first method, Key Cards, is not a secret move, but a location method that often makes sleights unnecessary.

KEY CARDS

Basic Use: To determine the location of a given card.

How It Looks: Invisible.

How to Do It: The magician notes the identity of the top card and has the chosen card replaced at the bottom of the deck, which is then cut. The chosen card will then be the first one above the noted card. Another way is to note the bottom card and have the selected card replaced on top. After the cut, it appears below the noted card.

Note: The use of key cards allows the deck to be cut genuinely in two piles as often as the spectators desire. The rotation will stay the same. Once in a long while, the key card and the chosen one will be split up. If this occurs and if the bottom card is the key and it ends up on the bottom of the deck, then the chosen card is the one on top. If the key card started on top and ends up there again, the chosen one will then be on the bottom.

THE THUMB PUSHBACK

Basic Use: To determine the location of a given card.

How It Looks: The cards are cut.

How to Do It: This simple move may be employed to get a chosen card onto the top or bottom of the deck, where it can be "discovered" or in some other way revealed. After the card is picked, the magician lifts off about half the deck and asks the spectator to put the chosen card on top of the *lower* pile. The magician then replaces the upper half, cuts, shuffles, and seems to thoroughly mix the deck. This is what really happens: when the magician is replacing the top half of the deck onto the chosen card, he sees to it that the upper cards jut forward about an inch from the front edge of the lower half. Meanwhile, the thumb of his upper hand is lowered onto the face of the chosen card. When the magician evens up the two portions by shoving the upper half back so it is flush with the lower section, the thumb automatically pushes the chosen card backward so it juts out from the back of the pack. (Fig. 12)

To Bring the Card to the Bottom: Stick the thumb under the jutting chosen card and cut the deck at this point. After the cut, the chosen card will be on the bottom. (Naturally, it is shoved flush with the pack during the cutting motion.) Do a false shuffle which leaves it on the bottom.

To Bring the Card to the Top: Follow the same procedure to bring it to the bottom, then shuffle it overhand to the top of the pack.

Forces are maneuvers that make the spectator pick a predetermined card. Here are several useful ones.

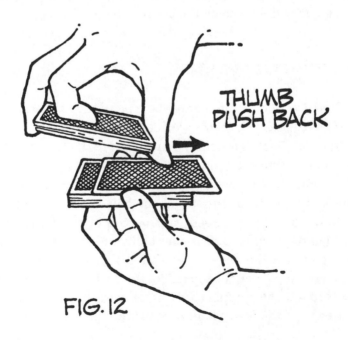

THUMB
PUSH BACK

FIG. 12

TOP COUNTOFF

How It Looks: The magician asks a spectator to name a number, perhaps between one and ten. He then tells the spectator to count off the same number of cards onto the table from the top of the deck and look at the last card. The magician demonstrates how to do it, then gives the deck to the volunteer, who proceeds as directed.

How to Do It: The card to be forced is on the top of the deck. After the magician knows the number—for example, five—he says, "Now I want you to count off five cards, like this," and does so. "Look at the fifth card." The magician casually holds up the fifth card, replaces it, then puts the five cards back on top of the deck. The force card is now fifth from the top.

CUT FORCE

How It Looks: The magician asks the spectator to cut the cards anywhere, but put the bottom half *diagonally* on top of the first. He then tells the volunteer to look at the card on the bottom of this new top portion.

How to Do It: The force card is on the bottom of the deck. When the cut is made, it will automatically be the bottom card of the upper, diagonal half.

Caution: This is an audacious move and works best if the spectator is temporarily diverted after making the cut and before looking at the force card. This is how it might be played: The magician has the volunteer make the cut. Then he says, "Now . . ." and pauses until the volunteer looks at him. "Are you sure I did not influence you to cut the cards at that point? Was it a free choice?" The volunteer concedes that it was. "Then," says the magician, "I am going to turn my back and when I do, please pick up the upper half, the one resting slantwise, and look at the bottom card. Then put the half back on the deck in normal fashion, shuffle the cards, and let me know when you are done." This helps to hide the obvious nature of the cut by distracting the volunteer with a sham question and by seemingly emphasizing how he may totally "bury" the card before the magician even turns around!

BEHIND-THE-BACK FORCE

How It Looks: The magician puts the deck behind his back, holding it with one hand. His other hand is high in the air, so it cannot touch the deck. He has the spectator reach behind his back and cut off as many cards as he wants and drop them on a table. Then the volunteer reaches back again and takes the very next card. The magician discards the remainder of the deck.

How to Do It: This move, one of the finest forces of the late Ted Annemann, seems extremely fair since it uses only one hand and the cut takes place out of the magician's sight behind his back. It is really a very bold deception. The force card is on the bottom of the deck *face up*. After the spectator cuts off a portion of the deck and drops it on the table, the magician just flips the cards over in his hand. The volunteer picks the force card—now face down—and the magician drops the rest of the cards on the table, turning them back over as he brings them from behind his back. Naturally, the spectator must execute the cut by feel, and not look at the cards. The natural way to suggest this is to say, "I'm placing the cards behind my back and want you to pick one by reaching behind. That way, neither of us can possibly know what it is. Then I will walk far away from you before you look at the card."

DEAL-OFF FORCE

How It Looks: The magician seems to deal cards off the top of the deck until the spectator tells him to stop. The magician then holds up the last card dealt for the spectator to memorize.

How to Do It: This is also a bold move. The force card is on top of the deck. Hold the deck in dealing position, and peel off the top card. Now slip the second card onto the *top* of the first card dealt. Keep doing so, and when told to stop, point out that the spectator could have stopped you at any time. (This is to divert him from the obviousness of the coming move.) Now hold the dealt cards up so he can see the bottom card of that heap. Naturally, this is the card that was originally on top.

COIN SLEIGHTS

The manipulation of coins is simple to master, and some of the moves may also be used when handling small balls and even slips of paper. Start by working with large coins and work down in size until you can handle even dimes. Most magic stores carry half-dollar-size "palming" coins, manufactured very thin for ease of handling. Try working with every kind of coin.

Palming a coin is much easier than palming a card and is the basic type of coin sleight. There are two essential kinds of coin palming.

BASIC COIN PALM

Basic Use: For producing, vanishing, and otherwise manipulating a coin or coins.

How It Looks: Invisible.

How to Do It: Hold the coin flat against the palm, which should be in a normal curved position. The coin is pressed into place by the heel of the hand and the "head line" (the uppermost crease in the palm of the hand). Very little pressure will hold the coin in place. (*Fig. 13*)

THUMB PALM

Basic Use: For vanishing, appearing, substitution, and other purposes.

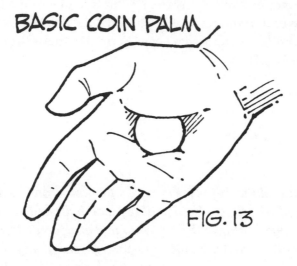

BASIC COIN PALM

FIG. 13

How It Looks: Invisible.

How to Do It: The thumb palm may be executed in various fashions. Here is a method that disguises the move. The coin is held at the fingertips between thumb and index and middle fingers. *(Fig. 14)* The fingers apparently put the coin in the palm of the other hand which closes over the coin. But the fingers really slide the coin into the crotch of the thumb. *(Fig. 15)* The fingers relax and the coin is lightly pinched between the base of thumb and index finger. *(Fig. 16)*

The following sleight is technically a maneuver, a sequence of moves designed to accomplish some aim—in this case, the vanish of a coin or ball.

FRENCH DROP

Basic Use: To vanish a coin or ball.

How It Looks: One hand holds the coin in its fingers. The other seems to take the coin away. When the latter hand is opened, the coin is gone.

THUMB PALM

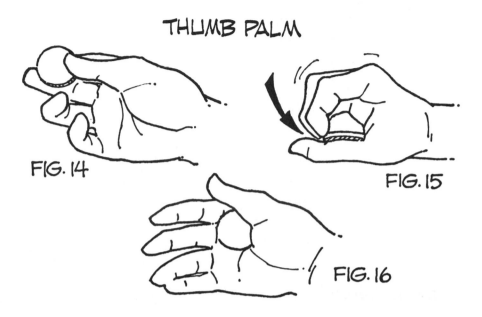

FIG. 14

FIG. 15

FIG. 16

How to Do It: The coin is held with its flat sides parallel to the floor. It is grasped by the palm-up hand, between the thumb and index and middle fingers. The other hand approaches it, palm down, and its fingers close over the coin, the thumb beneath. *(Fig. 17)* But as the upper hand closes, the lower fingers let go of the coin, which drops into the palm of that hand. The upper hand closes and moves away. The hand holding the coin turns over and palms the coin in its center. Its index finger points at the other hand, and the magician watches the empty hand, thus misdirecting the audience to watch the wrong hand. Meanwhile, the hand with the coin in it drops to the side and may get rid of the coin in a pocket. The empty hand dramatically and slowly reveals it holds no coin.

Here is another coin-palm maneuver for vanishing a coin without any difficult fingerwork.

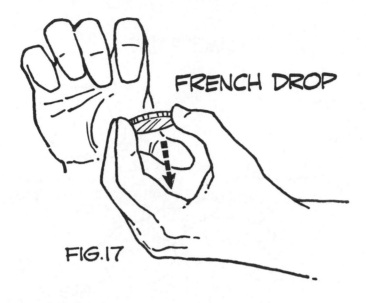

FRENCH DROP

FIG.17

HANDKERCHIEF COIN VANISH

Basic Use: To vanish a coin under difficult conditions.

How It Looks: A coin is folded many times in a handkerchief. When the cloth is shaken out, the coin has disappeared.

How to Do It: Open up a handkerchief all the way and put it on a table so it looks like a baseball diamond. Put a coin in the exact center and then fold up the cloth so the bottom and top points (second base and home) meet. The handkerchief now forms an equilateral triangle. *(Fig. 18)* Fold the cloth to the right so a right triangle is formed with the coin inside at the base of the ninety-degree angle. *(Fig. 19)* Fold the cloth once more so the top point lines up with the right-hand point, making another equilateral triangle. *(Fig. 20)* The coin is still inside, and can be felt in the left-hand point. Now if the right-hand points are examined, it will be found there are four: a set of one inside the other, and two separate ones below the nestled pair. Hold the two separate points, one in each hand, and very swiftly draw them apart. The handkerchief will now be stretched between both hands. The coin, apparently gone, will really be in a gutter formed by the folds. By tilting the cloth slightly to one hand, the coin will roll downward to

HANKERCHIEF COIN VANISH

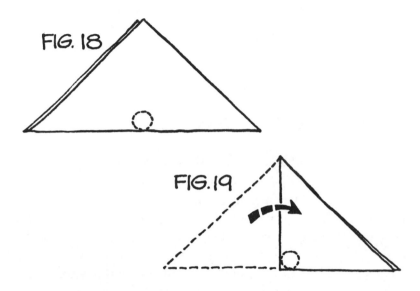

FIG. 18

FIG. 19

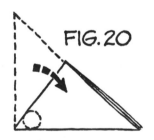

FIG. 20

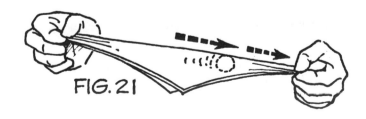

FIG. 21

that hand. *(Fig. 21)* Just before it arrives, that hand should relinquish its grip on the corner of the handkerchief. The coin falls in the hand and may be palmed. Meanwhile, the other hand whips its corner outward in a fast move to distract attention from the hand with the coin in it. The cloth is now given to a spectator to examine—which affords the magician ample time to dispose of the coin.

FALSE COIN COUNT

Basic Use: To make it seem as if the magician *or* the spectator had one more coin of any denomination than he actually holds.

How It Looks: The magician seems to count a certain number of coins into his hand, or into the outstretched palm of a volunteer. The hand is closed, then reopened, but one of the coins has vanished.

How to Do It: Simply clink each coin one on the other as they are counted into the palm. The last coin is clinked, but the magician thumb palms it and bears it away. This psychological ploy is quite convincing.

OTHER SLEIGHTS

There are various specialized sleights for use with different tricks. Of these, the following two are frequently needed.

BILLET SWITCH

Basic Use: To substitute one slip of paper for another, or to exchange dollar bills.

How It Looks: The fingers hold a slip of paper or a folded dollar

BILLET SWITCH

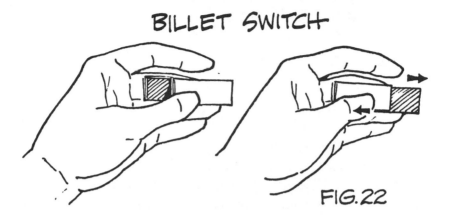

FIG.22

in one hand. The other hand takes it—or perhaps the paper is given to a spectator to hold.

How to Do It: It is necessary to have the paper folded. (The method for folding small slips of paper is outlined in the next chapter.) The dollar bill is folded lengthwise and creased to hold its shape, then folded again lengthwise and creased. Now fold it in the middle so the narrow ends meet. Crease to hold the fold; then repeat the latter folding process once. Now hold the bill you want to substitute in this folded fashion between the tips of the thumb and the index and middle fingers, with the back of the hand hiding it from the audience. The crease should be farthest out, *not* the ends of the bill. Now take the borrowed bill and have it folded the same way. Hold it at the fingertips of the *other* hand. Bring the latter bill to the hand that holds the hidden dollar. Grasp the innocent bill with thumb and fingers of the latter hand, making sure that it *overlaps* the hidden dollar and is on *top* of it. (This means the innocent bill is actually held between the index and middle fingers and the edge of the hidden dollar.) It is now easy to hand the innocent bill to someone else—but in the process the fingers slip it back, thumb palming it. Meanwhile, the hidden bill appears. *(Fig. 22)* The movement conceals the substitution.

Note: When handling paper money, always keep the bills as

much at the fingertips as possible and do not make fast moves, or the audience will become suspicious.

FALSE KNOT

Basic Use: To tie a rope with a knot that will later be removed in mysterious fashion.

How It Looks: The magician seems to tie a tight knot. But just by passing his hand over it, it vanishes.

How t. Do It: Most rope sleights are not hard to do, and this maneuver is no exception. However, it is not easy to visualize. Read the description carefully, observing the accompanying illustrations, then follow the moves with a piece of rope, one step at a time. (Cotton rope, also known as magician's rope, is the best kind to use. The center strands can be removed and discarded, leaving an unusually soft and pliable rope to work with.)

Pinch the end of a moderately lengthy piece of rope between outstretched index and middle fingers of one hand. Curl the ring finger and pinky of the same hand over the rope and then let a loop hang down. Grasp the opposite end of the rope in the other hand between thumb and fingers. *(Fig. 23)* The free end of rope is now crossed just over the place where the ring finger and pinky hold the other end in place and the free end is drooped over the crotch of the thumb of the other hand. *(Fig. 24)* Now the free hand reaches through the big loop formed and grabs the right-hand end of the rope to pull it back through the loop. *(Fig. 24; arrow indicates proper end.)* But as the free hand pulls the proper end back through the loop, the middle finger of the opposite hand bends and pulls back a small second loop in the opposite direction. *(Fig. 25)* The free hand continues to pull its end, thus making a tight knot. However, the little loop held back by the middle finger forms a slip knot. *(Fig. 26)* The free hand now pulls tightly on its end and the other hand now grasps the other end of the rope as if to make the knot as tight as can be. Actually, the purpose of this move is to *carefully* pull the slip knot loop smaller so it almost—but not quite—pulls all the way out. Experience will show when to stop. Now the rope seems to

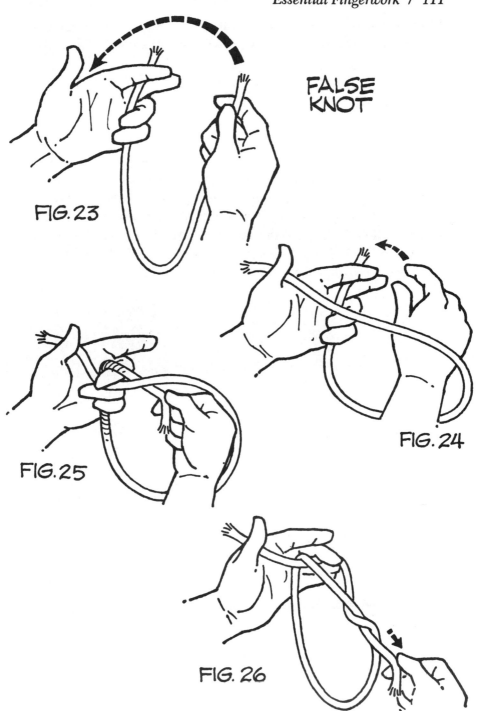

FIG. 23

FALSE KNOT

FIG. 24

FIG. 25

FIG. 26

have a real knot in it, but a quick pull of both ends—or simply sliding one's hand sharply over the "knot"—will cause the knot to fall apart.

REFERENCES

Additional explanations of sleights and how they are executed may be found in almost every magic text. Some of the more valuable are Jean Hugard's *Money Magic,* which deals exclusively with paper money; H. Rice's *More Naughty Silks,* which contains numerous silk sleights, many of which apply to rope as well. Dariel Fitzkee's *Rope Eternal* is the last word on cutting and restoring ropes, and W. B. Gibson's *Complete Illustrated Book of Card Magic* has clear photographs of virtually every card sleight.

7

Tricks with Sleights

COIN FLIP

Basic Illusion: One coin appears to turn into another.

How It Looks: Pretending to demonstrate his skill as a manipulator, the magician flips a coin, say a penny, from hand to hand. He makes it more difficult by keeping the receiving hand turned away and clenched till the last moment, and boasts that he can throw the penny so fast the eye will not be able to follow it. After a few trials with varying results, he opens his clenched fist to show that the coin has become, say, a quarter.

What You Need: Two coins, perhaps a penny and a quarter.

Sleights: Basic coin palm; thumb palm.

How It Works: The quarter is palmed and flipped the third time. The penny is palmed instead.

How to Do It: Conceal the quarter in basic coin-palm position and cover it with the curled pinky and ring fingers. Hold the penny between the thumb and index and middle fingers of the same hand. Clench the other hand and turn its back to the penny. *(Fig. 27;* but note that the pinky and ring fingers are not pictured folded in order to show how the quarter is concealed.) With the hands about a foot and a half apart, throw the penny toward the clenched hand—which quickly opens and turns to catch the coin. As soon as it grasps the coin, it closes again and snaps back to its original position. This flip should be executed rapidly as one continuous

113

movement so the spectator really will have some trouble seeing the coin fly from hand to hand. Repeat the flip. Start to repeat it a third time, but this time open the curled fingers and let the quarter fly into the other hand instead of the penny. At the same time, thumb-palm the penny. As the quarter is being shown, the hand with the penny can drop to the side to slip the coin into a pocket.

Tips for Presentation: 1. Practice the move until it is smooth; it is not hard to master. But when you perform the trick, pretend to be a little less deft than you are. Try to let the spectator see the coin on the first flip. On the second flip, you might even drop the penny "by accident." The third flip, of course, should be expertly performed. The spectator may be glad you have finally done it correctly—but will not be expecting the transposition, since he has been led to believe he is watching a simple show of dexterity, and not a very good one at that.

2. I usually reserve this effect for occasions when I am asked to "do some magic," but have no equipment available, not even a deck of cards. I remark that I can at least show a warm-up exercise that I use to get my fingers limber for doing magic. Then I dig into a pocket, palm the quarter, and come out with the penny at my fingertips.

3. If the spectator says he can see the coin being flipped, pre-

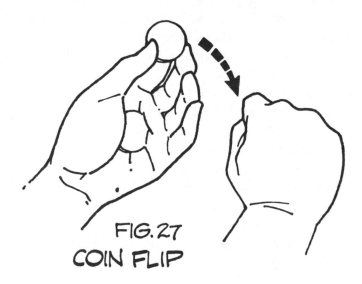

FIG. 27
COIN FLIP

tend dismay and ask for another chance. If he does not see it, act gratified and ask him to watch it again to see if you still can fool him.

SERIAL-NUMBER PREDICTION

Basic Illusion: The magician predicts the serial number of a borrowed dollar bill.

How It Looks: The magician has a volunteer take a dollar bill from his pocket and fold it in the manner outlined in the previous chapter for Billet Switch. Taking the dollar bill in his hand, the magician holds it to his forehead and predicts the serial number. The bill is handed back to its owner, who unfolds it and verifies the prediction.

What You Need: A borrowed bill. A second one hidden in the hand. Paper and pencil (optional).

Preparation: Learn the serial number of the hidden dollar bill, fold it in billet-switch fashion, and conceal it as described for that sleight.

Sleight: Billet switch.

How It Works: The magician gets the hidden bill in position and gives someone a pad of paper and a pencil. Then he borrows a dollar bill, has it folded, takes it, holds it to his forehead, and recites the memorized serial number. He returns the bill to its owner—but executes the switch and hands him the other. The bill is now unfolded and the number read off. The man with pencil and paper confirms its identity.

Tips for Presentation: 1. There is a legend that one soldier during the Second World War made a fortune in bar bets just doing this trick. The borrowed money must be handled at fingertips and in leisurely fashion. When it is raised to the forehead, the magician should seem to have great difficulty seeing the number. He affects great mental effort.

2. The bill's number may be predicted beforehand in writing, and the paper sealed in an envelope and given to another volunteer to hold. Then the magician switches the bill while handing it to the

person with the envelope. The only problem with this presentation is the need to fold the bill, which is unnatural since the prediction has already been written. One way to get around this difficulty is to have the man with the envelope stand several feet away from the rest of the audience. The magician passes out a bowl and has several people put dollar bills in it. Then he has someone pick a single bill and fold it in the prescribed manner before handing it to the magician, who, in turn, gives it to the person with the envelope. This handling seems to emphasize the absolute chance selection of the bill; the folding merely adds to the secrecy of the process.

CENTER TEAR

Basic Illusion: The magician reads the mind of a spectator.

How It Looks: The magician claims he can, under certain circumstances, read a thought. To prove this, he has a volunteer think of a short word and write it on a piece of paper which is then folded, torn, and destroyed by fire. After a moment or two of concentration, the magician divines the word.

What You Need: Paper. Pencil. An ashtray. Matches.

Sleight: The thumb palm.

How It Works: The paper is folded so the center piece with the word on it can be thumb-palmed and read by the conjurer.

How to Do It: If there is any maneuver the magician ought to learn to perfection, this is it. Though easy to do, the Center Tear is probably the greatest secret in mental magic. Volumes have been written about it. Here is the basic procedure: Invent a pretext to draw a circle on a small square of paper about four by six inches. Draw a second circle below it, but let the two intersect so there is an eye-shaped portion right in the middle of the paper. Tell the spectator to write his word in this "eye." The paper is folded in half by the spectator so that it is a four- by three-inch packet. It is folded again in the other direction—the paper is now one fourth its original size. *(Fig. 28)* The magician takes the paper and rips it vertically in half. *(Fig. 29)* He keeps his thumbs close together so that the ripping will be even, then puts the ripped-off pieces in front of the still

CENTER TEAR

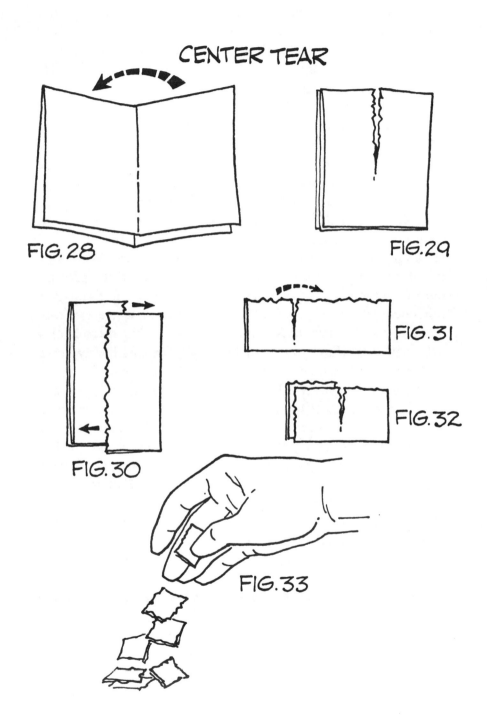

FIG. 28

FIG. 29

FIG. 30

FIG. 31

FIG. 32

FIG. 33

folded piece. *(Fig. 30)* Now he turns the paper packet one quarter rotation so the long sides run left to right. He rips off a piece a third of the way in from the left end and puts this fragment in front of the pieces in the right hand, but flush with the *left* edge. *(Fig. 31)* He makes a final tear, using the edge of the last-ripped piece as a guide. *(Fig. 32)* He puts the newly torn pieces in front of the pieces in the right hand and seems to drop all of them into the ashtray. But the folded piece—the one in back of all the rest—is thumb-palmed as the other bits are dropped. *(Fig. 33)* While the others burn, the folded square is secretly opened and read. Once that is done, the conjurer crumples the square and thrusts it in a pocket.

Tips for Presentation: 1. The drawn circles are not necessary. One could make a square in the center of the paper. But the linked circles provide a reason for limiting the writing space. When I do this effect, I draw one circle and say, "Let's imagine this represents my area of thought." I then draw the second circle. "Let's imagine *this* circle is *your* area of mental influence. Now we can see" —pointing to the eye-shaped middle section—"that there is only one small area where your thoughts may be tapped by my mind. Would you write a small word in that space?" and so on.

2. Though I have used the word "write" throughout, I generally instruct the volunteer to *print* the word, for some handwriting is virtually impossible to read, while printing is nearly always legible. I cover this by explaining that a printed word looks something like a neon sign—and this is exactly the way a word appears in my mind when I read a thought. After the paper is burned, I ask the volunteer to mentally "flash" the word to me as if it were a neon sign, visualizing it to himself the way he printed it. (The neon-sign image derives from genuine ESP research.)

3. To heighten the effect and make it easier to read the hidden word undetected, I have adopted a dodge recommended in one of the numerous texts on the center tear. After obtaining the slip of paper, I put it in a pocket and do not read it. Then I "concentrate" and claim to be "getting" a word of three or four letters . . . "but it is very, very hazy." I say that I have received an impression of roundness on the second letter of the word—*I think.* Then I look at the volunteer to see whether he confirms the statement. If he

does—and many, many words have rounded second letters—I nod with satisfaction and try to "get" the rest of the word but at last confess I cannot make it out clearly enough. If the "rounded" guess is denied, then I simply confess difficulty sooner. In either event, I ask the spectator to write down the word once more and burn it—*but this time I stand as far away from him as possible.* With back turned, I call out and ask him to tell me when he has finished. "I don't want to turn around until the paper is in ashes." Of course, with the back turned, it is now simple to take out the stolen piece of paper and read it at leisure. The volunteer generally remembers only the second writing and burning (because the first time it "didn't work").

4. The method of folding the billet permits the untorn piece of paper to be "billet-switched" for another piece the same size. In this fashion, a hidden blank substitute paper square may be burned while the entire untorn paper is unfolded and read. Some magicians prefer this method, especially in stage shows, where the tearing process is too small to be seen.

KICKAWAY PIP

Basic Illusion: The magician makes a mistake revealing a card—but magically alters the face of the wrong card so it is correct.

How It Looks: A spectator picks a card (the four of hearts) and mixes it in the deck. The magician shows another deck with a different back design and claims he has already removed the correct card. The deck is counted to show it only has fifty-one cards in it. The magician shows the fifty-second card—but it is the five of hearts. However, he rubs the center heart spot and it disappears, leaving the right number of heart pips.

What You Need: Two decks with different back colors. A pair of scissors. A dab of wax.

Sleight: Any force.

Preparation: Remove the five of hearts from one deck and *erase* the center pip with a clean pencil eraser. Take any heart card from the other pack and carefully clip out a single pip. Discard the rest of the cut card. Affix the pip to the center of the doctored five with wax. Put this card in a pocket and place its deck in another pocket. In the other deck, put the four of hearts in forcing position.

How to Do It: Tell the volunteer to pick a card. Force the four of hearts, and have the volunteer replace it. Set the deck aside and produce the other pack. Have the volunteer count it face down on the table. Now show the doctored five and ask for confirmation that it is the card the volunteer originally chose. When he says it is incorrect, ask how far off you were. When the four is named, brighten and say something like, "I can fix that easily." Then kick away the waxed pip with a flick of the index finger. To many, it will appear that the pip has vanished—and even those that see it fly away will be surprised.

Tips for Presentation: 1. Build the effect as if it were a real mental miracle, then undercut the serious tone with a happy smile and casual flickoff at the end.

2. Before flicking the pip, be sure the card is held high. Pause long enough to draw all attention to the card.

3. Onstage, this trick may be done with jumbo cards. The flick may have to be delivered with several fingers.

SUCKER ACE CHANGE

Basic Illusion: The magician claims he can change a three of spades to an ace of the same suit. But he begins so clumsily that the spectator is sure he knows the secret. He is wrong.

How It Looks: The magician holds the cards in one hand and shows the bottom card, which he *says* is the ace of spades. However, it is really the three. His fingers very clumsily hide the upper and lower spade pips. Furthermore, the center spade is small, not like the usual giant pip used for the ace of that suit. The magician claims he will change the ace to the three just by laying it face down on the table. As he says this, he turns the cards downward—but as he does so, his fingers let go too soon and the spectator clearly sees the card as the three of spades. The magician lays it face down on the table, and says it has now become a three. The spectator protests that it was *always* a three. The magician, "insulted," says it is an ace and suggests the spectator see for himself. Sure enough, when the card is turned over it is the *ace* of spades.

Preparation: Put the ace of spades second from the bottom and the three on the bottom of the pack.

Sleight: The glide.

How It Works: The three is pulled back and the ace put on the table.

How to Do It: Show the three with the hand in "glide" position. The thumb of that hand covers the top spade spot while the thumb of the other hand rests awkwardly on the other. Remove both thumbs too soon when turning the cards down for the glide. Pull out the ace and lay it face down on the table. Let the spectator turn it over himself; when he does, quickly cut the deck once to bury the three and put the deck on the table.

Tips for Presentation: 1. The opening moves are purposely clumsy so the spectator will be sure to see the three of spades. I have never known anyone, no matter how timid, to keep silent on this point. The magician is invariably called down for daring to foist off such a poor trick. The climax is a real surprise because of the setup.

2. I use this trick primarily as an ice-breaker. When someone tells a third party that I am a magician, and I am challenged to "do a trick," I often start with this one. The reason is simple: the challenger's tone often tells me that he has seen many poor conjurers and expects no better this time. By starting with this effect, I reinforce his initial impression—but at the end, he undergoes a corresponding reversal of sentiment and is impressed all the more for having been had. Naturally, the climax must not be played in smart-alecky fashion; the spectator must be entertained, not annoyed. When the magician pretends to be offended by the challenge, he should do so good-humoredly, clearly communicating that he has been spoofing the spectator.

ELIMINATING CARDS

Basic Illusion: A selected card appears in place of another card that has been placed on the table.

How It Looks: The volunteer selects a card and shuffles it back into the pack. The magician removes eight other cards, shows the first, and ascertains that it is not the chosen one. He deals it face down on the table, then puts the next card, unshown, back in the deck. He repeats the process till he has only four cards left. Squaring them up, he shows the bottom card to double-check that it is not the chosen card, then deals it face down, and puts the next one back in the deck. He shows the third card, which is still not the chosen one, deals it face down, and puts the last one back in the pack. Now the spectator picks one of the two remaining cards and discards the other. When the last card is turned over, it has apparently changed into the selected one.

Sleights: Either a force or the thumb pushback. The glide. Magician's choice (explained below).

How It Works: The selected card is either a forced one or is controlled to the bottom of the deck. The glide is then used to substitute it for the cards shown to the spectator.

How to Do It: This trick appears in one of Harry Blackstone's books of magic and is my favorite card effect. The final revelation is astounding to the spectator because the magician seems to be working with irrelevant cards all during the trick. The magician either forces a card or controls the chosen one to the bottom with the aid of the thumb pushback. He now seems to take a heap of cards at random from the bottom of the deck and counts off a few. What he really does is assemble a heap of eight cards, with the selected card second from the bottom. He shows the bottom card, is told it is not the correct one, and supposedly deals it face down. He really executes the glide and puts the chosen card on the table. He discards the real bottom card into the deck. Now he shows the third card, really deals it face down, and eliminates the next card and proceeds till four cards are on the table. He squares these up, examines these for a moment with some perplexity. (This helps disguise his deliberate placement of the chosen card back in second-from-bottom position.) He shows the bottom card again, does the glide, deals the chosen card, eliminates the next, and repeats so that there are now only two cards left on the table. (The magician must remember which is the chosen card.) Now comes a dodge known as the Magician's Choice—a force of the chosen card. The spectator is told he must eliminate one of the two cards, no matter which, and is asked to put his finger on one or the other. If he puts his finger on the chosen card, the magician says, "Good. Then we'll keep that one and eliminate *this,*" suiting the word to the action of burying the other card in the pack. If the spectator chooses the other card, the magician merely tells him to bury that one in the deck.

Tips for Presentation: 1. Though either a force or a pushback may be used, I would prefer the pushback because the spectator then may freely select any card from a fanned deck.

2. The magician might appear a trifle uncertain when he first squares up the heap of eight cards and again when he picks up the remaining four cards. This will make his actions appear random, rather than a deliberate ordering of the cards.

3. At the climax, one might confess defeat and ask the spectator to reveal the name of his card. When he does, the magician acts relieved and says, "Oh, *that* one!" and asks the spectator to pick up the last card.

TWO REVERSED CARDS

Basic Illusion: Two cards are selected and found reversed in the deck.

How It Looks: A spectator picks a card and replaces it on the top of the deck. The magician shuffles the cards and has a second spectator pick another card. The magician has him shove the second card into the middle of the deck. The pack is now cut and shuffled, then ribbon-spread along the table with backs up. The two chosen cards appear in the middle of the spread, both face up.

Sleights: Reverse sliparound. False shuffle. Card spread.

How It Works: The reverse sliparound is used for the first card, which then disguises the bottom of the pack as the top.

How to Do It: Have a spectator choose a card and replace it on top of the deck. Use the reverse sliparound to get it to the bottom facing the rest of the pack. Execute a false shuffle so the chosen card stays on the bottom. Fan the cards and have another volunteer select a second one. Now square the deck and in the process turn it over so the reversed chosen card is seen, disguised as the top of the pack. Have the volunteer put the second card in the middle of the deck—it actually goes in reversed. Turn the pack back over as you cut it, then shuffle it. Spread the cards on the table or fan them in the hands and the chosen cards will be seen reversed.

Tips for Presentation: 1. Use many shuffles in this routine so the deck seems well mixed. This also helps keep the pack in the magician's hands, where it must be turned over and back. These moves must be done casually while the hands fidget with the cards to cover the various moves. Meanwhile, the magician keeps up a stream of talk to keep the audience's attention diverted.

2. This trick works well in front of a fair-sized group. In such a case, have the two cards picked by spectators on opposite sides of the audience. The necessary crossover from one side to another gives the magician extra time and movement to hide the finger-work.

STOP ME ANYTIME

How It Looks: The magician writes a prediction, then begins dealing cards one at a time from the top of the pack. A spectator stops him at any time. The magician shows the next card on top of the pack. It corresponds with his prediction.

Sleight: Top glide.

How to Do It: The card to be forced is on top of the pack. The thumb keeps peeling it back under cover of the dealing hand, which pulls out the second card each time. When he is told to stop, the magician slowly grasps and turns over the top card.

Tips for Presentation: This effect works best with a "beeback" deck, which has red crisscross lines on it. These are very confusing to the eye.

CARD PUSHUP

Basic Illusion: A chosen card rises in the deck.

How It Looks: A volunteer picks a card, which is then shuffled back into the deck. The magician removes a group of cards, arranges them, and puts them back in the deck, then shows the pack to the spectator. A card is sticking out at the top, but it is not the selected card. The magician shoves it back into the deck, but another card immediately rises "by itself." It is the correct one.

Sleights: Any force or location.

How It Works: The manner in which the cards are sandwiched puts the chosen card in position to be shoved up.

How to Do It: Force a card, or control the one that the volunteer chose to the bottom. Remove five cards, including the chosen card, and arrange them face up so the chosen one is next to the bottom. Now jog both the chosen card and the fourth card up from the other three. *(Fig. 34)* Square them and place this heap in the center of the pack with the jogged cards sticking up. Only the wrong card is seen at this time. Hold the deck in one hand, with fingers wrapped around the width of the cards, back of the hand to the audience. The pinky should be at the bottom narrow edge opposite the up-jogged cards, and the cards should be gripped tightly. Now the other hand with one fingertip smartly pushes both cards down into the deck. *(Fig. 35)* This action causes a card to protrude from the bottom of the deck. The pinky shoves this card up (Fig. 36), causing the chosen card to rise from the deck.

DOUBLE-COINCIDENCE AND PREDICTION MIRACLE

Basic Illusion: The magician predicts the identity of two cards. The spectator locates one of them in a strange manner.

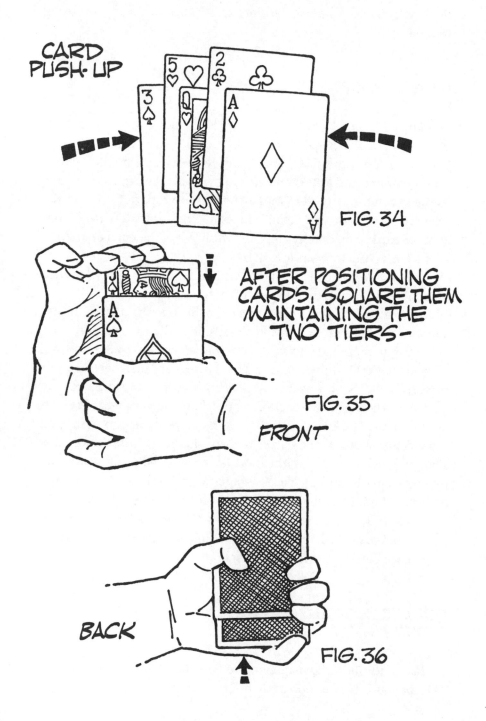

CARD PUSH-UP

FIG. 34

AFTER POSITIONING CARDS, SQUARE THEM MAINTAINING THE TWO TIERS—

FIG. 35

FRONT

BACK

FIG. 36

How It Looks: The magician writes the name of a certain card on a piece of paper and puts it aside; this is his "prediction." He takes a felt-tip pen and writes a second card prediction on the face of the bottom card of the pack, then buries the card. A second card is picked by the volunteer and memorized, then replaced in the deck and shuffled. The magician now hands the pen to the spectator and asks him to mark a large X on the back of the top card. After this is done, the marked card is shuffled into the deck. Finally the volunteer is asked to put the pack behind his back and, without looking, draw a circle on the face of any card. When this is done, and the marked card has been cut back into the deck to lose it, the magician takes the pack and ribbon-spreads it on the table. Finding the card with the X on the back, the magician turns it over to reveal that the spectator drew the circle on the face of the very same card. But that's not all: the name of the chosen card is written across the face of the marked one. Finally the written prediction is opened and it corresponds to the value of the marked card. It is an uncanny case of a double prediction and an odd coincidence.

Sleights: False shuffles. Forces.

What You Need: A slip of paper and a deck of cards. Two felt-tip pens.

Preparation: Throw away the ink supply of one pen, or use it until it has run bone-dry. Now draw a shaky circle on the face of another card with the second felt-tip pen. (Let us assume that the circle has been drawn on the ace of diamonds.) Now write in small script on the face of the same card the identity of any other card (for instance, the seven of clubs). Put the marked card second from the top and cover it with the card whose name has been written across it. (In our example, the top card is the seven of clubs; the second, the marked ace of diamonds.) Put both pens in an inside coat pocket.

How It Works: Both cards are forced and the critical writing is faked.

How to Do It: Take a slip of paper and write with the good pen "ace of diamonds"—that is, the name of the card with writing on it. Put the pen inside the pocket and fold the paper up. Give it to someone to hold. Take the cards from the case and take out the dry pen. Pretend to write on the bottom card and bury it in the pack. Put away the pen again and force the top card. (The top countoff will work well here.) Have it remembered and buried in the deck. False-shuffle the pack, leaving the new top card uppermost. Now take out the working pen and have the spectator draw an X on its back. Put the pen away and bury the top card, executing a genuine shuffle. Turn the cards face up and have the volunteer hold them that way behind his back. Give him the dry pen and have him "draw" by feel a circle on the bottom card. Take back the pen and the deck and proceed to make the several revelations.

Tips for Presentation: 1. You might patter about the difference between deliberate actions—yours—and the spectator's accidental ones.

2. Take time at the climax to explain how unlikely all the coincidences would be. Build up the tension before each revelation, never stopping till the end. This uncanny bit of magic was first shown me by the late Alwyn Stevenson, who demonstrated only the circle-drawing coincidence. Later it was marketed by Harry Lorayne in the same presentation and, at this writing, can still be purchased from many dealers under the name of Predict-O—a worthwhile investment, since it can get tedious waiting for a felt pen to run dry. The routine here presented is my own. I can attest to its overwhelming effect on small groups of people.

IMPOSSIBLE LOCATION

Basic Illusion: A spectator finds the card another spectator selected without any help from the magician.

How It Looks: The magician spreads the cards ribbon fashion with backs up and asks a spectator to withdraw a card *without looking at it*. Instead, he has the volunteer make a small pencil mark on the card's back, then replace it in the deck. The magician immediately ribbon-spreads the deck face up and asks another volunteer to put his finger on *any* card. He does so, and the card with the pencil mark is found.

What You Need: A pencil. A deck of cards.

Sleights: Key card. Card spread.

How It Works: A key card tells the magician where the chosen card lies. He causes the second spectator to choose properly.

How to Do It: All the magician needs do is note the identity of the bottom card. When the unknown card is drawn forth to be marked, the magician gathers the pack together, and has the unknown card replaced on the top of the deck. Then he cuts the pack so that the key card ends up just above the unknown card. (The cut also puts both cards roughly in the middle of the pack.)

The magician ribbon-spreads the pack face up, and looks for the key card. He knows that the card to the right of it is the one with the pencil mark. The magician carefully spreads the cards so that the faces of the key and chosen cards are more visible than any other. When the second volunteer is told to put his finger *immediately* on the first card he sees, chances are he will either pick the chosen card or one of the cards right next to it. If he does, the magician turns the card over; or, if the adjacent one was picked, he says, "I see you put your finger on the card right next to *this one*—" and pulls out the proper card, turning it over.

If the volunteer should touch a card several inches away from the right one, the magician will have to spell out its name, moving toward the marked one. He must estimate the number of letters needed and spell accordingly. (Example: The volunteer touches the three of spades. It is only five cards away, so the magician spells "three"; if, on the other hand, it is quite far from the marked card, he may have to spell out "the three of spades.") The spelling, if not properly estimated, can be corrected by pulling the card out and turning it over while the last letters are named. Other dodges will suggest themselves in practice.

Tips for Presentation: 1. This was also shown me by Alwyn Stevenson. Al told me he once did it in a pub and had a dart player throw a dart at the cards. He hit the marked one by pure chance—and a rare miracle apparently came to pass. (Al left right afterward; it was a tough act to follow.)

2. The imprecision of the ending is unfortunate. It *is* possible to make this trick fail-safe by holding the volunteer's hand and guiding it—actually pushing it right onto the card. This ending is less

effective, though, than allowing free choice to the volunteer. Though there is an element of chance involved at the end of the trick, it should be noted that the magician knows the identity of the marked card, but no one else does. So even if it is necessary to spell halfway across the deck, the finale is still perplexing. However, most of the time the volunteer will put his finger right on or near the marked card. Hurrying him along will help strengthen the likelihood that he will go for the central, most easily visible cards.

It is now time to consider a more ambitious form of magic, the routine—a series of effects which flow into a cohesive whole with dramatic shape and logical build of interest from the first effect upward to the climax. Below is a cut-and-restored-rope effect which I was taught by Alwyn Stevenson and later modified with a few opening moves. It is a routine that I employ often as an act-opener. The moves are not difficult but should be followed carefully with rope in hand.

CUT AND RESTORED ROPES

Basic Illusion: The magician ties and unties some magical knots in a piece of rope, then cuts it and restores it. He also "stretches" it.

How It Looks: There are seven distinct magical effects in this routine. In order, they are:

1. Appearance of a knot.
2. Unusually rapid tying of a second knot.
3. Disappearance of a third knot.
4. Restoring a cut rope.
5. Cutting the rope without scissors.
6. Stretching two pieces of rope to the same size.
7. Changing the two pieces of rope to one piece.

The magician shows the rope and flips one end into his other hand a few times, letting the end dangle down from it. On the third flip, there is a knot in the end of the rope. This is the first effect.

The magician unties the knot, takes the ends of the rope in both hands, and quickly brings them together and apart. A knot is in the

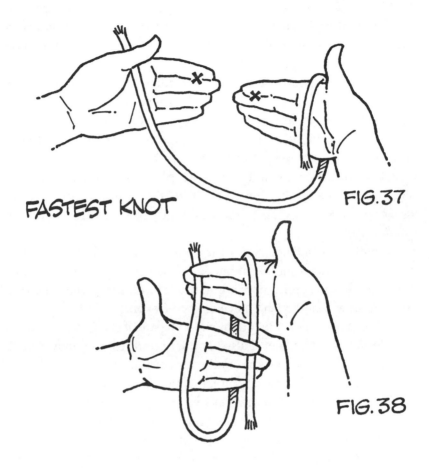

FASTEST KNOT

FIG. 37

FIG. 38

center of the rope. This is the second effect, and is called "the fastest knot in the world."

The magician unties the knot and ties another one in the center of the rope. Passing his hand over it, he causes it to disappear (third effect).

The rope is folded in half and the ends are held in one hand, with the middle hanging down. The magician takes the middle and holds it between the ends. He cuts the middle so there are four ends held in his hand. He lets the right-hand ends drop, and it appears that he is holding two short pieces of rope side by side in one hand. With the other, he takes hold of one of the dangling ends, grabs an upper end, and slides the rope through the stationary hand. The rope is now in one piece (fourth effect).

Tying the rope into a loop, the magician "sharpens" his fingers against his teeth and "cuts" the rope near the knot. The loop appears to be cut and the magician lets one end drop. He now seems to be holding a long piece of rope onto which is knotted a shorter section of rope (fifth effect).

He unties the knot and holds both pieces in one hand, side by side. One piece is long, the other short. By pulling smartly on the dangling lower ends, he "stretches" both ropes to the same size (sixth effect).

Finally, the magician ties the two ropes together and wraps them around the knuckles of one hand. He gets his wand and taps the rope. With a spiral unwinding motion, he twirls the rope free and it is now a single long piece of rope (seventh effect).

What You Need: A length of rope. A pair of scissors.

Sleights: Fastest knot. False knot. Cut and restored moves.

Preparation: Tie one knot in the end of the rope.

How to Do It: For the first effect, conceal the pretied knot in one hand. Flip the other end the first two times, then change ends and flip the *knotted* rope end the last time. Untie the knot.

For the "fastest knot in the world," hold one end of the rope between the thumb and fingers on one hand and let it hang down on the palm side in a loop. The other end of the rope is passed over the back of the second hand and draped loosely over the crotch of the thumb. It hangs down slightly behind the hand. *(Fig. 37)* Bring the hands together with the hand that has the rope draped on it *in front.* Pinch each end of rope between the index and middle fingers of the opposite hand. *(Fig. 38)* Draw the hands apart and the knot will automatically be tied. Untie knot.

For the disappearing knot effect, use the maneuver described in the previous chapter under "False Knot."

For the first restoration, hold the two ends of the rope in one hand and let the middle hang down in a long loop. Let this loop lay lightly on the thumb and fingers of the other hand and start to lift

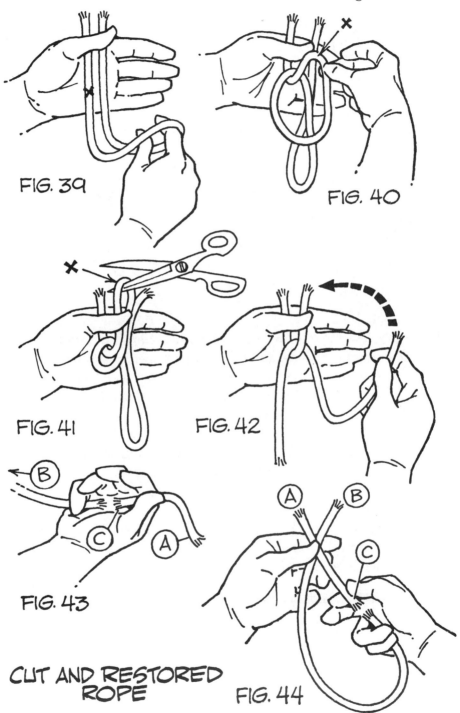

FIG. 39

FIG. 40

FIG. 41

FIG. 42

B

C

A

FIG. 43

A

B

C

CUT AND RESTORED
ROPE

FIG. 44

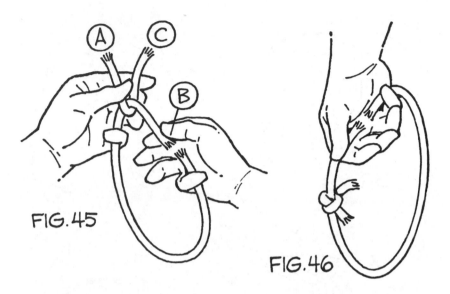

FIG.45

FIG.46

the loop towards the fingertips of the stationary hand. But in the process, grasp the left-hand end at a point X *(Fig. 39)* and pull a small loop through the big center loop. Put this small loop between the two ends of the rope and grasp it. The real middle of the rope will be concealed by the palm of the stationary hand. *(Fig. 40)* Cut the fake middle with the scissors *(Fig. 41)*, then let the two resultant right-hand ends drop. Put down the scissors and grab hold of either dangling rope end and bring it upward. With the same hand, grasp either upper end. *(Fig. 42)* Rapidly pull the linked short piece *(Fig. 42)* through the stationary hand and let that hand get a new hold on the extreme end of the longer rope. The rope is now apparently restored. Actually, one hand holds the end of a long piece of rope, while the other hand holds the ends of both the long and short pieces together, hiding the juncture to make it look like a single length of rope. *(Fig. 43)*

The cutting movement without scissors: For clarity, let us call the *free* end of the short piece A. The end of the short piece hidden in the hand is C. The free end of the long piece is B. The magician must cross ends A and B so that the rope is looped. *(Fig. 44)* He pretends to tie ends A and B together. But under cover of the fingers, he switches C for B and sticks B back into the hand so it is concealed with the other end of the long piece. *(Fig. 45)* The rope, once tied, looks like a single piece with the ends knotted. It is really a single long piece with a short piece knotted around it. The ends of the long piece are concealed in one hand. *(Fig. 46)* It is easy to pretend to cut the rope with the bare fingers. As the snipping motion is made, the other hand just lets one of the concealed ends drop.

Stretching the ropes: Untie the little knotted rope carefully and unfold it so it is linked with the long rope. The ends of the short rope stick up and the ends of the long rope dangle down. (This is the same position as Fig. 41, except that one end of the long rope is considerably higher than the other.) By grasping both dangling ends and pulling them through the linked upper rope, the long rope evens out. To the audience it appears as if the magician "evened up" two separate lengths of rope.

The final restoration: Reknot the short piece on the long piece. The audience will think you have tied two equal-length ropes together at the ends. While wrapping the long piece around the knuckles of the stationary hand, you will find that the short piece slides right off. (Let it do so under the cover of the hand doing the wrapping.) Palm it in the moving hand and dispose of it when reaching for the wand.

Tips for Presentation: 1. Execute all moves slowly and gracefully. The gratuitous twirling at the end adds to the slickness, and is a signal that the routine is ended.

2. The magician should not pause for applause after each effect. The routining of so many effects together builds to a single strong climax. I have found there are only two legitimate spots for applause in this routine—after the disappearing knot, and at the very end.

3. As an example of patter, I have set below the entire script *I* use in this routine. Let me repeat that another magician's patter should never be copied verbatim. It is better to find one's own things to say. Even if another script is particularly appealing because it fits the magician's style, it still should be tailored to an exact fit. The following script runs pretty much the same every time

I play this routine, yet there are small adjustments each time, depending on circumstances.

CUT-AND-RESTORED PATTER	ACTION
"I like to do tricks with ropes. Whenever I do, people never say I'm using trapdoors or mirrors or secret compartments. Besides, ropes are cheaper than trapdoors and mirrors and secret compartments.	Show rope.

Flip rope.

Flip rope. |
"Now here's a rope that likes girls. Every time I say 'Sophia Loren,' it ties itself in knots.	Flip knotted end. (Effect #1)
"Here's a little something that looks very easy but is really very hard. I call it the fastest knot in the world.	Tie knot. (Effect #2)
"There's only one trouble with this rope. It's fine for tying knots in—if it's in the mood. But if it isn't, then one, two, three—it disappears.	Tie false knot.
	Brush knot away. (Effect #3)
"Now we'll give our rope a little punishment. If I hold the ends here . . . the middle will hang down like this.	Hold ends with the middle down.
"Now I take the middle—so . . .	Pick up middle and cut the fake loop.
"Which leaves two ropes. *(Slight pause)* I can never remember if I use this end or that—well, whichever—I just give them a pull and restore the rope . . ."	Drop ends.

Restore rope. (Effect #4) |

(First applause)

"I now tie the rope in a loop. And cut it . . . wait a minute, I don't want to wear out my scissors . . .

Do so.

Hold fingers like scissors and "sharpen" by drawing over teeth.

"Here we go.

Making cutting action with fingers. (Effect #5)

"I cut it too near the end . . . because now I have one long and one short rope. But I can fix *that*.

Untie the knot.

Pull on the rope ends. (Effect #6)

"Now I have two equal ropes which I proceed to tie into a knot.

Do so, and wrap the rope around knuckles of the hand.

"With a little help from my magic wand . . .

Get wand, leaving knotted rope behind. Wave wand.

"Once again we have one rope."

Twirl rope free. (Effect #7)

(Second applause)

This patter is obviously the process type. It may not seem economical, but extra verbiage is needed to fill in while the various manipulations are executed. Note that the schematic arrangement is approximate. Some moves come a little before or after the cue words. Others are made *during* a certain speech. In any script the magician may follow, it will be necessary to experiment until the exact timing of motion and speech is found.

MORE TRICKS

Many excellent effects are available that rely wholly or in part on simple sleight of hand. Most are obtainable from any dealer. Here are a few that I recommend:

Coaster Coin Dazzler: This is a routine involving two beer mats and a small coin. The mats are placed over the mouth of a glass and the coin seems to penetrate the mats and fall inside the tumbler. The trick can be prolonged by using an Okito Coin Box (described below). An import from Holland, Coaster Coin Dazzler is based on the use of two identical magnetic coins. Each beer mat contains magnets. The trick requires skill in palming a small coin.

The Devil Box: This small box holds a coin which can be "stolen" via a false bottom.

The 4 Blacks: This splendid Dr. Jaks card trick involves four "blank" black cards. Two are picked and sandwiched together. The pips of a selected card are found on the face of one of these black cards. The method employs a simple sleight to conceal the preprinted card face from view. Naturally the chosen card is forced.

Mystic Coins: This is an excellent routine involving the vanishing and transpositions of several coins with a gimmicked cover which is able to wedge one coin inside it temporarily. Some palming is helpful.

Okito Coin Box: This is a useful tool for vanishing coins. It is a small metal box which has a lid that fits over either end. By putting the lid on the wrong side, the magician can let the coin drop into his hand. A moderately difficult sleight must be learned for handling the box, and palming is required.

Stretching Card: After forcing a ten, the magician pulls a card partway from his pocket. It seems to be a three. When the spectator says the card is wrong and should be a ten, the magician pulls out the rest of the card. It has ten spots, one beneath the other, and is over a foot long. This is a cute closing trick.

Svengali Deck: This basic tool can be used for forcing and many other purposes. Every other card is the same and cut short so that two can be lifted as one. The deck has many applications and requires little fingerwork to operate.

Tommy Windsor's Insurance Policy: The magician claims he will pay a sum of money to the spectator if he fails to name the chosen card. He even holds up an insurance policy which supposedly covers failure during performance. The magician does not get the correct card by name but when he opens the insurance policy, a giant picture of the right card appears, and the spectator cannot collect. A force is required.

Wild Cards: This is one of Frank Garcia's greatest effects. Eight cards of the same denomination are shown, and one "wild card" is also held up. After some very fair-looking moves, the eight cards all change to the same identity as the wild card. The trick employs specially printed cards and a false count which is moderately hard to learn, but is well worth the trouble.

Zip: A handkerchief stuffed in a pill phial is rolled into a piece of paper. When the paper is unwrapped by a spectator, the cloth is gone. An inner plastic shell to the phial slips out into the performer's hand as he is twisting one end of the enveloping paper. Palming of the shell is necessary.

8

Stacking the Deck

> The very best method of performing a given trick is the
> easiest method, and it is the method which should be
> used.
>
> Jean Hugard and Fred Braue, in
>
> *Expert Card Technique*

If you browse through magic literature, you may be struck by the preponderance of card tricks over any other kind. There are several reasons that could explain this fact, but the best is probably the simple fact that cards are available in practically every home.

Though I am a devotee of card magic myself, I have often felt uneasy about tricks which begin with the hoary command to "Pick a card, any card." Merely rephrasing the request is no solution. The trouble is that many people consider card tricks—especially in informal, close-up situations—a bore.

Naturally, a good magician who really knows how to amuse—and also knows *when to stop*—will surmount this difficulty. It will still be impossible for him to completely avoid having someone select a card, but sometimes he can vary the pace with a card effect that employs an entirely different scenario. Even when card selection is essential, a novel plot to the trick may also serve to liven things up. (In the previous chapter, Impossible Location and Dual-coincidence and Prediction Mystery have such out-of-the-ordinary plots.)

I am especially partial to card systems and setups, which often are associated with offbeat effects. Not only are they easy to perform—frequently automatic—but they often yield miraculous results. Though I can think of *one or two* setups that are popular with most conjurers, I suspect that the average amateur is too busy perfecting his sleight of hand to experiment much with this branch of card magic.

What are systems and setups? Both are ways of stacking the deck. A system is a secret method of arranging the cards so that the magician can perform a variety of locations, divinations, or other effects. In a setup, the pack is also set in a prearranged order, but usually in order to accomplish some specific trick or sequence of tricks.

The crucial test of any system or setup is whether or not it can be detected upon casual examination of the pack. The best systems are virtually undecipherable, while good setups are either equally invisible or at least disguisable.

The next several pages will describe a few systems and setups that I have found especially effective. Though none are difficult to master, some require a moderate amount of memory work and will not appeal to every conjurer. But those willing to do the requisite homework will be well rewarded.

LOCATION SYSTEMS

EIGHT KINGS

How It Works: The suits of the pack are alternated in the "bridge" manner: clubs, hearts, diamonds, spades. Thus the first card will be a club, the second a heart, and so on throughout the deck. There is a simple mnemonic device for remembering this order: *Cards Have Deceptive Skill.* (Or invent your own phrase.) The value of the cards is arranged according to an old poem which keys the sequence:

>   Eight kings threatened to save
>   Ninety-five ladies for one sick knave

The translation of this doggerel is:

>   Eight king three ten two seven (save-en)
>   Nine five queen four ace six jack

Thus the order of an "eight kings" pack would run:

8C	KD	3H	10S	2C	7D
9H	5S	QC	4D	AH	6S	JC
8D	KH	3S	10C	2D	7H

—and so on throughout the full fifty-two-card sequence.

By stacking the deck in this order and remembering the rhyme and suit arrangement, the magician can tell what card is above and below any card cut.

Example: The magician riffles the cards and has a spectator stick his finger in the deck at any point. The magician cuts off the cards above the finger and puts that heap at the bottom of the deck. The spectator looks at the card beneath his finger. Meanwhile, the magician notes the card now at the bottom of the deck. Let's say it is the queen of diamonds. Since this card originally was right above the card the spectator has looked at, the magician knows it must be the four of hearts.

SI STEBBINS

How It Works: This method of stacking is easier to learn than the Eight Kings arrangement. However, it is somewhat simpler for a spectator to detect, if anyone really wants to look *that* hard (which is doubtful).

The same suit rotation is employed in this system, but the order of cards works on purely mechanical intervals of three. Thus, if the first card of the pack is the six of clubs, the next would be the nine of diamonds, followed by the queen of hearts, followed by the two of spades (which "turns the corner" from king back down to ace). The cards are arranged throughout in this manner, so that the magician need only note where the pack has been cut, then count three back or forward, depending on which card he wishes to identify.

Here is a card trick with a "mental" plot. It can be done with either the Eight Kings or Si Stebbins systems.

TWO-CARD DIVINATION

Basic Illusion: The magician reveals the identities of two selected cards.

How It Looks: The magician shuffles a deck of cards, then hands it to a spectator and moves several feet away from him. He asks a volunteer to cut the pack and put it in his pocket. Then he suggests that the volunteer reach in, take the top card of the deck, and hold it up. The volunteer does so and the magician tries to divine its identity, but fails. Asking the spectator to concentrate more intensely, the magician has to repeat the experiment and succeeds the second time. Then he ponders for a moment and predicts what the next card will be. The spectator removes the next card on top of the pack, and the prediction proves to be right.

How It Works: The cards are arranged according to any system.

How to Do It: False-shuffle the cards and then give the pack to the spectator. When he calls out the first card by name, the system will automatically tell you what cards will come next.

Tips for Presentation: 1. Though one could read several cards by this method, stop at two—it is more than enough.

2. Perform the "mental magic" in the usual manner: as if you are trying to capture elusive thoughts.

3. When the spectator cuts the pack, try to glimpse the bottom card if you can. Then though you miss the first time, it can be a near thing—a two instead of three, for example. (*Do* miss: it builds the suspense.)

Mnemonic systems are entirely different in principle from mechanical ones. Though much harder to master, they are well worth the effort, since the results can be positively staggering.

BASIC MNEMONIC CODING

How It Works: A mnemonic system works on the principle that each card can be assigned a code word, while another set of code words can be assigned each number, in this case from one to fifty-two. By arranging the pack in any order at all, then forming mental pictures that use both code words, the magician can commit to memory the exact location of any card. With this information, he can then do anything a mechanical system offers. But he can also tell precisely how many cards are in a heap just by noting the bottom card and remembering its numerical value (as long as the deck is in the proper order and has not been cut). In addition he also can tell anyone how many cards down from the top any called-for card is.

A mnemonic system is built in several stages. Here is the way one works:

Stage One. Learn by heart an arbitrary group of symbols for the numbers one through zero. Here is a possible set (though the magician may substitute any other sound he wishes, the list below does relate the numbers to the sounds):

1	*l* (for "one stroke")
2	*n* (for "two strokes")
3	*m* (for "three strokes")
4	*r* (end of the word "four")
5	*f* (first letter of "five")
6	*p* or *b* (some similarity of shape)
7	*t* (some similarity of shape)
8	*sh* (similar sound to "eight-sh")
9	*k* (similar shape)
0	*z* or *s* (like start of word "zero")

Stage Two. Once the above has been memorized, it is a simple matter to build up and learn a system of code words for the numbers one through fifty-two. It is best to make up one's own words, but here are some examples:

1—ow*l*	20—*nose*
2—he*n*	32—*moon*
3—ha*m*	47—*rat*
15—*loaf*	52—*fan*

Now one must construct a set of key words that identify the

various cards. The easiest way is to start each key word with the same first letter as the card's suit, then end the word with a letter corresponding to the numerical value. Here are some examples:

4C—*car*	7D—*dot*	9H—*hug*	AS—*sail*
10C—*kiss*	3D—*dome*	5H—*huff*	2S—*sun*

All key words must be nouns or verbs that can be easily visualized mentally.

The picture cards can be given special names pertaining to their "sex," rank, and suit, or they can be treated in the same fashion as the other cards, giving them the numerical equivalents of eleven, twelve, and thirteen for jack, queen, and king, respectively. The proper method to use is the one that fixes the strongest mental picture in your mind. If the personality technique is utilized, the cards might be assigned such titles as:

JC—Caveboy	JH—Cupid	JD—Robber	JS—Gravedigger
QC—Cavewoman	QH—Bride		
KC—Caveman	KH—Groom	And so on	

The reasons for the names ought to be immediately apparent and easy to recollect; otherwise they are useless.

Stage Three. Once the magician has memorized key words for all numbers from one to fifty-two, as well as a second set of key words for every card in the deck, he must set about forging a series of memory links between each number and the card opposite it.

This is done by arranging the cards in *any* order whatsoever, then writing on a piece of paper the numbers from one to fifty-two and which cards correspond to each position in the deck. A correlation is made in the mind between each number-key word and the opposite-card key word. For instance, let us imagine that the first ten cards from the top of the deck are:

1—QD	3—7H	5—AS	7—8H	9—2C
2—3C	4—7D	6—KC	8—2H	10—JS

Let us assign arbitrary key words. For the numbers:

1—owl	6—bee
2—hen	7—toy
3—ham	8—shoe
4—arrow	9—key
5—ivy	10—louse

For the cards:

QD—princess	KC—caveman
3C—comb	8H—hash
7H—hat	2H—honey
7D—dot	2C—can
AS—sail	JS—gravedigger

With this information, we can forge the various memory links that will tell us which card is at each position—from one to ten—and later, for *every* position in the deck. For instance, we might visualize the following pictures for numbers one to five:

1—An *owl* is robbing the *princess'* jewels.

2—The *hen* lays eggs shaped like *combs.*

3—The *ham* wears a *hat.*

4—A man *dots* his *i*'s with an *arrow.*

5—A ship's *sail* is made of *ivy.*

It is best to form one's own mental pictures; they will be the most memorable. It is perhaps an unfortunate comment on human nature, but most memory experts agree that embarrassing, violent, and obscene mental pictures seem to have much greater staying power in the mind.

In the process of forging mental links for every card and position, it is essential to close the eyes and *clearly see* the mental image for a few seconds. Then dismiss it and go on to the next card and number. If the images are strong enough, they will be simple to recall.

Here is an example of the utility of this system: a spectator picks a card and cuts the deck at that point. The magician notes the bottom card, remembers its key word, instantly thinks of the mental picture (no effort is necessary if the link is strong enough) and in turn remembers the key word for the number. So if the bottom card is the seven of diamonds (the "dot"), the magician thinks of the dot being punctuated with an *arrow*—which is the key for the number four. He knows that the card picked was right below the seven of diamonds, so it must be the fifth card in the prearranged pack. The key word for five is *ivy.* He thinks of the ship's *sail* made out of ivy, and knows that "sail" is the key word for the ace of spades—the selected card. It sounds involved, but the process actually takes only seconds.

With any system of artificial memory, it is wise to review the order of the pack, mentally recalling the key word pictures a few times each week. The easiest way to do this is to hold the deck face down and go through it, one card at a time, trying to name each before it is turned over.

Here is a miraculous way to use a mnemonic system to its utmost.

SILENT CARD CODING

Basic Illusion: The magician performs three feats of mind reading under apparently impossible "test" conditions.

How It Looks: The magician explains that a true mind reader never has to ask the subject to write anything or in any way communicate with him; all the subject has to do is think of a word or object. A volunteer is asked onstage, and the performer picks up a slate and writes something. Then he explains that he has three possible ways to perform a mental test: choosing one of a group of coins; choosing a word from a dictionary; and choosing a card from a pack. The magician asks the volunteer to name one method, then turns the slate around to show that he has predicted the choice. Explaining that he tried this first test to see whether the subject would pick up the magician's thought, the performer now hands the pack of cards to the volunteer and asks him to shuffle it and put it in its case. After this is done, the volunteer blindfolds the performer, then is instructed to go into the audience and hand the pack to any other member of the audience. The volunteer receives these instructions aloud from the blindfolded magician, but is told not to answer aloud so no one can claim that a code is being used. Next the volunteer freely selects two audience members to think of a card; one thinks the suit, the other the denomination. The magician says they must whisper their choices to the original volunteer to make sure neither of them later changes or forgets the choice. When the volunteer has heard the cumulative choices, he silently places the blackboard in the magician's hands. This, the performer explains, is a signal to him that it is time to make a prediction. The magician explains that he will now attempt to divine first the suit and then the rank of the thought-of card. He does so, writing down his conjectures and showing them *before* they are named. As a final test, he asks the audience member holding the pack of cards to open it and count down from the top until he finds the chosen card. He is to think of this number. The magician concentrates again, and dramatically reveals the correct number.

How It Works: A combination of mnemonics, a confederate, and a special device for silent communication.

What You Need: A pack of cards set in an order that you've mnemonically memorized. A counting device (described below). A blackboard and chalk (or a pad and bold marker). A false blindfold.

Preparation: The cards must be mnemonically arranged and both magician and confederate must become proficient in using the system. The confederate must also be able to perform a false shuffle.

How to Do It: The confederate is called up to "volunteer." Selection of cards as the test medium has been prearranged, so the magician simply writes "cards" on the slate for the first effect. The pack of cards handed out is in the proper mnemonic arrangement, and the confederate pretends to shuffle them but does not disturb the order. The confederate has a small calculator device—the kind sold in many stationery stores—in his pocket. It should be small enough to be palmed. (A typical example of such a gadget is illustrated in Fig. 47.) After he has handed out the cards, the confederate casually slips a hand into his pocket and obtains the device. After he learns the suit and identity of the chosen card, he thinks of the number that corresponds mnemonically to that card and, as he goes back onstage, dials the number on the calculator. (Some calculators can be dialed one-handed with the thumb; others can easily be set by pushing buttons.) When the confederate hands the slate to the magician, he has the device in his open palm for the performer to see. The number keys the identity of the card, and also tells precisely where that card will fall in the prearranged pack. The blindfold, of course, is false. A simple handkerchief-around-the-eyes blindfold will not seriously obstruct vision down the sides of the nose.

Tips for Presentation: 1. This is a "talky" trick for two reasons.

CODING DEVICE

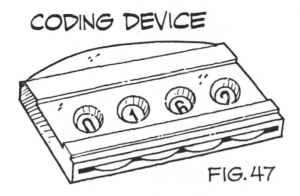

FIG. 47

First, the performer must tell the confederate what to do. Second, he must build up the suspense. The patter should be carefully honed to the essentials, so that the volunteer in the audience who holds the cards will understand what is wanted of him and count down properly to the chosen card. The suspense-building patter, however, must be fully developed. The real impact of this effect lies in the evident fairness of the test. Most mental tricks require the secret thought to be written down or in some way coded. By pointing this out in general terms, the magician helps set up the conditions by which the three divinations amaze the audience. They should build, too, from the first reading to the final location of the chosen card. Care must be taken to instruct the last volunteer not to open the pack before you are ready for the last effect. Then, just before you tell him to look for the chosen card, remind the audience that the deck has been shuffled and, since then, untouched.

2. Though handkerchief blindfolds are little trouble to fashion, the performer might prefer the professional look of commercially manufactured blindfolds. My favorite is Revello's Sightless Vision, which consists of a hood that completely covers the head and is tied around the neck. One side of the hood is opaque, the other transparent, yet the difference is indetectable. Another excellent false blindfold is made of cast iron, and can be obtained from some dealers.

S P E C I A L   S E T U P S

There are probably hundreds of card setups which accomplish various effects of more or less miraculous impact. Some may be found in nearly every important book of card magic, notably those by Walter Gibson, John Scarne, Paul Curry, and Theodore Annemann.

Following are three setups which produce memorable feats of magic.

PAIRED-CARD FORCE DECK

How It Works: This is an arrangement discussed at great length by Eddie Joseph in his manuscript "Bombay," an expensive explanation of an ingenious setup. Basically, the setup consists of discarding four cards of the same rank and substituting four identical cards for them in a strategic position. The rest of the cards are paired by color from ace to king in sequence, then the sequence is repeated.

Following is the exact order. Discard, for instance, the four queens. Then from four other decks obtain four identical cards, say fives of diamonds. Now put a black ace on the table face down and lay a red ace on top of it. On top of these two cards lay a black two, then a red two, and proceed in this manner up to king, always laying down a black card first. Two of the fives of diamonds are put on top of the other twenty-four cards (remember, the queens are missing, so the deck consists of forty-eight cards total, plus the four fives). Now the rest of the cards are assembled in the exact same order as the previous twenty-six: the other black ace, the other red ace, and so on until the remaining two fives of diamonds top the pack. Square all these cards and cut them once. The pack is now ready to be used for forcing the five of diamonds in a convincing fashion. If the spectator takes the pack and looks at the bottom card, doubles its value, and then counts down that far from the top of the deck, he will reach the force card.

Example: The spectator cuts the pack, sees that the bottom card is a six, and doubles it. He counts down twelve cards from the top of the pack—and gets a five of diamonds. The possibilities of such a deck are many—from mind reading and prediction to the simple forcing of a number that will lead the magician to a page of a book which he has memorized—and so on. The pack also can be arranged to force a second card in this manner: instead of four cards of the same denomination, take two pairs of two matching cards, and make sure one pair is red and the other black. When laying the cards down, be sure to put each red force card *over* each black force card. Now when the spectator looks at the bottom card to double it, he will count down to a black card *if he looked at one of that color.* If the bottom card is red, he will count to a red force card.

OUT OF THIS UNIVERSE

How It Works: Paul Curry invented an extremely popular setup called Out of This World. It is a magnificent trick and only suffers from being too well known. But while poking about in a pile of secondhand magic manuscripts, I discovered a repeated-run setup called Unbelievable! by F. Michael Shields and Bascom Jones, Jr. The effect, I believe, is even more astounding than Curry's setup. Since it is, to the best of my knowledge, out of print, I feel it a privilege to present a capsule version of the basic principle.

The pack is divided into the four suits and each red suit is paired with a black suit. Say, for instance, that clubs and diamonds are chosen. The two suits are shuffled together—which leaves twenty-six cards left on the table, the hearts and spades. These are assembled in the *exact random manner* of the first twenty-six and placed together with the other half to make one pack (it is not necessary to memorize this order). Example: the clubs and diamonds have been shuffled together and, from top to bottom of the twenty-six-card pack, are in this order:

7D	4D	10D	KC	5D	7C	AC	JC	QC
3D	8C	KD	AD	2C	3C	2D	4C	9D
9C	QD	5C	6D	10C	6C	JD	8D	

The hearts and spades are set in complementary order. Thus the first cards of the second half of the deck would be:

7H 4H 10H KS 5H 7S, etc.

The two jokers are needed at this point. One is put between the two halves of the deck as they are assembled, the other on the bottom. The magician executes a false shuffle that does not disturb the setup, then quickly ribbon-spreads the pack to show that the cards are different. He removes the joker from the middle, takes that half of the pack, and gives the other half to a spectator, who is told to discard the bottom joker. Now every time the spectator deals a card face down on the table from the top of his pack, the magician places next to it, face up, the card from the top of *his* pack. At the end of the deal, there are twenty-six piles of card pairs. The magician turns these over to show that every card has been matched up with the corresponding card of the same-color suit.

Tips for Presentation: 1. Shields and Jones wisely recommend covering a good deal of the table with the cards that are dealt by conjurer and volunteer. Place one pair far away from the last laid down, and continue so in order to build the psychological impression of a totally random deal.

2. In like fashion, the turnover by the magician ought to proceed from one far distant pile to another. His first remarks can center on the unlikelihood of coincidence bringing more than a few such pairs together. As he turns over more pairs, he steadily increases the tempo.

I will close this sampler of setups with one of my own effects—a force disclosure which provides an unusual triple climax.

MISSING BUT IN GOOD COMPANY

How It Looks: The spectator chooses a card by counting down from the top as many as he wishes. The jokers are discarded, the card replaced and shuffled into the deck, which is then cut. The magician asks for the denomination of the card and, when told, has the spectator deal the same number of piles as the number named, using a portion of the deck. He asks the spectator to pick a pile, and sets the chosen one aside. Then he puts the rest of the pack into the spectator's hands and asks him to deal four face-down piles until the cards are exhausted. When this is done, the magician asks for the name of the chosen card. When he learns what it is, he says it is a peculiar one that likes to go on jaunts away from its family—with that the first pile selected is ribbon-spread face up. It shows a consecutive run of the suit of the chosen card—but that card is missing from its place. Now the magician says that though the card is on a trip, it likes to travel in good company. With that, the magician turns up the top cards of three of the latter four piles dealt. Each has the same-number card as the one selected, but each is a different suit. The last pile is topped by the selected card itself.

How It Works: The setup makes this trick almost automatic. The weak spots are the "casual" showing of the cards early in the trick, and the burying of the chosen card, but these have been disguised. Here is the setup of the pack:

1. Let us assume the forced card is the two of hearts. (It *must* be a two.)

2. Set all four twos aside.

3. Discard ten black cards from the deck.

4. Remove the rest of the heart suit and arrange it in sequence with the ace on top. Place an indifferent card between each heart. Do not put one over the ace, but do put one beneath the king. Put a joker under this indifferent bottom card. Put the other joker on top of the ace.

Note: The discarded black cards make the trick work faster, and also disguise the preponderance of red cards in the second portion of the pack. When putting indifferent cards between the sequential hearts, do not be afraid to place a card of the same number and color next to any of the hearts. This will later help confuse the spectator as you quickly show the bottom portion while looking for the joker.

5. Place the three twos on top of the latter joker.

6. Place the rest of the pack on top of the twos.

7. Put the force card on the top of the assembled pack.

How to Do It:

1. Force the topmost card with the top countoff (see Chapter 6).

2. Turn the pack face up and throw away the bottom joker, announcing that you don't need it. Casually riffle the deck to show it contains unprepared cards. Now run through the pack swiftly from the bottom up till the second joker is reached. This will reinforce the idea that the cards are unprepared. The heart sequence, since it is interrupted by indifferent cards, will not be noticed in a rapid running of the cards. Cut below this card and have the two of hearts replaced here. (It will be placed on top of the ace of hearts.) Put the upper half of the deck on the two, but as you do, say you don't need the second joker, either, and discard it in a manner that does not reveal the face of the other two-spot above that joker.

3. Rapidly overhand shuffle the cards, *one at a time,* until the two of hearts appears on the bottom of the deck. Stop and false-cut the pack.

4. Ask the volunteer the denomination of the card he picked. When he says "Two," put the pack in his hands and ask him to deal it in two piles.

5. As he deals the two piles, remember which one contains the very *first* card dealt by him.

6. After he has dealt twelve cards into each pile, stop him. Tell him to pick one of the piles and execute a magician's force (explained in the previous chapter) so he selects the pile you have been remembering. Put a joker on top to mark it.

7. Now have him deal the rest of the cards, including the discarded pile he just dealt, into four heaps. (Make sure the discarded pile is added *on top* of the rest of the pack still in his hands.)

8. The heart suit now will automatically be found in sequence beneath the joker, while the four twos will end on top of the other four piles, one apiece.

9. The chosen card will be the last one dealt.

Tips for Presentation: 1. This works best as close-up magic, because it is important for the spectators to see the cards as the magician displays them at the outset (they must be convinced the pack is unprepared). The trick might be adapted to a modest-sized room with a small gathering in attendance, provided the general visibility is good enough to allow the pack to be seen as it is riffled and spread. Clearly, the effect is not suited to stage presentation.

2. There is a lot of dealing of cards in this effect, which can be tedious to watch. This drawback is partly offset by the strength of the climax, but should be further minimized through the patter. A theme has already been suggested—the selected card likes to travel, and is missing but in good company. To this may be added comment on the process itself—random selection and dealing by the spectator of the various heaps, which allegedly makes the "working" completely fair.

3. At the end of the trick, of course, the three "sister" twos are turned over first, leaving the chosen one as the final revelation.

MORE TRICKS

Menta-Match: This is a simplified "prediction" effect which allows the magician to claim that he has removed a card that was chosen long before the trick began. He shows red- and blue-back decks, puts one aside, has a card chosen from the other, then has the first deck counted. There are only fifty-one cards in it—and the chosen card is not one of them. The magician produces a sealed pay envelope with the chosen card in it. The packs employ simple setups; this is a virtually fail-safe trick.

The Paul Fox "Miracle" Gimmick: An elaborate mechanical system for mentally locating up to five cards chosen (even over the phone). The pack is prearranged and a small printed gimmick shows the order. The mentalist reads across the gimmick and by a system of cross arrangement is able to zero in on the chosen card(s) with very little trouble. Even if one knows the principle, Fox's gimmick is inexpensive and better made than any hand-fashioned one would probably turn out.

Synonymental: A card setup that does not involve playing cards. Each of many cards has a word on it, most of them the names of common objects. The subtle arrangement allows the magician to make three particularly subtle forces. At the climax three objects borrowed from the audience are placed on top of three "freely chosen" cards whose words turn out to correspond with the objects. A very strong effect.

REFERENCES

Paul Curry's Out of This World, though well known, is a must. It is available both in separate manuscript and in Curry's book *Magician's Magic*. (The latter version is more detailed.) Essentially, Out of This World is a setup of the red and black cards, one color on top of the other, so that when the pack is put in the spectator's hands and dealt in two piles, all of one color appears in one heap, the other color in the second pile, even though the spectator may choose freely on which heap he places each card. Curry's method of disguising the prearrangement is simple to master, being a false-shuffle variant; his routine contains many psychological subtleties.

In the area of mnemonics, the enthusiast ought to read Harry Lorayne's *How to Build a Super-power Memory*, a book-size treatise on various kinds of artificial memory systems. The best card mnemonic arrangement is "The Nikola System," an inexpensive booklet that is worth many times its price. The Nikola arrangement combines certain stacking principles with the mnemonic techniques so that an unusually large range of effects may be performed.

9

Controlling
the Audience's Attention

A magic trick is a little play, carefully built, detail by detail. It is devised so that everything is so obviously fair that the one or two small points on which depend the success of the deception may be slid over without attracting attention.

John Mulholland, in *Quicker Than the Eye*

Despite the old adage, the hand is not quicker than the eye. Not only is it impossible to manipulate quickly enough to escape visual detection, but as we have seen, rapid motions are out of place in a magic act.

The expert magician seeks to deceive the mind rather than the eye. As Sol Stein puts it, "A magical effect is like a seduction. Both are built through careful details planted in the minds of the subject."

Psychological deception is the key to good magic. The conjurer performs certain physical actions, but takes care to interpret them for his audience. In the French Drop, for instance, he wants the spectator to think there is a coin in an empty hand, so he treats that hand as if it really held a coin.

What makes psychological deception such an art is the fact that the spectators are aware beforehand that the magician intends to dupe them; thus they are on their guard. The skilled performer must be able to execute dodges, artifices, and maneuvers that enable him to circumvent the natural suspicion of the audience.

Magicians call this process misdirection—the deliberate diversion of the audience's attention away from something it is not supposed to see. But for our purposes, attention control entails much more than the drawing away of audience interest. It also includes the direction of attention toward the proper points of focus. This process takes place at every moment of a performance, whether deceptive actions are taking place or not. Thus, the process of polarization—the focusing of audience attention on the stage at the beginning of a show—is one aspect of attention control.

The direction of audience attention is governed by a few simple principles which hold true in any staging situation. The most important may be termed "point of focus" and "creative flow."

"Point of focus" means that there is one center of interest at any given moment of an act. This centralization of attention is to a certain extent a natural phenomenon, for a spectator cannot concentrate on more than one or two strong points of interest—and never on more than one if the two points are fairly far apart. The eye simply cannot see both. The wise magician will know what the point of focus should be at every moment, and will arrange his speech and actions to direct the audience's attention toward it.

Of course, the point of focus constantly shifts during performance. The linkage from one point to another is termed "creative flow." It is simply the smooth progress of an act from point to point, so that the audience's attention is redirected from one center of interest to another without disruption.

An example will help clarify these terms. In the trick Find the Ball (Chapter 3), the magician invites a volunteer to assist him. Let us imagine a third spectator watching the performance of the trick. As the ball and cups and cards are shown, the spectator's interest will focus on them. When the magician turns his back, attention will flow to the conjurer, then to the volunteer as he puts the ball under one cup. This creative flow is natural and unforced. Note that the spectator sees the magician even while the ball is being placed under the cup—but the full force of his attention is not directed toward the magician. The point of focus takes in both the cups and the hands of the volunteer as he moves them about, since they are close together.

In working out a skeletal structure that will take the audience from one point of focus to another in his act, the magician will employ many devices to focus the audience's attention. Movement by itself tends to draw the eye, as do color and noise. The personality of the performer helps establish the control, and the themes presented may further build the creative flow. Thus a magician who relies on comedy to sell his material will work to a staccato flow which breaks and reestablishes every time there is a sizable laugh. Laughter tends to give the audience a moment of relaxation, after which it can again focus its attention.

On the other hand, a magician who presents a serious or slick character, or who employs effects that stress danger and suspense, will probably work with a legato creative flow, one that moves from one point of focus to another without break. Such a performer must allow his audience time to relax its attention at the climax of each trick, in order to better concentrate on the succeeding effect. For example, if a performer is doing a guillotine trick, he would be foolish to plunge right into his next block of patter after the knife blade has dropped. Even after the volunteer has taken his seat, the audience will need a few seconds to settle down from the tension it has experienced. The magician might ask the audience to applaud the volunteer as he takes his seat. The applause serves as a release of tension, lets the audience relax its attention momentarily, and also serves as an automatic bridge to the next trick—for once it dies down, the audience will be ready to look and listen once more.

A careful reader will have already noted that laughter and applause can be valuable misdirective devices. If you need to get some secret prop into your hand during a magic act, there is no better time to do it than when the audience is laughing or applauding, thus allowing its level of attention to drop.

Misdirection—that portion of attention control that deals with the concealment of strategic business—is a kind of psychological disguise. Any magic act utilizes plenty of purely physical disguises—props that look innocent but have secret compartments, ropes that are disguised so an end looks like the middle, maneuvers that bring cards to the top or bottom of a deck while giving the appearance of genuine shuffles. Psychological deception is far more subtle and involves many more devices. The most comprehensive analysis of the subject is probably to be found in Dariel Fitzkee's overlong but brilliant *Magic by Misdirection.*

Following are some of the most important kinds of psychological disguise Fitzkee discusses:

Performer's Personality: An audience will relax its attention to the extent that the personality of the performer induces it to do so. The classic figure of the magician is the authoritative sorcerer with apparently unlimited powers. If a performer can portray this role convincingly, the audience's confidence will overcome its suspicions. For if the audience is sure the magician is too skilled to be caught, it may not even try.

Another kind of personality which may aid the magician in misdirecting the audience is the disarmingly uncertain type. By appearing to be pleasantly befuddled, the performer may lead the audience not to expect overwhelming results—until the climax is reached and the magician's real talents are suddenly revealed. Such a personality provides ample opportunities for misdirection. When showing Eliminating Cards (Chapter 7), I always pretend to be uncertain what comes next when I have to gather the packet of eight cards from the bottom of the deck. By fanning the bottom cards back and forth, apparently at random, and looking into space in a preoccupied fashion, I am able to delude the spectator into thinking I am trying to remember the next step. In reality, I am counting the eight cards and getting the chosen one into the next-to-bottom position.

Nature of Props: Because it is hard for the audience to maintain divided interest, the most interesting actions and objects will tend to attract its attention. However, although an unusual magic box will temporarily draw interest because of its pattern, hue, or shape, it often sustains less interest than a more normal-looking item. Penetrating a volunteer's body with a sword is less effective than an equally well presented trick in which the magician places razor blades in his mouth, simply because swords are rather exotic and unfamiliar to many people, whereas razor blades (and the very real danger involved in handling them) are familiar to almost everybody. A further advantage to using ordinary-looking props is that they also tend to allay suspicion. A cut-and-restored effect with a colorful silk handkerchief six feet square will seem less miraculous than the same illusion performed with a rope—even though the silk may be ungimmicked and the rope has been doctored. Nobody expects any physical tampering with a rope, while a large silk may look so "magical" that it is automatically suspect. Another advantage of normal-looking props is that they tend to be accepted at face value when there is a division of interest onstage and the audience has to choose where to look and what to suspect. So if an iron coin is put on a beer mat with a magnet in it, the coin apparently penetrates the mat and drops into an odd-shaped bottle below, the audience may wonder about the bottle, but probably won't even question the beer mat.

Suggestion and Inducement (Patter): The things the magician says or implies in his patter may lead the audience to false conclusions. The patter for the Coin Flip (Chapter 7) leads the spectator to believe he is witnessing a simple feat of skill. Thus his attention is diverted, and he does not look for a different coin to fly into the hand on the final flip.

Simulation and Dissimulation: Simulation means that the magician acts as if something were so when it isn't; dissimulation means he tries to hide the fact that something exists. In the French Drop, for instance, the hand that pretends to take the coin is held in such a way that it seems to hold the coin, and the magician looks at the hand as if it held the coin. This is *simulation.* In the same effect, the hand that has retained the coin drops to the side as if it were empty, and the magician ignores it. This is *dissimulation.*

Diversion: This device entails the substitution of a new and stronger interest for that which the magician wishes to hide. When a performer magically produces coins, certain absolutely necessary diversions are built into the trick itself. One hand may reach into the air and produce the coins while the magician turns nearly profile to the audience and with his upstage hand reaches under the edge of his jacket and plucks another batch of coins from a metal clamp pinned there. He pivots nearly profile in the other direction, raises the hand with the coins in the air, and produces them—while his now upstage hand reaches beneath the jacket for another "steal." In each case, the appearance of the coins provides a diversion for the next "steal." One of the most natural diversions possible is the calling up onto the stage of a volunteer from the audience. This action gives a magician plenty of time to execute secret moves.

Distraction: This technique generally entails a violent drawing away of spectators' interest from what they think is the correct point of focus. Harry Blackstone, Sr., used to have an assistant "accidentally" trip while walking across stage. While the audience was momentarily distracted, Blackstone obtained the object he was to magically produce. This was an ingenious use of distraction, but in general I would severely limit the use of this misdirective technique. The problem is that it breaks the creative flow. Once this has happened, the magician must reestablish his attention control—and though this can be done in a short time, it is still an undesirable kind of disruption. I would use distraction only when no other misdirective technique will work or when it honestly contributes to an effect. Suppose the magician slightly "cuts" his finger on one of the razor blades he is going to swallow. This minor distraction may allow fake blades to be substituted for genuine ones—and it will also add to the atmosphere and buildup of suspense.

Pointing: This is exactly what it sounds like—the deliberate indication of where an audience should look. It can be done with speech ("Look at this piece of newspaper"), gesture (pointing to a box which is about to yield a rabbit), or a look (the magician stares at a volunteer, awaiting the reply to a question; while the volunteer replies, the magician keeps "focusing" on him, meanwhile performing some secret move with his upstage hand).

Repetition: By performing a certain action several times in the same manner, the magician lowers audience interest in that particular detail. In the Traveling Coin (Chapter 3), several people feel the coin beneath the handkerchief. The confederate is last to do so, and by the time he spirits it away the repeated checks to make sure the coin is in place have allayed the audience's suspicions.

Confusion: Including a number of varied interests in the execution of an effect makes it hard for the audience to follow what is happening. The shuffling, cutting, and squaring up of cards are trivial details that serve to obscure the location of a selected card. Because so many things are done to the cards, the spectator probably does not even try to follow the precise fate of any given card. In the center-tear move, so many folds and tears are made that the spectator cannot hope to follow where the portion of paper with the word written on it has gone. Of course, confusion is valid only if a spectator is not consciously aware that he is being confused.

Anticipation: When people do not think the magic has yet taken place, even though it has, we say that the magician has "anticipated" the audience. In Card Elimination, the glide is used to substitute the chosen card for one which has been viewed. Since the magician appears to be working with indifferent cards, the audience thinks that the magic has not yet taken place.

Premature Consummation: The reverse of anticipation is when the magician has evidently brought a trick to a climax, only to reveal that there is a further wonder to come. The momentary relaxation of attention which results enables the performer to set up the final effect. Example: The magician produces a number of colorful rings from "nowhere" and shows them proudly. The audience begins to applaud, but as they do, the magician "steals" a large double chain of more rings and brings them forth—an unexpected climax which is possible through the momentary relaxation of attention.

Ruse: Fitzkee defines this as the employment of a crafty expedient for distracting attention. I would include laughter in this category. If, during a children's show, the magician pretends to get his hand caught in a piece of equipment, he will probably get a hearty laugh. During this moment, the hidden hand might well be obtaining some hard-to-grasp magic device. A classic ruse occurs in the famous Egg Bag Trick. The magician removes his hand from a small bag in which he has placed a wooden egg. His hand steals to his armpit, which snaps closed in an unnatural position. Meanwhile, the magician shows the bag empty—but the audience does not care, because they are sure the egg is under his arm. Of course, it is concealed in the bag but the ruse misdirects attention from that possibility.

The skilled magician will study attention-control techniques and strive to build a framework of devices into his act. By so doing, he will ensure that the audience looks where it is supposed to, and not at the magician's secret moves.

Some tricks have built-in misdirective devices, while others require the magician to use his ingenuity to cover up weak points.

An example of nonautomatic misdirection is the climax of the Cut-and-restored Ropes (Chapter 7). At the final restoration, the magician has a short piece of rope palmed in his hand. How does he get rid of it? He may employ a ruse by picking up a magic wand from a table, meanwhile dropping the rope behind some object.

Another possibility would be to use the repetition technique. Have a small quantity of colored confetti in a trousers pocket. Call it magic woofle dust and explain that it enables various kinds of impossible things to take place. Take a pinch of the confetti and sprinkle it over the ropes every time a magic effect is about to happen. The repeated sprinkling can be amusing in itself, especially to an audience of children. When the climax of the trick approaches and the small piece of rope has been palmed, all the magician has to do is reach into his pocket for more confetti, at the same time leaving the telltale rope inside.

The Center Tear (Chapter 7) employs nearly every misdirective technique—both built-in and otherwise.

When the volunteer prints a word in the middle of the slip of paper, the magician uses a ruse to explain the necessity of doing so—he draws two linked rings and compares the central portion to the "one area of your mind that I can read."

Tearing the paper several times makes the carefully executed tears seem random. The pieces of paper which drop into the ashtray are an example of confusion—there are so many that the audience does not suspect the vital center piece is missing.

Likewise, dropping the paper pieces brings in simulation (the center piece is supposed to be there), dissimulation (the hand that palms the center is supposed to be empty), and pointing (the magician physically indicates that the torn message is in the ashtray, thus drawing the spectators' eyes there).

When he actually reads the message, the magician needs to exercise powerful misdirection so no one will pay any attention to him. Having the message burned is a diversion which accomplishes this. People are fascinated by fire; they automatically stare into the flames.

In Chapter 7, it was suggested that the magician might "fail" to figure out the secret thought at first, and consequently have to ask the volunteer to write it again and burn it. While the volunteer does so, the magician has lots of time to read the stolen center. Since the audience thinks the trick didn't work at first, it assumes that the magic has not yet taken place when, in fact, the magician actually is doing the "dirty work." This presentation employs the principle of anticipation.

Premature conclusion is another valuable technique. Suppose there are so many people in the room that it is difficult to read the message without being observed. A solution might be to have someone blindfold you and have the folded message written secretly and placed into your hand. Handle the folded note, finger the paper, crumple it, then tear it apart, feel the edges, and proceed in like manner until all the tears are made. After the pieces are burned touch a finger to the ashes, walk about blindly trying to sense the whereabouts of the unknown (to you) writer of the note. At last, touch the ashes to the forehead of the correct person. Before anyone can comment on the remarkable occurrence, you then apparently read the volunteer's mind on the spot—telling him what his message was. The revelation that you know who wrote the message makes the group think the trick is done. In that moment, the contents of the note may be learned.

The blindfold should be fake, so that the identity of the writer is observed as he puts down his message. The rest of the effect is pure showmanship. But while the paper is burned, the performer unfolds the slip of paper. If it is still too dangerous to read it, he simply carries it unfolded and palmed in his hand. He glances at it just as he touches the volunteer's forehead with his ash-coated finger. No one will look at anything but that smudge.

Misdirection, it should be evident, is a difficult subject to master. It requires continued application, study, and experimentation on the part of the serious entertainer.

Remember what Dariel Fitzkee says: the spectator is able to draw upon the acquirements of a lifetime when he first watches you exhibit a piece of magical apparatus. It demands exceptional skill to overcome this obstacle and turn a group of potential skeptics into an enthusiastic audience. This is the greatest challenge—and fascination—of being a magician.

10

In Search of Personal Style

Never tell the audience how good you are; they will soon find that out for themselves.

Houdini on Magic,
edited by W. B. Gibson and Morris Young

When I first studied creative writing back in high school, I used to worry about the word "style." Its meaning eluded me. Grammar, punctuation, vocabulary—all these were definable according to rules and traditions. But style? A free-form term—its tenets and characteristics refused to be pinned down, and even a dictionary did not help.

The problem with style is that it is not a measuring device for evaluating quality. It is a subjective method of analysis according to manner. Everyone has a style, no matter whether good or bad. Style is the way we talk, walk, and express ourselves in a fashion peculiarly our own. We dress a certain way, we use certain idioms of speech, we adhere to a certain speed and rhythm of movement. Whether consciously or not, we all have style.

The important question is, Does the style we possess accomplish the effects we wish to put across when we perform? Do we please and amuse the audience? If not, we must take a close look at the ways we move and talk onstage, our attitudes toward the audience, and the kinds of magic we present best.

Style is really the chief concern of this book. We have already discussed the kinds of magician that do not please—these individuals have flaws in their performing styles. It is the business of every magician to constantly evaluate each performance to see if anything in it did not come off. A magician must keep reappraising his performing style to make sure it continues to fit the staging and audience situations he encounters.

In discussing the style of a magic act, there are two variables to consider: the personality of the performer as it is projected to the audience, and the quality of the show itself. Each, of course, is intimately interrelated to the other.

The cardinal rule to observe when determining style is to *be original.* This is not as simple as it sounds. I considered one of the first short stories I ever wrote terribly original until I realized that the idea for it had originated in a comic book I'd read years before. Everyone makes a mistake like this once in a while, but all should consciously strive to bring something different and personal to the act being shaped.

The variables of personal style include many options in areas of dress, delivery, makeup, and the character one decides to play. The first three will, of course, be largely determined by the latter. For instance, if the magician decides to portray an elderly wizard, he may choose clothing that is somewhat out of fashion. His delivery may be leisurely or, in the case of a humorously decrepit character, decidedly halting. His makeup will rely heavily on facial lines and shadows, perhaps a sallow complexion, possibly a beard, mustache, or bushy white eyebrows.

On the other hand, if the performer wishes to play a slightly inebriated magician, his delivery will alter accordingly and his gait will be unsteady. Perhaps his clothing will look unpressed and rumpled. His makeup may make his cheeks look flushed, his nose red. However, it is important to note that the magician, like any other artist, should represent his character with selective reality —that is, the artist picks out salient details and centers on them, perhaps exaggerating them for effect, but his representation is not the same as the actual thing itself. So a rumpled suit onstage must be deliberately made to seem so. There is no excuse for wearing really dingy costumes—only *apparently* dirty ones.

Theatrical makeup is an important subject for a magician to study. There are several good texts on the topic, including those by Yoti Lane and Norman Corson. However, the best way to become familiar with the possibilities and limitations of makeup materials is to study with a theatrical expert, especially a skilled actor. Second best is buying a variety of greasepaints and hair stuff, reading about the chief principles of making up, then *experimenting*. Beginning magicians tend to err on the side of smearing too much on the face. Except when a very distinctive character is being played, the performer should only apply "corrective" makeup—just enough to bring out his face to best advantage.

What kind of character should one assume? The choice is legion, and should be dictated only by the capabilities of the magician. But one thing is essential—be *consistent*. Don't build up one impression, only to ruin it with an inappropriate trick or gag.

Try to avoid the clichés. Oriental magicians are quite passé, unless they are genuine, or so novel as to give new life to the role. The omnipotent-wizard characterization is difficult to sustain because one cannot make a mistake in this guise. Also, there is some absurdity in the "genuine" magician who goes about covering objects with silks and having people count cards. If he were real, he would need no such artifice.

Make no mistake about the character you choose to portray. To be effective, you must be an actor first and a magician second. Even when a magician decides to "be himself" onstage, he is still playing a character: that of a magician.

I have several characters which I employ when doing my acts. In a small room, as I've already mentioned, I tend to assume a slightly befuddled pose. On a platform, I strive for an amiable delivery mixed with wry remarks. I modify the latter to a somewhat more serious delivery when doing mental magic. For children, I become "Count Emkay the Miraculous," a comic takeoff on the late Bela Lugosi—with bowler hat, bizarre makeup, broad Hungarian dialect, and plenty of slapstick.

But the one quality that I try to establish in all of these characterizations is "personal proof." This is the art of making the audience like the performer on sight. It is achieved by having a genuine regard and affection for the audience, and involves a great degree of unforced self-confidence and a willingness to sell oneself rather than the equipment. The hallmarks of personal proof are neat dress, assured comportment, and plenty of *genuine* smiles.

Ken Griffin observes that there are three major styles of show—those played "naturally," those with a humorous slant, and those that stress mystery. There are many variations and combinations of the three, and to some extent, the choice is dictated by the size of the audience and the room being worked in. But each presentation style naturally limits the sort of tricks that can be shown. A slapstick trick might be out of place in a mysterious act, while slick manipulative work is generally bad policy in a humorous act—especially for children.

The hardest thing to learn is what kind of tricks to purchase. Selection is a matter of trial and error, and will be mastered only as the individual becomes more familiar with his own strengths. The "secrecy syndrome" which most dealers and magicians endorse makes it even harder to make wise purchases. But if you find yourself stuck with a piece of equipment, *do not put it in your act.* Even if you are hard pressed for funds, you cannot afford to perform magic that does not suit your style. Dariel Fitzkee even recommends dropping whichever number you do least effectively, since such a move will automatically ensure a better act.

The best course—just as in building patter—is to invent your own effects, or at least find new ways to present the ones you do. Sometimes by combining two pieces of equipment in a new form, a novel presentation will evolve—and it will be all your own. For instance, there is an effect on the market in which the magician magically changes a solid chain to a group of separate links. Another piece of equipment changes separate links into a chain. Using both tricks in one act might provide a pleasing way to open and close the performance.

The magician simply must search for his own way of selling himself as a conjuring entertainer. This is a hard thing to do, and though it is advisable to seek the help of outsiders in viewing one's work, ultimately improvement can come only when the magician learns to see himself as the audience does. Then by *realistically* evaluating the effect he makes, the magician can make the best use of his particular strengths and limitations.

Maturity is the key factor. One must master the ego to build the ego; one must be both instrument and player, puppet and puppeteer. Self-awareness is the hardest task the interpretive artist must master. But concentrating on it consciously is a sure step in the right direction.

11

Putting Together an Act

I do a great cut-and-restored rope trick! You ought to see
it—it runs half an hour!

Typical magician's boast

Though a magician must ultimately rely on his own taste and
judgment in developing a personal style, he does not have to
wander totally in the dark. There are certain guidelines of good
showmanship (many of which have already been discussed) which,
if observed, will ensure that his performance will be at least acceptable.

The areas in which many amateur (and some professional)
magicians draw failing grades are timing and routining. Too many
would-be wizards don't know how to put an act together; some do
too much magic at one session, or fail to provide enough variety
within the act. Worst of all, some do not understand how to build
toward the climax of a trick; as a result, their miracles fail to mystify
as fully as they might.

When we talk about theatrical timing, we are referring to two
general types: *interlinear* and *overall* timing. Each is governed by
the principles of *restraint, proportion,* and *adaptation.*

Overall timing is concerned with the length and shape of the
magic act as a whole. It involves total length, as well as *pace* and
tempo. Total length simply means, How long is the act? In most
cases, the answer is, Too long. The mere fact that the magician is
fascinated with his gadgetry is no assurance that the audience will
be. A little magic usually goes a long way. The principle of *restraint*
should be ruthlessly applied to the length of an act. If a magician is
in a program with several other performers, he should expect to
perform no longer than ten to twelve minutes, or at most fifteen,

and then only if the producer requests it. In some cases, the magician will be told to perform for less than ten minutes; if so, he must do as he is told or run the risk of never being asked to perform with that group again. If his material simply will not fit the allotted time span, it is probably better for the magician to drop out of the show than to go on too long.

A solo magic show gives the performer greater leeway in total playing time. A club or after-dinner act may last twenty-five minutes or more. But some bookers, in their desire to get their money's worth, require a magician to play for forty-five minutes to an hour. Anything over half an hour is too long for most performers, no matter how accomplished they are. A magic act ought to be kept to about twenty-five minutes, if at all possible; if you simply cannot avoid playing longer, stretch your act with nonmagical effects or other presentations that vary the pace and theme. A manipulator might bring in mental effects; a mentalist might conduct a spiritual experiment; a children's magician may bring along a clown or mime to do a turn.

Restraint must also be applied to the length of individual tricks in a routine. Never let a trick run on too long. I am always amazed and horrified to hear magicians boast about entertaining children with some simple trick for ten minutes at a time. *This is too long!* No trick or illusion should run longer than five minutes; most should last between three and four minutes. Anything longer than five minutes will run a very real risk of boring the audience.

Another reason to keep each effect relatively short is the principle of *proportion.* In the average act, the magician will perform perhaps four to nine effects. If one trick is abnormally long, it will stand apart from the rest of the show and seem poorly integrated. A careful balance of playing times gives the show a pleasing, artistic sense of balance.

This brings us to the crucial terms *pace* and *tempo.* Tempo refers to the actual speed of speech, movement, or manipulations which a magician employs in performing a trick. When appearing before young children, for instance, the performer will probably speak slowly and distinctly, and keep all gestures broad, slow, and visible. Thus he adopts a slower tempo than when he appears before adults.

Of course, no two tricks should be played at precisely the same speed. The appearance of several handkerchiefs from an apparently empty box may be performed more briskly than the cutting and restoring of a piece of rope. The reason is that the rope routine requires manipulations which may be suspected if executed too quickly; a slow tempo makes everything appear fairer. On the other hand, the handkerchief production employs nothing stranger than reaching a hand into an empty box. Since the movement is not naturally suspect, the magician may perform it more rapidly.

The deliberate alteration of tempo in order to achieve stronger trick presentations is called *pace* or *pacing*. When an act is well paced, it means time has been artistically distributed and utilized. Some tricks develop more slowly than others, so the magician may juxtapose tricks with varying pace in the order of his act. If he does, the faster tricks will appear even brisker by contrast, and the slower ones will seem even slower.

Even within a single trick, pacing can be used to good effect. During Invisible Flight (Chapter 3), the magician may wrap up the silks carefully and slowly. But at the climax, he quickly strides to each chair and rips open the newspapers to reveal the color change. The speed of the final actions will appear more thrilling in contrast to all that has occurred before.

The system of tempo variation employed in an act, combined with the actual times of each trick, may be varied infinitely. However, the interest of the audience should heighten as the act goes along until the final effect tops everything that has been done earlier. It may be possible to shape a short act steadily upward, attaining a higher pinnacle of excitement with each ensuing step. But in a longer routine, it may be necessary to drop the level of tension once or twice in order to build to several peaks, each higher than the previous one. Thus, a twelve-minute routine might begin with a short trick, continue with a longer effect followed by a still longer third trick, and then close with a shorter effect. Timing in minutes might be: two, three, five, two. A longer act would alternate short and longer running times in a peaks-and-valleys approach to the pinnacle of the act. Possible timing in minutes for a twenty-five-minute show might be: one, two, three, two, five, two, three, five, two.

It should be evident that it is almost impossible to maintain a rapid pace in any fairly lengthy performance. "Building too fast" is a technical term which means a performer starts at such a rapid tempo that there is no way for him to "top" himself. It is important to begin an act slowly enough so that there is somewhere to go later. In certain cases, such as in nightclubs, where the audience is inattentive, it may be necessary to begin on a high point to capture interest. But once the audience is caught, the tension should be gradually relaxed, so that the next climax can be prepared.

Applause can be an effective method of lowering the level of suspense. In planning an act, the magician must decide on the points when he wants applause, and then strive to attain it only at those times. In general, it is wise to avoid getting too many hands in any one trick, since the final effect may suffer from too much early enthusiasm.

There are a few purely mechanical things to avoid in planning the timing of an act. Any time a volunteer has to be selected from the audience, the tempo falters while everyone waits for him to come onstage. Similarly, borrowing objects from the audience, selecting and identifying cards, and examining magical equipment lower the level of interest. A trick which requires one or more of these things should be sandwiched between effects that do not require any.

We have noted the importance of restraint and proportion in the timing of an act. The third governing principle is *adaptation,* which also might be called adjustment. Timing is a flexible concept and will vary with the kind of show and audience the magician faces. I have heard nightclub comics complain that they cannot work for hospital audiences because they are so low in spirits that they won't laugh. The real fault lies in the performers who don't know how to vary pace and energy to motivate such audiences to enjoy their shows.

The magician must appraise the kind of situation he will be facing in any given show and make appropriate changes in his pacing. An excellent trick called Book of the Mind involves passing out three books to audience members who each choose pages and look at the top word. The magician mind-reads then the thought-of words and writes them on a slate, one at a time. The performer concentrates on each word individually, so the trick plays at a moderate tempo which accelerates slightly at each minor climax until the final word is reached. One time when I was preparing for a hospital show, I noticed that the audience was unusually despondent. Realizing that the full five-minute Book of the Mind would be too slow for such a house, I immediately determined to play the entire act at a more rapid tempo than normal, and when I reached the mental test, I "read" all three thoughts at once, instead of one at a time. Though some of the effect may have been lost, I succeeded in cutting out two minutes of playing time, and as a result, the audience's level of interest quickened for my act—and the remainder of the show.

Up to now, we have been considering overall timing. The other variety the entertainer must master is *interlinear* timing. This is the art of letting the audience know you are leading up to punch lines, or climaxes of tricks. Essentially, the technique depends on learning how to emphasize the moment when a pinnacle of interest is reached.

Magicians should study the way a good professional comic delivers his material. The tempo of delivery, the pacing, and the pauses all help the comic set up the situation unmistakably so the audience knows when a laugh is expected. A good comedian can make an audience laugh even when his material is not especially clever, as long as he understands the mechanism of interlinear timing well enough to structure the kind of response he desires.

Such a structure may entail a gradual acceleration or deceleration of speech as the climax nears. Verbal pointing may also utilize pauses to separate the gag line from the rest of the material that has gone before. Once a pinnacle of interest is reached, the performer may "freeze" the pose momentarily to create a visual tableau.

Whichever device is employed, the magician must signal the audience in subliminal fashion that the climax of a trick or act is approaching. Let's again consider Invisible Flight. This trick has a double climax—two handkerchiefs change places from a distance. Until the final revelation, the magician has performed with a slow tempo. But after both silks are wrapped and placed on opposite sides of the stage, the magician picks up a magic wand and begins to speak more rapidly and a bit louder. The change in dynamics and tempo tells the audience that a climax is coming. Then the magician swiftly strides to one packet, rips it open, and shows that one silk has changed. Before any applause can reduce audience tension, the magician drapes the cloth on his shoulder, quickly strides to the second packet, rips it open, and reveals the other silk. He holds them both up and freezes for a second, then bows. The refusal to accept applause after the first revelation quickens interest. The magician's final pose clearly tells the audience that the trick is completed. The bow is a signal for applause, which releases the magician for his next effect.

Adaptation is of prime importance in planning interlinear timing, and there is no substitute for playing before as large a variety of audiences as possible. Each group will differ, and each must be worked to in distinctive manner. The mechanics of building climaxes may stay the same, but the tempos employed will constantly have to be adjusted. In general the performer will find that he is able to relax tempo when an audience is alert and responsive. When it is not, he will have to speed up tempo accordingly.

The length and pacing of the act are prime considerations in routing—the deliberate selection and shaping of material to suit a specific performing engagement. The suitability of various tricks to "problem" audiences will be discussed in later chapters, but for now, let us observe a few ground rules in the general choice of material.

Avoid using several effects that are markedly similar in nature. Three tricks, one after another, in which the magician produces a handful of money would be repetitious in most cases. The magician who builds his entire routine around the production of coins and bills deliberately sacrifices variety of effect for unity of theme, and his act would almost certainly be a short one. It is also a good idea to vary the kinds of materials used in a single act. If you do a rope trick, it may be well to follow it with a silk effect, since ropes are colorless while silks are eye-catching. Though some magicians prefer to limit themselves to one prop, it is generally true that a variety of props builds visual interest.

In routining the act, seek to build a curve of interest up to the climax. After gaining the audience's attention with a trick that is startling or amusing, the magician should forge a chain of effects to take the audience from climax to climax until the ultimate miracle astounds it utterly. (Or, if the presentation is primarily amusing, the build should be toward greater hilarity.)

In a short act, the first effect generally must establish the magician's credentials. The next effect may be used to exploit the performer's personality. The third trick will fully employ the performer's abilities in bringing about some especially remarkable effect. The closing effect will reestablish the wizard's skills and leave the audience totally impressed.

A typical four-trick humorous act might consist of the following effects:

> X-Salted
> Clatter Box
> French Arm Chopper
> Soft Soap

Each of these is a commercially marketed effect. Let's see why they might work in the above order.

X-Salted involves the production of a continuous stream of salt from a supposedly empty shaker. When I perform it, I patter at first about a new breakthrough in hypnosis which now makes it possible to hypnotize inanimate objects. Then, I "put the salt shaker to sleep" in broadly comical fashion and after some byplay, proceed to pour the salt into a partially folded handkerchief. The initial patter helps amuse the audience and also leads it to doubt that the magic to come will be all that effective. As a result, the pouring salt is doubly surprising. The pacing of the effect is deliberate and the tempo remains slow until the climax, when the shaker is suddenly dropped into the handkerchief. The cloth is immediately shaken out; both shaker and salt have vanished.

Now that the audience is impressed with the performer's ability, he treats it to an amusing interlude *(Clatter Box)* which builds upon the mild humor of the first trick's patter. This time, a volunteer from the audience watches the magician take a red silk from a box, put it in a bag, and tap the bag with a wand—whereupon the silk disappears. The volunteer attempts to produce the cloth from the empty box, but in the process he "breaks" the fan, the wand, and finally, the box itself (though he does succeed in bringing back the handkerchief). This trick comes off as very humorous and gives the performer ample opportunity to act more and more disgusted as each piece of his equipment is "wrecked." Since I find it easy, as an actor, to express frustration, the trick is a good one for exploiting my stage personality.

Using the disasters of the previous trick as a link, the *French Arm Chopper* can be performed next as a "punishment" for the clumsy audience volunteer. In this effect the spectator sticks his hand into a hole through which a large knife blade will be forcefully passed. The tempo of *Clatter Box* is necessarily rather slow, since the audience member handles many of the props. But in the chopper routine, the magician controls the performance and has most of the lines, so he can build the tempo to a climax that is both funny and suspenseful.

After the volunteer is dismissed, it is time to wrap up the act quickly and effectively. *Soft Soap* is a "sucker" trick which allows the magician to have a final laugh on the audience. He shows three dirty handkerchiefs and stuffs them into a laundry-detergent box. After shaking the box, he takes the cloths out—clean. But the audience suspects that the dirty ones are still in the box. The magician, feigning disgust, declares he'll never do this lousy trick again. He rips up the box (proving that it is empty), throws down the pieces, and walks offstage.

How does this act pace out? The salt-shaker effect begins slow, speeds up slightly when the salt is produced, slows down while the salt pours, then reaches a sudden conclusion as the shaker and salt vanish. The clatter-box routine begins slow as a volunteer comes onstage, proceeds somewhat faster while the magician makes the silk vanish, and slows again as the volunteer "breaks" the props. The arm chopper picks up quickly as the device is shown and the danger is recognized, then builds at a gradually faster tempo until the blade chops down on the arm. The tempo drops slightly between tricks, but is quickly built again until the clean silks are shown in the closing trick. The tempo slows momentarily while the audience protests, then reaches a final peak as the magician tears up the box and storms out.

The variety of props contributes to the effectiveness of this brief routine: white salt and glass shaker with metal top; red silk, cloth and wood fan, black and white plastic wand; large yellow and black wooden guillotine with black bag; metallic knife blade; cardboard box with commercial design on it; dirty-gray cloth handkerchiefs.

The variations that a magician may work into his routine are legion. I am sure a capable performer already will see ways to improve the above routine. As long as he keeps in mind the principles of restraint, adaptation, and proportion, he won't go wrong. But beyond everything else, the magician should strive to be economical. If his audience is left wanting a little more entertainment than it has been given, then the performer's timing and routining will have been successful.

12

Magic of the Mind

The most impressive tricks are those which require
little or no equipment to perform.

Sol Stein

Tricks and routines that feature mind reading, prediction, and
other ESP effects are the aristocrats of the world of wizardry. Next
to children's magic, mentalism is probably the ultimate test of a
performer's talents. While the secrets on which mental tricks
depend are often deceptively simple, performing them requires
flawless showmanship on the part of the entertainer. The quality of
patter, precision of timing, and artfulness of misdirection make
demands on the magician unequaled in other branches of the mystic profession.

A mental act, says Dariel Fitzkee, shows perfect unity of theme.
The performer who restricts himself to mental tricks automatically
unifies his act since he is, in effect, claiming certain mental powers
which are in themselves interesting.

Bold device and subtle artifice are the keys to most great mental
effects. One magic text actually suggests that the magician detect
the identity of a chosen card by ribbon-spreading the pack *face up*
on a table. The identity of the chosen card is immediately known to
the performer by simple visual inspection. However, the audience
is not aware of the ruse, and it is unlikely that the volunteer will call
attention to it if the magician's personality is strong. In another
bold mental effect, the magician reaches into a paper bag full of
cards and "feels" the spots on each pasteboard before removing it
to prove he has made a correct identification. The secret? The bag
has a small hole in one corner, and the performer holds each card
against the gap before removing it from the bag.

It takes plenty of nerve to get away with such simple deceptions. Obviously, atmosphere and suspense play the crucial role in
such tricks—a statement that holds true to some extent for all
mental effects. The magician must learn to dramatize mind-reading
tricks for all they are worth. If a message is to be revealed, he must
never just come out with the answer. He must seem to experience
great difficulty in revealing it word by word, sometimes letter by
letter.

This apparent strain serves a double purpose, for while the
magician makes his answers look like real work (thus building the
suspense), he also allows an out for himself when a mistake sometimes occurs. Perhaps he intends to reveal three thought-of words,
but one spectator honestly forgets his, or even deliberately changes
his mind. If the magician has succeeded with two out of three
thoughts, he may claim to have become mentally fatigued in the
process. Or he might suggest that it is difficult to attune himself
with the last spectator's thoughts.

In all other branches of conjuring, it is practically imperative
that the performer succeed 100 percent of the time. But in a mental
act, the performer may actually benefit from an occasional mistake;
it makes the act appear more genuine. In fact, it is often wise to
program some deliberate error into a mind-reading act, one that
may somehow be rectified to the entertainer's credit.

Henning Nelms puts his finger on the reason for the legit-
imate-failure factor in mental acts when he notes that most tricks
may be classed as demonstrations, while mind-reading tests are
experiments. A demonstration, by definition, is supposed to show
something happening, but an experiment is only an *attempt* to
make something happen and allows the possibility of failure.

Of course, the performer must do everything in his power to
make sure any mistakes which occur in a mental routine are
deliberate ones. One of the things that make airplanes safer than
automobiles is reserve instrumentation; similarly, a seasoned
magician safeguards his act with reserve preparations. In a mental
act, for instance, a magician may need to secretly read a written,
sealed message. His insurance should be to have several methods of
doing so. If the initial line of attack fails, he must be able to set up

the experiment again with some other device that won't let him down. Another safeguard is to have extra tricks on hand with effects similar to the ones planned. Keep this additional "hardware" out of sight but ready to work in case something goes wrong with a scheduled effect.

The most likely source of error a mentalist must face is the spectator's recollection of thought-of words, cards, etc. Learn to size up the alertness of a volunteer swiftly; if there is any doubt as to his reliability (or honesty), be sure that he writes down his "thought" for later verification. Or, if writing would be suspect, have him whisper it to another audience member. If he picks a card, it might be possible for him to show it to the audience without letting the performer see it.

In general, effective mind-reading tricks and acts are designed to persuade the audience of the authenticity of what it sees, at least for the duration of the performance. However, some performers seem to feel no compunction about claiming to be genuine psychics—a dangerous practice and, in my opinion, downright dishonest. There probably *never* has been a "real" mind reader on any stage at any time in history. Even though I believe in the existence of telepathy, I doubt that any genuine telepathist can go onstage and have his power work regularly enough to be both convincing and entertaining. Let us be honest and admit we are performers. While we may give the illusion of infallibility, I do not think it wise to boast of paranormal powers in private, unless the boaster is prepared to prove himself on the spot.

Look at an average mind-reading effect and logically analyze what happens. A prediction is sealed in an envelope. A number of books are passed out to the audience and a page is "freely" chosen in each. A word is chosen. The performer has the envelope opened to show he predicted what the word would be. Honestly, now—if the mind reader were genuine, why would he need any such artifice? He would simply reveal a spectator's thoughts without fooling around with any secret messages or props that he himself has brought to the theater.

Following is a selection of mental effects, principles, and suggestions, some of which I have used successfully in my own act.

Look upon each succeeding trick as a challenge to your show-manship skills. What kind of patter theme would best suit you when performing it? How would you misdirect the audience's attention at the critical moment? How long should the effect run in perfor-mance, and where would it fit best in a routine of mental magic?

In order to compare the honest ESP test with the magic trick, this section begins with an experiment which is absolutely genuine. It is not intended for formal shows, since there is a real failure factor involved, but for private get-togethers where the performer doubtless will take pains to point out that there is no trickery whatsoever. The workings of the test are so fair that it is unlikely that anyone would seriously question what he sees after the experiment has been demonstrated a few times.

ESP CARD LOCATION

Basic Illusion: A spectator picks the card predicted by the magician from a group of five.

How It Looks: The magician holds up a fan of five cards and asks the volunteer to sit next to him, close his eyes, and clasp the mentalist's hand. Next the volunteer is told the identity of one of the five cards, all of which are held with the faces away from the volunteer. The volunteer, eyes still closed, reaches up one finger and touches a card. He takes it out of the fan and generally finds he has selected the named card.

How It Works: This is what is known as "contact" mind reading. It works automatically in nearly every case.

What You Need: A pack of cards.

How to Do It: The only thing the performer needs to do is stare intently at the card he names, and *will* the volunteer's finger to touch it. The volunteer must let his finger wander freely above the card for some time. The subtle messages transmitted to him from the magician's clasped hand will guide him to the proper card. The magician must not try to "signal" when the finger nears the correct card; the subconscious does all the work.

Tips for Presentation: 1. Since this is not an infallible test, it should be reserved for private occasions such as family get-togethers. Some subjects simply will not have the proper rapport to find the card, though most of the people with whom I have tried this effect show an astonishing percentage of accuracy. If the subject succeeds in detecting the first card, it may be well to repeat the experiment with four cards, then with three, and so on.

2. Try to have a witness when this trick is performed, because the subject will probably think you are deliberately moving the correct card under his finger. If the subject does very well on this test, give *him* the cards and explain how it works, then try to find named cards in turn yourself. Let your finger hover freely over the cards and move it in diminishing arcs until the *tip* of the index finger touches a card.

3. If the subject scores very high in accuracy, try the test without holding his hand. If it still works, you will have undergone a genuine ESP experience. (My father showed me this effect many years ago. We achieved such a high level of accuracy that eventually he was able to lay the cards face down on a table and influence me to choose the proper card just by walking across the room to the table and touching the first card I felt drawn toward.)

LAST-MINUTE MESSAGE READING

Basic Illusion: The magician divines a message thought of by a volunteer.

How It Looks: A spectator is asked to think of a word, a short phrase, or perhaps a question that can be answered easily. To set it in his mind, the spectator is asked to print it on a stiff white card (about the size of a wedding invitation). Now the card is put into an envelope and sealed so there won't be any suspicion of trickery. The magician squirts the envelope with lighter fluid and sets the whole thing on fire. After it burns itself out in an ashtray, the magician reveals the word, phrase, or answer.

How It Works: The alcohol of the lighter fluid makes the envelope temporarily transparent.

What You Need: Ashtray. Envelope and stiff card. Pen. Container of lighter fluid.

How to Do It: The magician notes which way the written side of the card is inserted in the envelope, then squirts the same side with the fluid straight from the container. The writing will appear through the envelope. Once the envelope begins to burn, the face of it will turn opaque again.

Tips for Presentation: 1. This effect is ready-made for impressive presentation. It is *clean*—that is, the handling of the props seems absolutely fair, and the method is perfectly disguised. The performer should stress this apparent fairness in his patter, and he should be as far away from the envelope as possible when the writing takes place. The only time the performer handles the envelope is when he burns it, and he should do this casually, without the least appearance of having thought out his actions ahead of time. The performer must conceal by his acting ability the fact that he glances at the writing; it will be wise for him to speak while he is squirting the fluid, in order to divide the audience's attention between his words and deeds. Further, the audience will be watching his mouth as well as his hands, and if he holds the envelope far enough away from his head, it will be impossible for anyone to focus on both places at the same time.

2. It is not essential to ask the spectator to *print* his message, though it will be much easier to read if he does.

3. Do not let the trick's simplicity lead you to believe that it must be a short one. It can easily play between three to five minutes, depending on the magician's skill in building suspense. The better actor he is, the more miraculous the message reading will seem.

Note: In any trick involving fire, take every possible precaution. Have a container of water or some other sure fire quencher handy. This trick should not be taught to or performed by the very young.

A FAST PREDICTION

Basic Illusion: The mind reader predicts in writing the card a spectator will freely choose from a pack.

How It Looks: The magician shows a deck of cards, then looks around for some paper but cannot find any, so he writes a prediction on the face of a card. He drops the card into a hat, then walks over to a spectator and holds the hat high above the spectator's head. Handing him the deck, the magician now asks the volunteer to pick a card, then drop it into the hat. After this is done, the magician points out the absolute fairness of what he has done, and has another spectator remove the two cards. On one card is the magician's prediction—the name of the other card, which was selected by the volunteer.

How It Works: The pack is prepared beforehand, and the magician only pretends to write the prediction.

What You Need: A pack of cards. A felt-tip marker that has run dry.

Preparation: From a deck of cards, remove one card. On the faces of all the other cards, write with a felt-tip marker the name of the card that was removed. Place the removed card on the bottom of the pack and put a joker beneath it. .

How to Do It: Casually show the deck, perhaps even riffling the edges to show the sides that are not written upon. False-shuffle the pack after discarding the joker, then "write" on the bottom card with a dry marker. Drop this card into a hat. The spectator takes any other card and drops it unseen into the same hat (thus not seeing the writing on the chosen card). Naturally everyone will assume that the spectator had picked the card that has no writing on it, and that the magician wrote on the other.

Tips for Presentation: This is the most obvious of tricks, yet it succeeds in fooling audiences. It is important to emphasize the fairness of the selection after both cards are in the hat. While doing so, you may gently agitate the hat, as if mixing the cards. Of course, there is no need to mix the two cards in this effect, but the

186 / The Creative Magician's Handbook

movement will divert the audience's attention for a few seconds. Otherwise, an astute spectator may reason out what has happened.

ONE-AHEAD MESSAGE READING

Basic Illusion: The mentalist answers several questions sealed in envelopes.

How It Looks: The performer passes out paper, pencils, and envelopes to a group of people and instructs them to write words, phrases, numbers, questions, or whatever they wish, then seals them in the envelopes. The envelopes are passed up to the performer, who holds each to his head, one at a time, and reveals the contents. He rips each open to confirm what he has read, and asks the various audience members to acknowledge their messages as they are divined.

How It Works: A confederate fakes the first answer. After that, the conjurer reveals the contents of the various envelopes that he has torn open, always staying one ahead of the message he is supposedly reading.

What You Need: A confederate. Enough pencils, papers, and envelopes to distribute to a generous number of audience members.

How to Do It: The confederate does *not* pass up an envelope. In a large group, no one will notice the omission. When the magician gets the envelopes, he holds one up and pretends to read the contents. No matter what kind of bogus answer he delivers, the confederate acknowledges it as his. Now the magician "confirms" the answer by tearing open the envelope and "reading" the message aloud. He actually makes up the wording of the confederate's message—but while he is doing so he memorizes the actual words written on the card! Now when he holds up the next envelope, the magician "reveals" the message he has just secretly read. Tearing open the new envelope, he pretends to confirm his findings but really has an opportunity to read the next message. In this fashion, he stays one ahead of the audience. Since the confederate has not passed up an envelope, the magician finally will exhaust the envelopes and still have one message in his mind. He must ask if he "got" all the thoughts of every audience member that passed up a message. One will say that his thought was not divined. The magician looks about for an extra envelope, cannot find it, asks the audience if there is an envelope lying on the floor anywhere. But since no one will be able to find it, the magician finally says that he will try to "read" the last thought *directly* from the subject's mind, even though this is a much more difficult feat to accomplish. The subject comes forward, the magician places his hands on or near the spectator's temples, concentrates, and after much internal "struggle" succeeds in getting the final thought. This is a very strong ending for an easy effect.

Tips for Presentation: 1. The final reading without an envelope offers great opportunities for the actor and should be built up to a great peak of interest. If the nature of the message allows, the magician should "draw it forth" in bits and pieces, as if catching hold of small "corners" of the thought with great difficulty. Here is a possible line of patter for an imaginary message: "I was married this morning."

MAGICIAN: Your thought seems to concern a person . . . no, it is more than one individual . . . I would venture to say that you are one of the principals, is that correct? *(At this point, get an acknowledgment from the spectator; the more "yes" answers drawn forth from the spectator en route to the ultimate revelation, the greater the impression made on the audience.)* The other person involved is of the opposite sex, I believe? *(Affirmation from spectator.)* I also seem to see some other individuals connected with your thought . . . but they are rather shadowy . . . they seem to be watching you. Does that make sense? *(Affirmation.)* Yes, it's coming clearer—they are watching you *with* the woman in your thoughts. It's some kind of event . . . *(with sudden determination, as if the thought just crystallized)* I think I have it! *It's a wedding* . . . the woman is your wife, is that right? *(Affirmation.)* The guests are the wedding party . . . but . . . *(show some confusion)* . . . there *seems* to be another part of the thought, something else I haven't gotten. *Is* there something else? *(Affirmation.)* Please concentrate on this part of the message . . . *(Pause.)* Time? Does it have to do with time? *(Affirmation.)* You want me to tell you when the wedding took place? *(Affirmation.)* *Note that this partial failure to read the thought only sets up heightened anticipation for the final revelation. The magician has done so well thus far that the audience wants to see him succeed.* The wedding was quite recent, that's obvious from the vividness of the mental picture you are flashing at me . . . within the last week or two . . . no, wait! . . . More recent than that. *(Brief pause, then with cheerful, total confidence.)* You were married today! Is that it? *(Affirmation—but come in quickly and stifle premature applause.)* Would you please tell the audience the *exact* words you wrote?

VOLUNTEER: I was married this morning.

MAGICIAN: I'm sorry—would you say that a little more slowly? *(Repetition hammers the point home.)*

VOLUNTEER: I was married this morning.

MAGICIAN: Congratulations . . . *(shakes his hand)* and thank you very much!

(Applause will probably begin here. Get a second round by asking the audience for a hand for the newlywed as he takes his seat.)

2. This effect is known in the magic world as a "question-answering act." There are myriads of books dealing with the subject, many of them concerned with codifying the kinds of messages audiences tend to write, together with suggested answers. The trouble with "question answering" is that it casts the performer as a fortuneteller rather than as a mentalist. I believe the nature of this kind of act should be to show how sealed messages can be "read"; but this ability should not carry with it the claim that the performer can give advice to the audience and/or predict its future.

INDETECTABLE-OBJECT CODE

Basic Illusion: The "medium" is able to divine various thoughts pertaining to selected objects.

How It Looks: The magician introduces a "medium," who is taken out of the room with a committee to vouch for the fact that the medium and the magician do not communicate with each other. The magician shows several objects resting on a table, and proposes to set up some tests for the "medium." For instance, a number of coins may be put into a change purse, which is then closed. A card may be *mentally* chosen from a pack. Perhaps a wristwatch is set to a certain hour, then turned face down on the table. Various other tests are possible once the principle is understood.

How It Works: The necessary information is coded to the "medium" by the manner in which the objects are placed on the table.

Preparation: The "medium" and the magician must practice the coding principle by rehearsing various sample tests. The "medium" must strive for accuracy and reasonable speed in obtaining the necessary information during rehearsal.

How to Do It: The table should have a large rectangular top to allow greater space for coding. Also, this shape will be easier to mentally divide into areas. Each test will require the magician and "medium" to imagine the tabletop divided into areas. (Since the boundary lines are invisible, the system is virtually indetectable.)

For instance, the mental choice of a card can be coded by imagining the tabletop in twelve large sections, four along the top edge, four along the bottom edge, and four in the middle. Each section will "read" from stage left to stage right. Thus if the magician sets down the closed deck of cards in the upper left corner of the table, the "medium" will understand that an ace has been chosen. If the pack is in the middle of the table, but left of center, it will be considered to rest in the sixth imaginary block and a six will be the card that was picked. In this way, the denominations from ace to twelve may be coded. A king may be coded by placing the pack on the very edge of the table, with a little bit of the box protruding over the edge. (Anywhere along the edge will do.) A joker may be coded by retaining the card pack in the magician's hands and not setting it on the table. (In this application, the "medium" would walk to the magician and take the deck from him.)

To code the suit of the chosen card, the magician also takes care to set the pack down so that the top of the deck (the part that opens) points either to an imaginary three-, six-, nine-, or twelve-o'clock position with reference to the table edge. So if the pack is in the lower left-hand corner of the table and the top of the pack points right, the "medium" will know that the card is a nine of whichever suit the three-o'clock position signifies. (It is probably easiest to code the suits clockwise in the bridge order: clubs, diamonds, hearts, spades.) When the "medium" enters and notes the coded card, she picks up the pack, opens it and looks through the cards until she finds the chosen one. (This provides a reason for using the whole deck even though the choice was a mental one.)

In the case of the coins in the purse, the magician may code any amount up to a dollar by mentally dividing the tabletop into nine areas. By placing the purse in the upper left corner, the magician tells the "medium" that the amount is at least a dime. If the purse clasps are pointed up, the amount is exactly ten cents. If the amount is eleven cents, the clasps are pointed to an imaginary one o'clock. In this fashion, the nine areas code from ten to ninety cents while the clasp positions take care of the odd pennies. If the amount is under ten cents, the clasps may communicate the amount in clock fashion; the purse is placed on any edge of the table. Coding the hour on the wristwatch, it can be seen, is now a simple matter with this principle.

Tips for Presentation: This method requires considerable showmanship. The various tests must be programed into a rising series of climaxes. The only thing the magician must practice is the instantaneous mental recollection of where the object to be coded should be placed. The actual placement also should be sufficiently rehearsed so the magician can place the object correctly without appearing to deliberate where to put it. It should look like a random movement.

CODE FOR ANY ROOM

Basic Illusion: The "medium" is sent out of the room. The magician has the company select an object and place it beneath some knick-knack or article of furniture. The "medium" returns and slowly walks about the room, narrowing down her search to the specific vicinity where the object is hidden. At last, she finds its place of concealment.

How It Works: The room is divided into imaginary sectors, which are coded silently by the magician.

How to Do It: Rooms roughly square in shape fit this system best. Mentally divide each room into four large segments, and agree beforehand with the "medium" which direction to use for orientation. Let the upper left-hand section be numbered one, the upper right section two, and so through to four. Note in which sector the object is hidden. When the "medium" reenters the room, the performer unobtrusively clasps his hands together, the fingers of one around the fingers of the other hand—but grasps only as many fingers as needed to code the correct room sector. Thus, sector one might be keyed by clasping the index finger with the other fist, meanwhile curling the rest of the fingers backward into the fist. Practice so the posture is casual and unobtrusive.

Once the "medium" learns which general sector to look in, she begins veering toward that quarter of the room. Now the magician must mentally divide the coded sector itself into four subsectors, oriented in the same way. He relays this sector to the "medium"

ROOM CODE

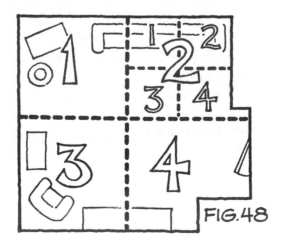

FIG.48

with the code. In this fashion, the "medium" draws ever closer to the correct corner of the room. A final subdivision using the same system will so limit the amount of space that the "medium" will have very few places left to consider. Some shrewd estimation at this point should discover the hiding place, though it is possible to still further subdivide sectors (even portions of furniture) until the correct spot is reached. (See Fig. 48 for a graphic representation of how a room is mentally divided.)

THE ULTIMATE PREMONITION

How It Looks: Any card is called out by the audience. The magician shows a pack of cards, and it is counted. One card is missing—the called-for card. The magician takes a sealed pay envelope from his pocket. The named card is within.

How It Works: Pocket indexes and subtly prearranged packs are used.

What You Need: Three packs of cards, all with the same back design. A set of pocket indexes, which can be purchased from most magic dealers. Pocket indexes are cloth-and-cardboard files which hold all fifty-two cards in sequential order, twenty-six in each of two indexes. One index is put in one pocket; the other half of the deck in its index is put in the other pocket.

Preparation: Put one pack of cards in the proper order and position in the indexes and place these in two pockets according to the instructions which come with them. In one of the remaining card cases, assemble only odd-numbered red suits and even-numbered black suits. In the last card case, put only even-numbered red suits and odd black suits. From each pack, remove one card. (The jack is considered odd, the queen even, the king and ace odd.)

How to Do It: There is a manuscript called "Premonition" which is supposed to tell how to accomplish the above effect, but it is so overpriced that I never purchased it. However, the effect has long intrigued me, so I eventually worked out what seems to me to be the basic method that has to be used. The pocket indexes are files small enough to be placed in one's pockets, and since the cards are sequentially arranged in them, the magician may "count down" by the fingers and extract any card by feel. To the audience, the magician has reserved only one card in his pocket. In this effect the fifty-two cards are sealed in pay envelopes, but this does not hamper the working of the indexes. The two prepared packs are placed in opposite jacket pockets. When the card is called out, the magician immediately determines whether it is odd or even, and what its color is, then reaches in the pocket that holds the pack of cards which *excludes* the suit/number combination in question. Thus, if the nine of spades is called, the performer would take out the pack that holds only even-numbered black cards and odd-numbered red cards. When counted, the pack will seem to be missing one vital card—and the called-for card will naturally not be in the deck. Assumption: the magician removed it earlier. During the counting-seeking process—which a volunteer does—the magician has ample time to obtain the correct card from the proper pocket index and hold it for all to see. By the time the attention returns to him, the presence of the pay envelope will have registered.

Tips for Presentation: In the above plot, an even more startling effect can be achieved by using a mnemonic code in connection with a set of pocket indexes. After the card is called out and the pack counted, the magician secretly substitutes a mnemonically arranged pack for the counted one. (He does so while the pay envelope is being opened and the chosen card is shown.) Now he places this card back in the pack, then brings it to the top while false-shuffling to keep the pack in order. He palms the card away from the pack, and hands the deck to a spectator. Predicting how many cards into the deck the card will appear, the magician can then "mind-read" the cards directly above and below it.

The following—my own elaboration of an Alwyn Stevenson trick—has a great impact on audiences. Though it takes some time to prepare, it is well worth the effort. It is a parlor trick, but can easily be adapted for the stage by increasing the size of the equipment.

SUPER SUCKER SPIRIT SLATES

Basic Illusion: The identity of a selected card is revealed with the aid of "spirit" writing.

How It Looks: The magician shows a small stiff rectangle of odd-looking blank white paper. Claiming it to be sensitive to the "spirits," he places it between two palm-size slates or blackboards, wraps a rubber band around them, and places the packet on a table or asks a spectator to hold it. A card is selected by another member of the audience, noted, and replaced. The magician now states that he has a spirit friend who will divine the identity of the card. Taking the rubber bands off the slates, he shows the square of paper. The image of a strange-looking person is now faintly outlined on it. In the image's upheld hand are two giant cards, one with its back showing, the other with its face showing. The face of this card is the same suit as the one chosen, but the number is one off. When the audience mentions the discrepancy, the magician shrugs and notes that his spirit friend often does things backward. Turning the card over, the magician reveals another faint picture—the image of the same person, this time with his back showing and the two cards still held high. The card whose face showed in the first picture now has its back to the camera; the other card's face is now revealed—it is that of the chosen card.

How It Works: The chosen card is forced. The paper with the images is switched for the blank paper via the "Spirit Slates" flap principle.

What You Need: A "Spirit Slate" trick, easily obtained from most dealers at little cost. (If a stage-size version of the trick is planned, then large slates must be used.) A pack of cards. Rubber bands. Cardboard. Access to a Xerox machine. A Polaroid camera. Two giant cards of the same suit but separated in number by one step.

Preparation: Setting up this effect will take a little time, but once it is done, the equipment will always be available. First, dress up in an outlandish costume. Hold the two giant cards in one hand—one face out, one back out—and have someone take a

Polaroid photo of you facing the camera with the wrong card face outward. Now turn around so that your back is toward the camera and keep the cards at the same height and in the same position. Have a photo taken of this pose. Take both photographs and place them on a Xerox machine. Make Xerox impressions of each picture, and also get some blank paper from the same machine. Take a piece of cardboard and cut two small rectangles about the size of the Polaroid photos. (These rectangles must fit in the center of the Spirit Slates, so the pictures may have to be trimmed down considerably.) Cut out two blank pieces of paper the same size as the trimmed photos. On either side of one cardboard rectangle, paste the two blank rectangles of paper. On either side of the other rectangle, paste the two Xerox photos. Set the pack to force the card showing on the "turned-around" photo. Place the photo-paper rectangle in the Spirit Slates so it is covered by the flap. Lay the blank rectangle casually on top.

How to Do It: The working should be clear from the nature of the preparations described above. The Spirit Slates trick consists of two miniature slates with a black flap which fits just inside the recessed writing surface of either slate. By putting the flap over a message written on a writing surface, the performer makes the slate appear blank. When the slates are bound together, the magician reverses them so that when they are taken apart, the flap transfers to the other slate's writing surface; this action reveals the hitherto concealed message. In the present trick, the flap is used to switch the photo paper for the blank one. Use any force of the necessary card. The working of the rest of the trick is automatic. Care must be taken, of course, to handle the slates so the edges of the photo paper are not revealed prematurely. While the switched photo is first seen by the spectators, there will be ample opportunity to spirit away the flap and the blank piece of paper beneath it, thus leaving the remaining equipment innocent and examinable.

Tips for Presentation: Presentation of this effect is pure process, and no atmospheric buildup is necessary or desirable. The sucker aspect of the finale is enough to spoil any spooky mood. But more important, the equipment itself generates enough atmosphere. The Xerox copy is very strange-looking, and the photo impressions will be hazy in outline. Even with the cutesy climax, the audience will be duly impressed by the bizarre quality of the effect.

Following are two effects known as telephone tricks. While the opportunities for performing them will be limited by the availability of a speaking instrument, they will be worth keeping in mind for special occasions when they can be introduced. Each effect makes use of common trick card decks.

THE FREE-CHOICE TELEPHONE TEST

Basic Illusion: A card is chosen by anyone called on the phone at random. The magician shows a pack of cards and reveals that one card was reversed much earlier that evening. Not only is it the chosen card, but it turns out to have a different-colored back from the rest of the deck—proof that the magician already knew which card would be named.

How to Do It: This stunning phone trick is one of Tony Corinda's easiest, yet most amazing ideas. The only thing needed is a Brain Wave Deck, available from most magic dealers. This trick deck pairs off every card, face to face so that only backs are seen either way the cards are held. One half of the pack has red backs facing out; the other, blue backs. The cards are treated with a substance known as Roughing Fluid, which makes them adhere to one another face to face. Thus the magician is able to push off two at a time. He knows the sequence of the cards, so that he can easily find any card named just by running the cards through his hands. He also knows which have red or blue backs. Say the ten of hearts is selected: the magician takes the cards out of the box so that the blue backs are face up. He runs through them till he finds the place where the ten will appear. Gently adding pressure to the blue-back card adhering to the face of the ten, he slides the cards apart so the ten shows face up. He withdraws it and turns it over, revealing a red back—apparently, the only one in the deck. The spectator, naturally, may call anyone he wishes on the phone and ask him to name any card, since the magician can locate any one named.

Perhaps the most unusual feature of the previous effect is the freedom of the audience participant to phone anyone he wishes. Most telephone mind-reading effects require the performer to name the number to be called. Here is an example of this genre of magic, with a trifle more subtlety of coding than is usual.

ULTRA-MENTAL PHONE CODE

Basic Illusion: A card is selected, and the volunteer is told its identity by an unnamed individual he calls on the phone.

How It Looks: A pack of cards is produced from its case, spread to show various card faces, then shuffled. A spectator takes a single card and shows it to the group. The magician claims he knows an expert mind reader and proposes to phone him in connection with the current test. He does so, but does not communicate to the person he calls by any spoken word. As soon as the party answers, the magician hands the phone to the volunteer. The party on the other end almost immediately divines the name of the card.

How It Works: A combination of the Ultra-Mental Deck, an auditory signal, and some simple pumping for information.

What You Need: An Ultra-Mental Deck, easily obtainable from many retailers. An assistant willing to be at a given phone at the proper time.

How to Do It: The Ultra-Mental Deck repeats several card combinations throughout, though its system is not easily detected when the pack is casually spread from hand to hand. Thus it is easy to give the impression that the deck is unprepared and all cards are different. Actually, the spectator is able to choose only a few cards in each suit. The magician and the "ESP expert" both know which these cards are. The magician codes the suit when he makes the phone call; this is done by quietly clicking the nail of the middle finger against the thumbnail directly into the phone's mouthpiece. (No clicks for clubs, one for diamonds, two for hearts, three for spades.) The magician calls the number *but holds the mouthpiece away from his ear.* When the assistant picks up the receiver and says hello, the sound will be discernible to the magician even though no one else in the room will realize the other party has answered. As soon as he knows the assistant is listening, the magician clicks his nails into the mouthpiece. After he is finished, he must act as if he just then heard the party pick up the phone; he puts his ear to the earpiece, listens briefly without saying a word, nods his head, and calls the volunteer over and has him say hello. The assistant takes over; he knows the suit and realizes that the spectator could have chosen only two or three cards because of the deck used. He proceeds to pump for information in the manner described in the Ultra-Mental Deck instructions. For example, he may know the suit is spades, and the only available cards in that suit are the three, ten, and queen. His first remark on the phone may be, "Yes, I see you have chosen a black card. I think it is a high number, is it not?" If he gets a negative reply, he knows it is the three. If he gets an affirmative, he then might remark, "Yes, I thought so—a high number. In fact, a picture card, is it not?" If the answer is affirmative, he knows it is the queen; if negative, he knows it is the ten. Then he proceeds to correct the impression, or capitalize on his right guess—whichever action is appropriate.

There is one great difficulty in most coded mental acts: it is hard to find an assistant willing to spend time learning the code. The following card code system is a partial answer to the problem; it employs several easy-to-learn coding techniques.

TWO-WORD CARD CODE

Basic Illusion: Names of mentally selected cards are divined by the "medium."

How It Looks: The "medium" is blindfolded and the magician goes into the audience, where he asks people to think of cards. First, he has someone determine the suit color only. The choice is whispered to the magician, who writes it on a slate. A second volunteer determines the exact suit within that color, and the magician also writes this for the audience to see. Finally, the rank of the card is named and written down. Attempting to pick the thought from the collective consciousness of the audience, the "medium" announces first the color, then the suit, and finally the rank of the card.

How It Works: The *sound* of the information being written, together with either of two word combinations spoken by the magician, codes the card to the "medium."

How to Do It: When the magician writes the color, he scrawls *red* in one continuous effort. But if black is chosen, he prints the *B*, so that he makes two distinct sounds with the chalk. (This is much easier to discern than might be imagined, especially to the blindfolded "medium," whose entire sensory awareness is concentrated on hearing.) The suit is communicated in like manner: if either clubs or spades, the magician makes a deliberate separated stroke on the *C* of the former, and writes the latter in one continuous line. *Diamonds* takes two attacks on the *D*, and the *i* is dotted last, while the *H* of *hearts* is formed with three distinct chalk marks. The rank of card is a bit more complicated, but is still easy to learn, as follows.

If ten, ace, jack, or queen is chosen, the magician should audibly ask the audience member to repeat the name of the card to him. This action tells the "medium" it will be one of these four ranks. *Ace* is then written in one line; *jack* is written in one effort, but the *J* is distinctly dotted at the end of the writing. The *Q only* is written to signify the queen, and it is formed with a circular motion and a stroke, easily discernible by ear.

If the ten is chosen, ask for the name to be repeated, then *print* the word. The staccato sounds will be easy to identify.

If the king is chosen, say nothing and print the name.

If one of the odd numbers is chosen, after writing the name, ask the spectator if you have it right by saying "OK" in one of the following forms:

3 = OK.   5 = OK then?   7 = Is this OK?   9 = OK?
Observe that 3 is different from 9 in its vocal inflection.

Note: OK is chosen for the odd numbers because the *O* signifies the word "odd."

If one of the even numbers is chosen, the code words are "all right":

2 = All right. 4 = All right then? 6 = Is this all right?
8 = All right?

Tips for Presentation: 1. Once the card is coded, wipe the slate clean. This will signify that the coding is completed, and the "medium" may begin to divine the card without being told to start—a subtle point.

2. Another ending might be to hand the slate to the "medium" and let her "play" the scene with much mental strain, finally inscribing the three pieces of information (color, suit, rank) on the slate.

Mental routining is probably more difficult than arranging a regular magic act, because of the limited kinds of effect that are available. A prediction may make a good opening effect, especially if it is relatively short in playing time. A mind-reading test involving several persons often makes a good climax, but one should strive to end the routine alone on the stage for maximum effect. It may be well to have some brief mechanical card force ready to close the routine, something with a strong climax but little time needed to play. The Brain Wave Deck is especially useful in this regard.

MORE TRICKS

There are many valuable effects on the market in the area of mentalism. Some of the ones I have found especially rewarding are noted below.

Dictionary Mentalism: Al Baker is credited with this splendid book test. A page is chosen in a dictionary and the performer tells which word is so many lines down on it. He repeats the effect, but predicts which word will be selected the second time. Though it is not in the printed instructions, I have found it possible to tell (by "giant memory") which page any word is on by the same method, which informs the performer which word will be picked on each page.

ESP Color Rapport: A stand with five compartments on it bears five colored circles within each compartment. The magician shows five cards, each with a corresponding circle on it. He turns the cards back to audience and mixes them, then asks various audience members in which compartment each card should be placed. After he complies with their wishes, he shows that each color has been properly matched. Relying on magnets, this excellent effect is one of the few mental tricks that can be worked well before children.

Hoodoo Voodoo: This is a beautifully crafted set of white and black magic effigies of a man. The spectator sticks a pin in one—only to find that the magician has predicted his move by marking a white magic X on *his* copy of the effigy.

Mental Epic: This sophisticated application of the "one-ahead" principle permits one to "read" three thoughts—a selected word, a number, and a chosen card—by writing the thought on a divided blackboard. The effect is strong, the equipment attractive. I work it with a blindfold to build an impression of fairness.

Note: The pocket-size version of this effect is ridiculous. One cannot see it used without wanting to ask, "But why not just write the answers on a pad of paper?"

Popsy Pegs: This is a lovely and rather rare demonstration of psychokinesis (PK)—the ability of the mind to physically influence inanimate objects. Four large cards in a stand are shown, and one is selected. The card has a colored circle on it which the magician has "not seen" (there is a subtle coding device in the stand which is tripped when the card is removed). The magician now produces a framework that holds four colored streamers corresponding to the circles on the cards. Everyone concentrates on the chosen color and the appropriate streamer suddenly leaps high into the air.

Revello's Sightless Vision: This is a hood that fits over the head but permits the performer to see clearly. It is a fine, well-made piece of apparatus.

Will Power: This may be the most unusual piece of equipment in all mental magic. A long wooden stick has a ridge that holds several small cards. Three are picked and shuffled back into the pack. Then they are positioned under the ridge so that each card is separated from all the others by several increments of space. The spectators who picked the cards in turn balance the stick on the crotches of both hands, then bring the fingers together. The hands meet in different places each time, and the cards beneath the fingers on each "run" are plucked forth. They are the chosen cards.

Among the mentalism texts that I would call indispensable are Annemann's *Practical Mental Effects*, Corinda's *13 Steps to Mentalism*, and Nelson's *Hellstromism* and *The Art of Cold Reading*. Other valuable texts: Milbourne Christopher's *One-man Mental Magic* and *More One-man Mental Magic*, Will Dexter's *Identity Parade*, Ron Baillie's *Universal Mind* and *Extra Sensory Perfection*, Don Tanner's *Grant's Fabulous Feats of Mental Magic*, Grant's *25 One-man Mind-reading Tricks*, Corinda's *Tele-trickery*, David Hoy's *Psychic and Other Party Games*, Shiels' *13!!!*, *Something Strange*, and *Daemons, Darklings and Doppelgangers*, and William W. Larsen's "Spook Show in Your Parlor" (pamphlet).

13

Preparing for the Stage Show

Until now, we have been discussing principles of showmanship which are generally applicable to any staging situation. But platform- and stage-sized shows have certain characteristics all their own, and these will be examined in the next few chapters.

Before producing a magic show of any size, it is essential to plan and rehearse very carefully. The basic character you will portray must be determined. The pacing, patter, and routining must be worked out in detail. The tricks chosen must not exceed the limits of your technical ability, and the duration of your act or show must be dispassionately considered and, if necessary, ruthlessly cut.

In addition to the esthetic values of the act, the magician must consider the physical characteristics that will be involved. If possible, he should try to visit the staging facility on which he will be expected to work. Then he must determine his furniture placement. Does he have his own tables and stands? If so, where should they be placed on the stage? Does he have to borrow tables on which to set his props? If so, will they be available at the theater, school, or club in which the show is scheduled?

Every detail must be planned carefully beforehand. The magician must know where every piece of furniture is to be placed, and he must know where every essential piece of magic equipment will be when he needs it. Moreover, he needs to plan the blocking—the patterns of stage movement that will characterize the visual aspect of his show.

Earlier, we touched upon some of the fundamentals of stage movement, but now we must examine the subject a bit more thoroughly. Certain mechanical principles tend to govern the placement of furniture onstage, as well as body positions, and the magician ought to be familiar with a few of these basics in order to construct a pleasing, theatrically logical *stage picture* for his audiences.

Anyone working onstage should familiarize himself with the various imaginary areas into which stages are traditionally divided. We have already mentioned the terms *upstage, downstage, stage left,* and *stage right.* (Remember that left and right always relate to the actor's viewpoint as he faces the audience.) Using these four terms as guides, it is possible to divide the stage floor into several imaginary areas. Some texts stress nine subdivisions, but for most purposes, the following six will do.

1. UL—*Up left,* the left side of stage away from the audience.
2. DL—*Down left,* the left side of stage toward the audience.
3. UR—*Up right,* the right side of stage away from the audience.
4. DR—*Down right,* the right side of stage toward the audience.
5. UC—Center stage away from the audience.
6. DC—Center stage toward the audience.

A diagram of the six stage areas from directly above is shown in Fig. 49. The curved portion of the outline represents the apron of the stage—that part closest to the audience and usually in front of the curtain.

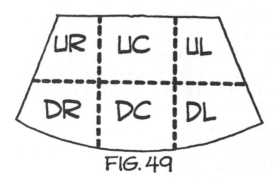

FIG. 49

We also speak of center stage, the geographic center of the playing area. In Fig. 49, center stage would occur at the halfway point of the line dividing UC and DC.

When theater directors speak of these stage areas, they note that the areas do not share equal worth or strength. The level of audience interest may be heightened by simply planning an act to take place in a stage area of greater strength.

The six areas in order of blocking strength are: UL (the weakest), DL, UR, DR, UC, DC (the strongest). As may be seen, the center positions are the strongest of all, with stage right claiming the next strongest impact. Center stage is the natural focal point for the spectator's vision; it is the place where anyone sitting in the usual theater seating arrangement normally would look. In addition, the occidental eye is used to reading left to right. Therefore, it will naturally look first at stage right when the curtain opens, then center, and finally, stage left.

Downstage is a more commanding position than upstage because it tends to have better visibility and physically brings the performer closer to the audience—which in itself is more visually arresting than a position that keeps the performer at some distance. Also, downstage sometimes improves the performer's audibility.

The positioning of furniture and props onstage is a fine art. Many magic acts utilize a table at center and two balancing ones DL and DR. Such an arrangement takes advantage of three areas of contrasting strengths, but keeps the center of attention (the middle upstage table) where it ought to be. Simply by moving from table to table, the magician is able to draw the audience's attention from one area to another, thus giving variety to the visual aspect of the show. Yet the central table will ensure that he always returns to the strongest part of the stage. Other magicians work only from one table at center, but this arrangement restricts the variety of their movements.

In an earlier chapter, we talked about the body positions that a performer may assume in relation to the audience (full front, one quarter turned, profile, three quarters turned, and full back) and noted that each is associated with a different degree of strength. Therefore, a performer standing full front DC will automatically command a higher degree of interest than the same individual standing at one quarter left in the UL area.

When there is more than one person onstage, a new set of guidelines comes into play. A magician must be able to draw attention even when a spectator or assistant is standing with him onstage. Likewise, he should be able to give the attention to the volunteer when he wishes.

There are three fundamental positions that two people can assume onstage in a magic act. The two positions of shared strength, in which each person attracts a nearly equal share of audience attention, are one-quarter L and R, and profile. In the one-quarter L and R shared position, the two people face one another in one-quarter turn stances, left and right. In the profile position, the two face one another on the same plane in a profile or half-turn stance. In the third position, audience attention is focused on one individual to the near exclusion of the other. The person commanding most attention faces the other in a one-quarter turn position left or right, and the other adopts a three-quarter turn stance facing him.

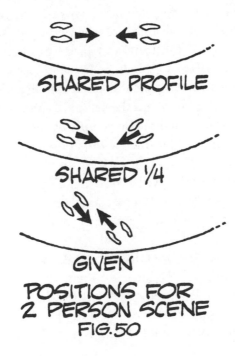

SHARED PROFILE

SHARED ¼

GIVEN

POSITIONS FOR
2 PERSON SCENE
FIG.50

The individual who stands with part of his back to the audience will attract very little attention. (These three two-person positions are shown in Fig. 50. The arrows indicate the direction each person faces. It should be noted that these positions are only examples and do not depict the full range of possible placements.)

There is one other principle of stage blocking that is very important to the magician, and that is the *triangle*. When more than two individuals are onstage and it is desirable to focus audience attention on one of them, the triangle method may be used. Even when only two persons are involved in the act, the triangle may still be formed by using a piece of furniture for the third point.

The principle of the triangle hinges on the fact that three focal points, or centers of visual interest, onstage are almost never placed on a straight line because it is a most uninteresting arrangement. To add variety, at least one should be on a different plane. When this arrangement is formed on a stage, an imaginary triangle is formed between the three persons or objects. Generally, the individual at the point of the triangle away from the audience commands the greatest attention. An example of such a simple triangular stage picture may be seen in Fig. 51. The arrows indicate that the downstage persons are looking at and facing at three quarter turns to the upstage actor.

Complex arrangements based on the triangle principle may be made when forming a stage picture. In general, the point farthest upstage will tend to take greatest attention. However, a triangle in

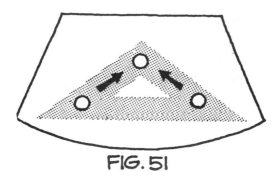

FIG. 51

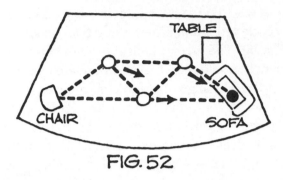

FIG. 52

which one leg is DR, while the persons at the apex and the other leg stand UL and DL, would tend to focus attention on the DR person (particularly if the others are looking at him).

In Fig. 52, an interlocking series of triangles is shown. Note how the focus of attention is directed to the person sitting on the sofa. How might the body position of each individual be changed to alter the focus of attention?

Let us see how a pattern of stage movement in a magic trick can take advantage of the principles discussed, using Invisible Flight from Chapter 3.

In Fig. 53, we see a stage setup consisting of the UC table and DL and DR chairs mentioned earlier. On the table are the two sheets of newspaper needed. The two handkerchiefs to be transposed are draped, one apiece, on the backs of the chairs. The magician begins the effect standing behind the table, thus taking the apex of the triangle formed by his body (and the table) and the chairs. He picks up one piece of paper and walks to the DL chair. Note the slightly curved line of movement. He stops just upstage and right of the chair to pick up the handkerchief. (If he came down level with the chair, he would have to turn away from the audience momentarily to get the silk; the position shown is stronger.) After wrapping the handkerchief up, he places the parcel on the seat of the chair.

In Fig. 54, the magician crosses to position 2, the table, where he picks up the second sheet of paper. Without stopping, he continues to position 3, just above and left of the DR chair. Here he wraps up the second silk and puts the parcel on the chair seat. Note

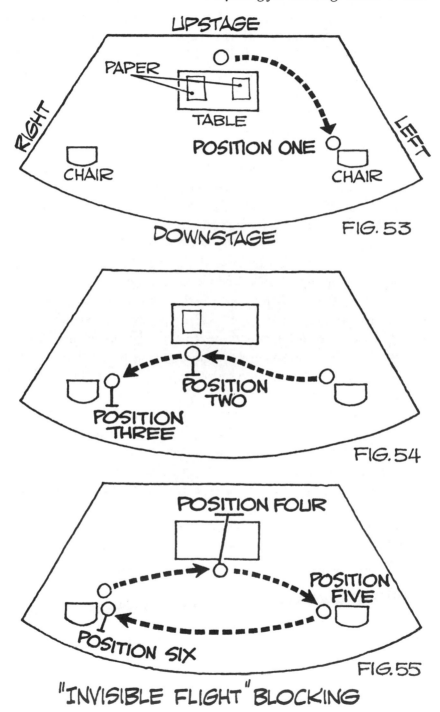

FIG. 53

FIG. 54

FIG. 55

"INVISIBLE FLIGHT" BLOCKING

that the second position puts him below the table and in a weaker body position for a moment. This is unfortunate, but the only alternative would be to cross to the upstage side of the table to get the paper, which would be too far out of the way. Generally, the shortest distance from one place to another onstage is the one a performer should take. Since the performer can pick up the paper while moving, the disadvantage of position 2 is a minor one, and is quickly corrected by the stronger posture of position 3.

In Fig. 55, the magician crosses to position 4, *but turns* so he is facing the audience. Here he makes some kind of cabalistic pass or says magic words to make the transposition "happen." He then proceeds to position 5, where he opens the first packet and reveals the exchanged silk. He crosses almost directly across to position 6, holding the first silk before him in a kind of flourish as he crosses. At position 6, he rips open the second packet and completes the trick.

Note how the positioning in this trick keeps the magician in relation to a triangle at all times, while the two climaxes occur in strong stage areas. Just before these climaxes, the magician assumes the strongest position since the beginning (position 4 in Fig. 54), thus drawing all attention and suggesting by pure mechanics that the finish is about to take place.

When planning any stage or platform show, the magician should keep these fundamentals of blocking in mind and pattern his stage movements to take maximum advantage of the strong areas. In addition, he will find blocking and also choice of material governed in part by the sight lines of the house, theater, or auditorium in which he is playing.

The term *sight lines* means exactly what it says: the lines of visibility from any seat in the house to the stage. If you have any doubt whether the audience will be able to see any part of your show, have someone sit in the following seats to check for visibility: the center of the first row, the extreme ends of the first row, and the extreme end seats of the last row. If everything is visible from these five seats, there are no sight line problems in the act.

Magicians must also consider a unique problem in the matter of sight lines or angles. Some equipment and/or moves must not be seen from the audience, so the magician must also check sight lines from the five seats named above to make sure hidden details will stay concealed.

The wise magician will block his movement beforehand but will not be so rigid about it that he cannot adapt during performance. Unexpected occurrences do take place, especially when volunteers are onstage, and the performer must be flexible enough to modify his staging to encompass the unforeseen.

The problems of blocking become more complex when the magician is asked to perform in staging arrangements other than proscenium (the traditional arrangement of most theaters and all movie houses) or proscenium-style floor plans. The most difficult arrangement would be the arena theater, also known as theater in the round. Arena staging setups make possible a pleasing rapport between performer and audience, but the accompanying angle problems are nearly insurmountable for a magician. When there are people on every side, it becomes impossible to show illusions that require a "blind side," where secret work may take place. Furthermore, even if the magician uses so-called angle-proof tricks in his act, the poor visibility for the people behind the performer's back proves a drawback. If a magician is forced to play in arena fashion, he should try to insist on blocking off one side or the angle of an aisle so he can give himself a substitute for a wall to play against.

If a magician cannot escape a staging situation that is less than satisfactory (and sometimes, when giving a show at a new location, one does not know until the last minute), then he must carefully choose his tricks and play different parts of the act to various sides of the audience. If he is facing one group of people during one trick, he may occasionally turn to include others, but constant pivoting should be avoided. Once he begins a new effect, the magician can play it for another group or side of the audience.

Such alternation is an unhappy compromise, but if it must be used, then the magician should simply make up his mind that some parts of the act will always be missed by some people. He must strive to apportion this liability fairly among the different audience sectors. The more he can play in or near an aisle, the more people will be able to see him at a time. It is also possible in some tricks to hold the equipment high enough so that even the people behind the magician's back can see.

Once the magician has planned what he will do and has thoroughly rehearsed it, he should decide what production values are needed to enhance the act. Are assistants necessary? If so, how will they be dressed? Will music build the dramatic atmosphere of some effects? If so, the magician must find a way to reproduce the sound. A live musician is the best method, but it is not always easy to find one who will always be available when needed at a realistic price. If the music is put on tape or a record is used, the entertainer must find out whether a tape or record player will be available. He also must be sure there is someone reliable to work the machine. Even if the magician brings his own sound equipment, he must double-check the stage to make sure there will be convenient electric outlets. If there are not, he may have to pack extension cords with his gear.

Lighting is another production value that can greatly enhance a magic act. The magician should remember that the greater the intensity of light onstage, the higher the audience's interest may be built. If one area is dark and another well lit, the well-lit section will attract more attention. Sometimes an entire effect may be played in uniform light which slowly grows brighter as the climax of the effect nears, subtly pointing up the unfolding drama. On the other hand, dim lighting will sometimes be of great value in building atmosphere, as in an occult theme. Just as in the case of sound effects, the magician must be sure the physical facilities he needs are available for lighting the show properly.

Whenever there is technical work that must be executed by stagehands unfamiliar to the magician, it is important to write out all cues clearly beforehand. Sound cues should get a separate sheet from the ones that involve lighting, and if a curtain must be pulled, that cue should be clearly written down on a separate piece of paper.

On a cue sheet, the exact nature of the cue must be spelled out, along with the dialogue, stage action, or signal from an offstage colleague which immediately precedes it, so the technician will know just when to do what he is supposed to.

The magician must also prepare a detailed checklist of all tables and props, and where each prop is placed (whether on a table or backstage). He should have a master list of all technical cues, and if necessary, costume and makeup checklists as well. The more he is able to put on paper, the less likely he will be to forget something important.

Before leaving for a show, the magician should be sure that all props are clean, and that his costume is neat and pressed. He should arrive early for every show so he can take care of any last-minute problems that may have arisen. Early arrival also ensures extra time to set up and go over the technical cues with the backstage crew.

Just before the show starts, it is wise to make a final inspection of all properties, to be sure that everything is where it should be, and every piece of magic equipment is in working order.

If there is a master of ceremonies, the magician should not trust to chance that his introduction will be made properly. An introduction serves as the performer's polarization; if it is unsatisfactory, the magician will have a great obstacle to surmount in the early moments of his act. It is wise to coach the emcee as to what kind of introduction you prefer. In some cases, it may even be a good idea to give him a *short* written introduction, or at least a list of vital points to make in his remarks to the audience.

We are now at the point where the curtain is ready to rise, or the performer is about to walk out onto the stage. It is important that the magician's voice and body be loosened up beforehand. I have met no entertainer, amateur or professional, who does not greatly benefit from a few moments of warm-up exercises.

I have already mentioned vocal exercises for improvement of projection and diction. These exercises also serve to get the speaking equipment tingling and ready for the performance. There are many useful bodily warm-up exercises that can be adopted: deep knee bends, flapping the arms about loosely, waggling the hands loosely from otherwise stiff arms. My favorite warm-up technique is to imagine tension in the forehead and eyes, then the jaw, then the neck, and so on down the body, part by part, until the whole body is tight. Then, one area at a time, I release the tension.

Some performers worry about stage fright, and others seem to think that unless a showman is scared before a show he will give a poor performance. This is ridiculous. The only kind of legitimate stage fright is that which stems from being unprepared to do a good job. Anyone who is guilty of giving an underrehearsed show deserves to be worried.

I think what many entertainers mean by "stage fright" is really a natural condition of exhilaration and heightened awareness that can come before a show. The nervous system is stimulated by the anticipation of the upcoming performance; perhaps the breathing is more rapid, and the pulse races. Rather than call this "stage fright," I would term it "concert pitch"—that is, the tuning up of a performing instrument to the proper level. Some of this tingly feeling may be controlled by deliberately taking deep slow breaths, and perhaps stretching slowly. Before I walk onstage, I prepare an "offstage beat," a mental attitude to show what kind of person is entering. I think how pleasant it will be to entertain such a fine audience, and I enter smiling. As I start out, I take one quick deep breath and don't exhale until I'm onstage. As a result, I enter in high spirits, feeling quite buoyant.

Before we take up the performance of the stage show in greater detail, a word should be said about a magician's postshow performance. If he has much equipment to break down—pack up and put away—he should rehearse this portion of the show as carefully as the setting up and performance. It may be important to get out of the auditorium at a certain hour, or the magician may have to travel a great distance to another show. Speed may be essential: if so, advance planning will help tremendously. (See Ken Griffin's excellent *Illusion Show Know-how* for much valuable information on the mechanics of quickly breaking down a large show.)

A final word: leave the auditorium, dressing rooms, etc. the way you found them. Refuse, cigarette butts, milk spills, torn paper—all should be properly disposed of. Apart from the ecological considerations, tidy stage habits often prove quite practical. A school or auditorium may think twice about rebooking a performer who has turned the stage facilities into a pigsty.

14

Assistants and Volunteers

Conjuring is a profession in which no one errs
through excess of modesty.

Robert-Houdin

Magicians often achieve certain kinds of effects through the help of
other people. Such helpers may be classified as assistants, who
travel with the act or show; confederates, or secret assistants; or
volunteers, recruited from the audience.

Some conjurers believe that the only important person onstage
is the performer himself. This view is shortsighted, for it can lead to
audience antagonism. Further, it is hard for such magicians to get
and keep good assistants. Their attitude persists at the expense of all
other egos; as a result, the assistant can find no joy working for such
a show.

Fitzkee aptly calls this the servant-master relationship, and is
correct in saying it is no longer appropriate. The all-knowing seer
whose mute helpers are simple functionaries is an anachronism.
The performer must subjugate his ego and learn respect for the
individual abilities of each person who sets foot on the stage with
him.

The usual haphazard choice of volunteers from the audience is
also a mistake. The person who leaves his seat to assist a magician
has become part of the act, and should add to its entertainment
value. Selection of audience volunteers can be a tricky business, and
sometimes an unfortunate choice will occur. But if the magician
looks over the group carefully beforehand and mentally picks out
likely prospects for later use, he will at least avoid last-minute
surprises.

There are no hard and fast rules for picking volunteers.

Experience will teach a showman instinctively what to look for, though he will not always get it. Basically, the qualities I look for are amiability, intelligence, and just a trace of shyness. The last quality is particularly important, since it will make it easier to influence the volunteer's actions.

In general, it is wise to choose pleasing-looking individuals, though I would interpret this in the broadest possible sense and find beauty in many ages and types. A pretty girl may be an asset onstage to some extent, yet a dazzling beauty may draw attention away from the effects (this distraction could be a valuable mis-directive device as well as a handicap). Certainly a smiling elderly man or middle-aged woman presents just as nice an appearance onstage as do the so-called beautiful people.

Though the choice of a volunteer ought to appear free and off the cuff, the magician must really choose in advance the person who will stand onstage with him. The easiest way to draft the person you want is to ask for volunteers while looking vaguely about, then stare straight at the individual you have mentally selected. If there is any reluctance on his part, and if physical circumstances permit, you might walk forward and hold out a hand to the spectator—few can resist such a direct "draft." But if an audience member strongly resists, find someone else. Don't embarrass or upset that spectator.

When I perform the French Arm Chopper—the trade name for a particularly effective wrist guillotine trick—I select my volunteer before the show and brief him. I have found that while the equipment is perfectly safe, it can give the wrist a nasty knock unless the volunteer is prepared. There may be other occasions when a magician should forewarn his volunteer. In such cases, it may even be necessary to tell just what is going to take place, *even the method;* if you have picked your assistant wisely, you need have no fear that he will reveal the secret prematurely. Prechecking the volunteer is valid at any time when it will heighten the effect of a trick. Once the volunteer is onstage, treat him or her with respect and friendly firmness. Show that all action and direction in the show originates with you. But at the same time, remember that the volunteer does not know what you want, so be sure to give explicit, simple instructions. If by chance you get a slow volunteer, whose thought processes move sluggishly, be especially patient and accommodating in explaining what you want. This is common courtesy, and besides, it will make you look good to the rest of the audience. If, on the other hand, you err and draw a smart aleck, do *not* try to outsass him! Be polite, pleasant, and friendly, no matter how much you'd like to send him back to his seat. Firmly insist on following *your* script, in spite of his digressions or comments. If you can top his remarks in a witty manner, do so, provided you show no rancor. The audience will probably sympathize with you all the more because of the volunteer's freshness. If possible, speed the tempo, even eliminate details if you can, and get the smart aleck back to his seat as soon as feasible. Then proceed in a more leisurely manner to your next *solo* trick.

Remember, the first thing you are selling when you do an act is your own personality. If you do not respect and like the audience or *any* of its members, chances are you will not entertain anyone. The audience may begin to resent you as a person, and if this happens, you might as well break your wand and catch a magic carpet home.

One more extremely important piece of advice regarding treatment of volunteers: make sure that the equipment they will be involved with is in no way physically uncomfortable to them. My first experience as a volunteer to a magician took place in the Catskills, where a third-rate performer called me up to assist in the Human Hen Trick, in which a seemingly endless series of eggs is produced from the volunteer's mouth. The trick involves a hollow metal shell whose rounded exterior resembles an egg. The volunteer is prepared beforehand by the magician, who tells him to slip the shell in his mouth while going offstage after a preliminary trick. The volunteer then pretend- to be ill and holds his stomach; the magician holds the assistant's head over a hat, and the volunteer opens his mouth, showing the "egg." The magician drops a palmed egg into the hat, and the spectator closes his mouth, only to repeat the routine again and again. When I aided in this trick, the metal shell was rusty, and its taste was so awful that I hardly had to feign sickness at the proper time.

There is no excuse for giving a spectator an unsanitary prop to handle. Not only is it uncouth, but it can be a threat to the volunteer's health (and to your finances, if you get sued as a result).

Let us now consider the professional assistant who works with the magician during the show. There are all sorts of functions that an assistant can fulfill in a magic show, though many performers use them only to dress up the stage, hand the magician props, and sometimes do concealed business necessary to a trick. While these functions are important, they are not interesting enough in themselves to ensure the loyalty of a good assistant. The magician who limits his helper's role to such humdrum chores will probably spend much of his time finding and breaking in new assistants.

Some books warn against the assistant who mugs too much and tries to steal a scene from the magician, but this problem will never come up if you find an ego-satisfying role for the helper.

When I perform my children's act, Count Emkay the Miraculous, I often use one or two assistants, and I always give them something interesting to do onstage—either a character to play or some other vital role which permits them to react, show emotion, and take an active and *noticeable* part in the show. I have used a number of female assistants at one time or another for my ·comedy version of the Bullet Catching trick (described in a later chapter); though these assistants are essentially a target in the effect, the increasing nervousness they show at my false blunders is the primary reason the effect builds to its peak of interest. Sometimes a girl assistant will take the voice and movements of Melville, a dragon puppet I trade gags with. Other times, especially when I produce objects from a hat (but *never* the thing I am trying to find), the assistant will be the reactive link with the audience, showing embarrassment and impatience at my ineptness. Such reactions are vital to the act.

Another way I have used assistants is to cast them in comedic roles, to which I play straight man. The bumpkin who wants to learn magic but gets everything wrong is a viable character for a children's show and it permits the assistant to get laughs and be an important part of the program. One time I used an assistant in a character of a much more competent magician than Count Emkay.

When I entered in a black cape, I called attention to a sign on an easel which read "Count Emkay the Miraculous" in simple black letters. But when the assistant entered wearing a bright red satin cape, he turned my sign around to reveal the words "Mazza the Assistant" in fancy script with letters made of glittering spangles.

At least one magician who has written a pamphlet on magic showmanship holds that assistants should never be part of the magician's curtain call at the close of the show. This is a selfish and useless attitude. If the assistant has worked hard, he or she should be recognized for it. The shape of the show may dictate that the assistant stand onstage in the background for the call, but this is better than excluding him entirely. And if the assistant has played a vital character, he or she must by all means garner a share of the applause.

When looking around for a permanent assistant to work in your act, keep only one thing in mind: the effectiveness of the show. It is no time for you to do favors for unqualified friends or to seek the gratitude of some individual you admire. Find a personable, intelligent person who is willing to *rehearse* until every cue and every piece of timing is precise. More than most other theatrical arts, magic requires flawless execution; every seemingly random movement of an assistant should be carefully rehearsed to occur in the smoothest manner possible. One strives for an illusion of artlessness, but considerable technique is hidden beneath that disarming veneer.

If an assistant must come onstage and set or take away a prop, the movement must attract no more attention than the magician's purpose requires. More than about three steps taken onstage will draw considerable audience attention; if the magician does not want to lose the spectators' focus, he should arrange for the assistant's movements not to take place at times when the attention must be elsewhere. On the other hand, sometimes it may be useful to divert the audience's attention to the assistant, in which case a longer cross or sequence of movements may be just the thing.

A good assistant must have the same degree of poise as the magician. He should possess graceful carriage and good posture. If he speaks, he must be able to project and enunciate as well as the chief performer. The assistant should also be able to smile as easily and genuinely as the magician. In short, the assistant must have "personal proof"—to be liked by the audience practically at first sight.

Even if you obtain the services of a thoroughly professional and competent aide, it is wise to make comprehensive cue sheets of every action and speech the assistant will be required to execute, whether onstage or off. Both magician and assistant should swear by their cue sheets; even though the contents are known by heart, the sheets should be trotted out and carefully reviewed before every single performance.

Costuming can be a vital consideration in preparing an assistant for stage work. Do not leave the choice up to the assistant, but talk it out with him or her and decide on some wardrobe that is both theatrically appealing and comfortable for the helper to wear. Never insist on a dress or costume which will embarrass or annoy the assistant; you need to maintain high morale in order to give a good show. If a woman is helping you, permit her to choose a style which flatters her figure. If she likes to wear short skirts, let her do so (unless you are playing for an audience that might be offended by such a costume). If she is self-conscious about her legs, do not insist on putting her in a miniskirt; she will be too ill at ease to do a good job onstage, and chances are you will retain neither her loyalty nor her services.

Jewelry sometimes "dresses" up a costume nicely, but bear in mind that cufflinks, bracelets, rings, and other gewgaws may catch on the magical equipment with which you or your assistant are working. Permit jewelry only if you are certain that it can in no way interfere with the smooth working of the effects.

One final piece of advice when choosing assistants: seek polite people with a sense of decorum and plain good manners. Whether you are touring from town to town or simply doing a show at a local social club, you will be associated with your assistant in the minds of the sponsors. A surly helper can displease a client so much that you may lose any chance of a return date with that organization.

In small towns, this is an especially keen danger. Townspeople talk to one another, and since many Americans retain an unpleasant suspicion of theatrical folk, it is most important to behave in a manner which will temporarily suspend their prejudices—at least as far as you and your show are concerned. Never permit an assistant to enter a town where you will be playing and display ill manners or slovenly dress. If you do, you will surely lose business.

We have discussed many do's and don'ts pertaining to assistants and volunteers, but if problems should arise not discussed in this chapter, one piece of advice will go far toward solving them.

Do not treat your assistant or a volunteer like a magic wand. He or she is not a prop, but a human being with feelings that need to be considered. Do so, and you will be rewarded with loyalty and, ultimately, better performance.

15

Tricks and Routines
for Stage and Platform

Routining a longer show for stage or platform requires a fine sense of pace. The effects must generally build toward a pinnacle of interest at the close of the evening. If the show includes more than one act, each curtain must represent a climax of excitement, with the last act reaching greater heights than the previous ones.

But though the shape of the stage show should be an upward curve, there must be careful and subtle variations within the show's framework. Momentary let-ups of suspense must be carefully programed so the audience has an opportunity to catch its breath before the next demand upon its attention and concentration is made.

Careful use of musical and lighting effects may facilitate this buildup, with stage lights growing progressively brighter throughout the evening, until the finale is a blaze of illumination. Similarly, the areas of the stage may be so blocked as to use more and more of the playing space as the evening proceeds until the ultimate effect fills the full stage with color and spectacle.

At the end of a successful performance, the magician will take a certain number of curtain calls. This final appearance should not be haphazard; it should be blocked out and timed as carefully as the rest of the show. There is an all but universal temptation to see how many bows can be milked from the audience; it is a practice that should be scrupulously avoided. Too many curtain calls merely weary the audience and subject the performer to the danger of still being onstage when the applause stops. One or two bows are sufficient; in the case of a very successful show, perhaps three. I cannot conceive of a reason for exceeding that number.

Following are a number of routines and tricks suitable for stage and/or platform shows.

THE DRUNKEN MAGICIAN

How It Looks: The magician enters to music and, in pantomime, portrays an inebriated wizard trying to get into his house and go to bed. He enters in disarray and tries to find his house key. Instead, he produces fans of cards, coins, balls, silks—any unlikely object imaginable. At last he finds his key and tries to insert it in an imaginary door. But it vanishes from his hands. After some bleary-eyed fumbling, he produces the key again, only to have it disappear again as he reaches out toward the door with it. The third time he simply breathes at the door, and it seems to open; at least, he pantomimes walking through.

Now he tries taking his jacket off, but finds a miscellany of strange objects in its pockets. At length, he discovers a rope up his sleeve, pulls it, finds it is some thirty feet long and is stuck to one ankle. He pulls the rope back through the pants leg, hoping to release the other end. But when the first end disappears through his sleeve, the magician finds it has now apparently gotten stuck to his other ankle. (In other words, the audience has seen three ends of the rope.) He pulls the latest end, and again the entire length is produced. Once more, it seems stuck. But with a triumphant yank, the magician at last frees it, to find the last end attached to a pair of shorts. He is now able to remove his jacket.

Going to a table, he mimes hunger. He takes out a giant pocket watch, checks the time, and opens it, finding a sandwich inside. Taking a bite, he puts it back in the watch and sticks it in his pocket again. He finds a banana in his pocket, tries to unpeel it, but the peels keep snapping shut again. Finally he puts it down in disgust, produces another banana, and *unzips* it. Taking a bite, he zips it back up, and puts it back in his pocket. Lighting a candle to see what he is doing, he absent-mindedly bites off the lit end and chews and swallows both wick and candle.

Then he becomes aware that he is thirsty. Taking a piece of newspaper, he wraps it into a cone and produces an uncapped bottle from it, then proceeds to pour some liquid into a glass. As he pours, he yawns, taking away the hand that holds the glass to cover his mouth. The glass remains suspended while he pours. Then he grasps it again, drinks, and puts the bottle and glass down; he yawns again, decides to go to bed. Taking a jug from the table, he pulls out the top—it is a nightcap. He dons it, then reaches into his pants and pulls his shirt out. It drops to the floor, and is as long as an old-fashioned nightshirt. He picks up the jug again, pulls the top—it is a lit candle. He turns the jug around, and it is seen to be a chamber-pot. He walks off with the candle showing the way, yawning.

How to Do It: This routine requires considerable acting ability on the part of the magician. It is really a series of sight gags with a magical slant. Most performers who use the "drunk" idea concentrate on gentle humor and lots of mystification. In this routine, broad comedy is the keynote, and the magician should be adept at playing for laughs. Chaplin's short film *One A.M.* is a comedy classic which might be profitably studied before undertaking this routine. The actual effects are stock ones that may be purchased at most magic shops; some few of them, such as the One-two-three Banana (the one whose peels snap together) may be difficult to find, but the performer may substitute many other effects into the general framework. As described, the routine employs the following devices:

Production of Objects: Load the jacket and sleeves with as many kinds of cards, coins, balls, and other objects as possible. There are so many varied kinds of equipment available that the individual must decide for himself what kinds he can handle best.

Vanishing Key: Either attach a key to a piece of black elastic and hang it just beneath the jacket so it can easily be grasped, or else purchase a Vanishing Key with a sharp hook that will pin it to the pants leg as the hand swings backward.

Objects in Pockets: Load the jacket pockets with a variety of rubber production items that can easily be squeezed into a small space: oranges, apples, hot dogs, chickens, fish, pizza, etc. Stick in a few packets of artificial flowers that compress into a small wad but open out into colorful bouquets when released. (They are known as Spring Flowers.)

Rope Routine: Ask for the Professor Cheer Rope Trick. It is a popular, rather overpriced item long used in comedy acts and by circus clowns. Despite the price, the effect is worth it, and the threading of the rope on the body is so complicated that one really must invest in the instructions. The rope comes threaded with the attached shorts. I have found that the fifty feet provided in the equipment is too much rope for good comedic timing; I suggest cutting the rope back to thirty to thirty-five feet.

Food Gags: The Sandwich Watch is a standard comedy prop, as is the Zipper Banana. The One-two-three Banana, as noted, may be difficult to obtain, but is worth looking for. The candle eating is a well-known effect: cut off about an inch and a half of the candle end, stick a pin upright, then fashion a fake candle end from a piece of apple. Stick it onto the pin, and in its center force a sliver of almond (the "wick"). The almond will light. As he brings his mouth toward it, the magician blows out the flame, and immediately pops the end in his mouth. It will appear that he has swallowed a flaming candle. Let the mouth be hollowed around the candle till the wick cools; it will not be very hot anyway. Then bite off and swallow a piece of the apple and almond. *Caution:* This trick, which involves fire, is not to be performed by young magicians. Even mature entertainers must be extremely cautious when using flame in a trick. The burned almond is easily extinguished, but the trick must be handled with great care and rehearsed extensively to get the flame blown out in the same motion that places the candle in the mouth.

Bottle Production: This is the inexpensive Soda Pop Production in which the bottle is stolen from the pants by hooking the thumb into a strong loop attached to a bottle cap. Under cover of the newspaper, the thumb pulls the cap off the bottle and takes it away while the paper is discarded. The uncorked bottle remains.

Suspended Glass: This is an effect known as the Airborne Glass. A central post in the middle of the glass has a catgut loop attached to it. The loop is slipped over the end of the bottle, which pours right over the loop into the glass. The loop is indiscernible.

Going-to-bed Gags: This is an effect known as And So to Bed. It is available from a few Midwestern suppliers, and other magic dealers probably could order one on request. The equipment consists of some cloth that can be sewn to the bottom of any shirt to transform it into a nightshirt; a cutout board shows a jug on one side, a chamberpot on the other. The cutout holds the nightcap and has a wooden stick that looks like a candle, into which a safety match may be stuck. A piece of striking paper is pasted on the side of the cutout.

Tips for Presentation: 1. There are many effects which may be added to or substituted for those outlined. This routine would play, I believe, about five minutes and might make an act in itself, or could be an interlude in a longer show. In either case, the fact that they are about to see a portrayal of a drunken magician must be explained to the spectators, either by the magician or by a master of ceremonies.

2. Music is essential. There are many standards associated with inebriation that could be used: "Sweet Adeline," "Three o'Clock in the Morning," "One More for the Road," "How Dry I Am," etc. It would be preferable to work with a pianist or other live musician. Recordings may be employed, of course, but a sound track will make it necessary to perform the act the same way every night. With a pianist on the scene, the magician can experiment with the timing of each individual gag to see which may be developed further and which must be played short.

3. The magician should react to the things happening as though he were as surprised as anyone watching. He should act as if his magic has gotten out of hand, and he is no longer in control. Study the way a good comedian or humorous actor does a double-take, then strive to find an original way to do so yourself.

4. Before playing this act, considerable rehearsal will be needed. Since there is a huge quantity of material that will have to be concealed upon the magician's person, he must adopt a mode of dress that will hold the various pieces of apparatus; if possible, large secret pockets should be sewn into the garments themselves. A cape

would be the easiest piece of costume to adapt to such purposes, though baggy, sloppy evening dress would also serve. Not only must the costuming accommodate the props, but it must permit the various effects to work without being hampered. The Professor Cheer rope production in particular should be repeatedly practiced to make sure the rope does not get caught on other pieces of magic equipment hidden in the performer's clothes.

ELECTION-DAY BLUES

Basic Illusion: The magician produces various liquids from "empty" containers.

How It Looks: After complaining that election day closes all the bars, the magician says he does not mind, because he has a Think-a-Drink gadget which works as follows: he holds up a small jug, thinks of wine, and pours out a red liquid, which he swigs. A policeman shows up at the polls at that point, and the magician shows that the jug is empty. But as soon as the cop turns away, the magician thinks of crème de menthe and pours a green liquid from the jug. The policeman turns around, but the magician has drunk the liquid and the bottle is again empty. The magician uses it a third time, thinking of whiskey; a yellow liquid is produced and drunk, but the jug is still shown empty. The magician now says that the trick is over, but he dares not return home to his wife in such a condition, or she will never believe he has been doing a magic show. So he holds a large glass under the jug and thinks "milk." Nothing happens. Acting embarrassed, the performer explains that it has been so long since he thought of milk that the jug does not know what it is. Perhaps he does not need any after all . . . he will make a test. Taking a large red flower out of a vase, he breathes on it. It wilts. "I guess I do need the milk," the magician says, reaching for a can of evaporated milk. He tilts it over the glass, but it is also empty. To save the day, the performer takes a rubber glove from his pocket, blows it up to look like an udder, and "milks" it into the can of evaporated milk. Now he is able to pour a full glass of milk from the can—which he sets aside, with a wry face, "for later."

How to Do It: This, too, is a gathering of several existing pieces of equipment into a single routine.

Color-changing Liquids: Into three shot glasses place one drop each of food coloring: red, green, and yellow (which may be blended into an amber hue by mixing with other colors; see the food-coloring package for details). Even if the drop dries out, it will be enough to tint the liquid properly. The jug is filled with plain water.

Empty-full Jug: This is a device known as a Lota Bottle or Bowl. Many styles and sizes may be purchased in a wide range of prices. Essentially the device consists of an inner chamber where most of the liquid is stored. An air hole on the lip of the jug may be stopped up by putting a finger firmly against it; this stops the flow of liquid.

Wilting Flower: This is a mechanical device with a wire threaded through the artificial flower. At the end of the wire is a ring which any finger can pull down; this action pulls the blossom of the flower sideways and downward.

Empty-full Milk Can: This uses an item known as a Foo Can—a can with a wall dividing its middle so that, turned one way, the liquid will be retained though the can is inverted. Turned the other way, the liquid pours out. The milk can and rubber glove can be bought together under the name Invisible Bovine. Instead of using milk, it is wise to put a few drops of OOM into the glass and keep plain water in the Foo Can. (Milk will shorten the effective life of the equipment.) OOM stands for "Oil of Milk." It is an oily substance which will make water look exactly like milk. It cannot be imbibed—hence the last gag about leaving the milk "for later."

Tips for Presentation: 1. This is an amusing routine, provided the audience does not mind tricks involving alcohol. It plays perhaps four minutes, and should build in tempo till the final pouring of milk gets the sole round of applause of the trick. The action of placing the glass aside is enough of a transition to make it obvious that a new trick will soon be begun. I have found that this effect fits well in the second slot of a four- or five-trick act, or may be used early in a longer show. It gives the performer a chance to warm up to the audience in the role of a narrator. He is telling a story for their amusement, and this relationship should knit closer the bond between spectator and performer.

2. To be safe, it may be wise to pack a thermos of water to fill both Lota jug and Foo Can, in case there is no water faucet handy where you are performing.

IMPROMPTU SAWING A WOMAN IN HALF

Basic Illusion: A woman is bound with ropes or ribbons or silks. They are "pulled" through her without injury.

How It Looks: The magician introduces his assistant and asks two audience volunteers to help. Taking two sturdy pieces of rope of equal length, he has the assistant stand in front of the middle point of both ropes, then hands two ends to one audience member and the other pair of ends to the other volunteer. Showing that the ropes cannot pass onto the other side of his assistant's body without halving her, the magician takes one end each from the two audience volunteers, ties a knot with them, and pulls the knot tight around the assistant's waist. Then he hands the now crossed ends back to the volunteers. Building the suspense as effectively as he can, the performer instructs the volunteers to pull sharply on the ropes at the count of three. As he says the number, he fires a shot, and the assistant shrieks. The ropes seem to pull through her and can be seen unknotted and still held by the two volunteers—but now the rope is in front of the assistant's body.

How It Works: The ropes are doubled and loosely tied together so that what appears to be the true middle of both is really the juncture of the two folded ropes held together by a loop of thread.

How to Do It: Fold each rope in half and attach them with thread as explained. Make sure the thread you use is easy to break. The central strands from a piece of magician's rope are well suited to the purpose; they break very easily. Show the two ropes draped casually in one hand, the ends hanging down. The audience will think you are holding two long lengths of rope by their middles. In fact, you are holding two folded pieces of rope and concealing the connecting thread in your hand. If the thread were cut at this time, the two ropes would drop from either side of your hand. The folded ropes are placed behind the assistant's back so the two loops held together by the thread loop are concealed by her body. The action of taking an end from each assistant and knotting them in a simple square knot around her body automatically sets up the trick. When the assistants yank the rope, the thread will break and the ropes will unfold in front of the assistant's body.

Tips for Presentation: 1. The entire effect is built up by careful details, patter, and the acting of the assistant. She must appear nervous, perhaps quite scared. The gunshot and scream may be used together, or the shot may be eliminated, but some kind of sound must be made at the climax—even if the magician just shouts something cabalistic. After the ropes are "through," the magician should pose for a second or two so the audience sees just what has happened.

2. When I play this effect, I use a variant on the market called Visible Walking Through Ribbons. In this version, the assistant conceals the false middle of two colorful ribbons in front of her body, holding the place with her hand. By tugging on the ribbons after they have been circled around the assistant's waist, I am able to show that the pressure forces the helper to move forward slightly, thus building the impression that the ribbons solidly circle the assistant's body. At the time of the three-count, I make a few false starts to delay the effect and heighten the suspense. For example:

MAGICIAN: One! Two! (*He pauses and faces the audience.*) I hope this works . . . I never tried it before . . . (*He turns around.*) One! Two! (*Sneezes.*) Excuse me! *Three!*

The last count comes suddenly, when the audience is off guard.

3. Sol Stein plays this trick using giant colorful silks instead of ropes. At the outset, he reminds the audience that most magicians only saw in half women who are concealed in boxes. Instead, he plans to do so in the open. When the silks are knotted about the assistant's middle, the audience volunteers are told to "saw" the silks from side to side to do the "cutting." The actual moment of cutting is built up with a suspenseful countdown, and the volunteers are ordered to pull the silks through *"fast."* As soon as the penetration is completed, Stein calls out *"Stop!!"* in a commanding tone of voice—which effectively halts the movement of the volunteers, sets the tableau of the effect, and freezes the audience's

attention before anyone can respond. This presentation is an excellent example of the way a climax is prepared, achieved, and terminated. At all times, the audience's reactions are under the performer's strict control.

SILK ESCAPE

Basic Illusion: A rope held by a volunteer penetrates a silk tied about the magician's hands.

How It Looks: The performer's wrists are tied together with a silk. A *long* piece of rope is dropped behind the silk and the ends are drawn above and below the silk passing between the wrists. The volunteer stands on the other side of the stage and holds both ends of the rope. With a simple swing of his wrists right and then left, the performer steps away from the rope. Though his wrists are still tied, the rope has fallen free.

How It Works: A loop of rope may be worked over the hands so as to release it from the silk.

How to Do It: The magician keeps the heels of his hands far enough apart when his wrists are bound to leave a little space

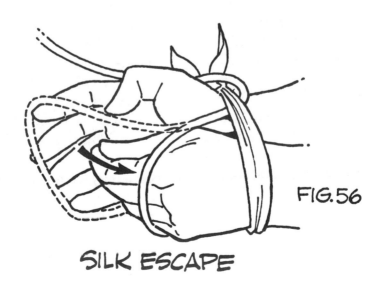

FIG. 56

SILK ESCAPE

between them. While swinging side to side, he grasps the center of the rope with the fingers of one hand and pulls it through the center of the tied silk and between the heels of his hands. This loop he then places over the fingers of his other hand so it lies against the back of that hand (*Fig. 56;* the dotted line shows the rope about to be slipped over the other hand; the solid line shows the rope after it has been so positioned). The rope will automatically pull away when the magician steps back or the volunteer pulls on the ends.

Tips for Presentation: This simple trick is very mystifying to most people. It can be built up by emphasizing the strength of the silk and the rope, and by delaying the moment of release. Perhaps the volunteer could be instructed to pull hard on the count of three. The actual release can be concealed easily with the ostentatious swings of the body. The extreme length of the rope will help mask the movements and allow an easier release for the magician.

UNDERCHAIR ESCAPE

Basic Illusion: The magician escapes from an especially uncomfortable-looking rope tie.

How It Looks: The magician hands a short piece of rope to a volunteer and asks him to tie it to one of the magician's wrists. After this is done, the magician sits in a straightback chair and, bending forward, places his bound hand alongside of the chair's seat. He places his unbound hand on the opposite side, then tells the volunteer to run the rope underneath the chair and tie it to the other wrist. This is done, and the magician appears to be entirely helpless, bent double in the chair with his hands bound so that the chair itself interferes with any possible escape. A screen or other obstruction is placed in front of the magician. After a few moments, he tells the volunteers to remove the screen. He is still tied, but his jacket has been removed. If desired, the screen may be replaced and, after a moment, the magician may step forward, free of the rope.

How It Works: The way the magician allows the rope to be tied makes it impossible for the second wrist to be secured with anything but a slip knot.

How to Do It: This clever principle may be found in one of A. C. Gilbert's old books of magic. The magician uses a short piece of rope that will just reach onto the other side of the chair. But when he places his bound wrist by the side of the chair seat, he keeps it a little higher than the lower edge of the seat, thus giving himself some unsuspected slack to work with later. The other wrist only can be bound with a slip knot, and once the magician is concealed, he will be able to employ the slack to get his other hand over to the slip knot-bound wrist and loosen the knot so that wrist may be removed from the loop. This release is not always easy, and should be carefully practiced until the optimum rope length and amount of slack is worked out.

COMIC ROPE TIE

Basic Illusion: The magician is securely bound, yet in seconds he is able to release himself. But when the concealing material is taken away, he is found to be as tightly bound as ever.

How It Looks: The magician calls two volunteers to assist him, at least one of whom must be wearing a jacket. The magician hands one volunteer a pair of scissors and gives a long length of rope to the other, then asks one volunteer to remove his jacket and take everything out of the pockets and put the contents on a table. While this is being done, the magician exits and immediately returns with a straightback chair, which he sits in. Taking the rope, he circles it under his legs and crosses the ends above his thighs, handing one end each to the volunteers. Putting his wrists together, he has the ropes recrossed and tied onto his wrists, so that a square knot rests tightly above the middle of his wrists. The ends of the rope are trimmed a few inches on either side of the knot, and any audience member may add a further knot with these ends. The two volunteers now stand on either side of the magician. One covers his arms and wrists with the jacket he has removed—like a barber's towel—and then both volunteers turn away from the magician. The performer claims it will take him three minutes to get out of the ropes, but as he does, he holds up three fingers of one hand, taking it out from under the coat. Putting his finger to his lips, he indulges in some comic byplay with the assistants, tapping each on the shoulder in turn. Each time, he whips his hand back under the jacket, so that when the volunteers turn around, each blames the other. At length, the magician complains that he cannot get free from the ropes because the volunteer did not remove everything from his pockets as he was told. With that, the magician brings a large, ludicrous object from beneath the jacket, perhaps a plucked chicken. He flings it away, then, gesturing with his free hand, tells the volunteers to get the scissors, remove the jacket, and cut him loose. They do so, but he puts his hand back beneath the jacket just before it is removed. When it is taken away, the audience sees the magician as securely tied as ever. He has to be cut loose from his bonds.

How It Works: The method of passing the rope around the thighs fashions a large loop with lots of slack that can be passed onto the loop of rope that encircles the wrists.

How to Do It: The method of binding the magician automatically leaves much slack free in the rope, and since it is really a figure-eight loop, the entire rope could easily be slipped from the body (though it is more mystifying to leave everything intact at the end of the trick). This particular routine was shown me by Alwyn Stevenson, though the principle is well known. The only adjustment that must be practiced is the amount of slack to be permitted the wrists. By circling the thighs with the rope, and by keeping the knees slightly apart, there should be plenty of extra rope. Under cover of the jacket, the knees are clenched together, and the loop around the wrist becomes loose. One hand slips out, while the other holds the loop in place. (For a clearer picture of the way the rope encircles the wrists and thighs, see Fig. 57. The loop is exaggerated for the sake of clarity.) The rest of the trick is pure comedic byplay. The plucked chicken or whatever item used is kept offstage on the top of the straightback chair. When the magician goes off to get the chair, he quickly slips the item inside his jacket, then picks up the chair and comes out holding it high enough to hide the unnatural way his arm is pressed to hold the item against the body.

Tips for Presentation: 1. This trick runs about five minutes, and

COMIC ROPE TIE

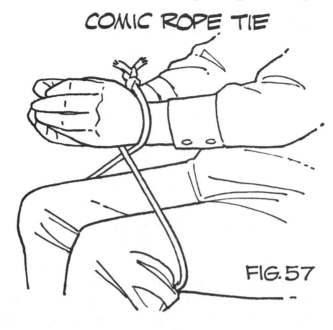

FIG. 57

the tying of the performer's hands will occupy a good part of that time. However, the tying occupies legitimate time, and the careful procedure will enhance the impression in the audience's mind that the knots are tight. The magician should instruct the volunteers to pull the ropes so tight that they cut into his wrists. Then he may have another member of the audience step up for a moment—if there is not much space between the front row and the platform and it is easy to reach the performer. This volunteer may test the ropes by tugging at the portion around the performer's wrists. This slow buildup is essential to make the knots appear genuine. The rapid removal of the wrist once the jacket covers it is made all the more impressive because of the reversal in pacing.

2. The timing must be split-second at the end for utmost effect. The hand must dive back into the loop just before the jacket is removed. It is better to play this trick a bit leisurely at first, then shave seconds off the final revelation.

KNOCKOUT CARD PREDICTION

Basic Illusion: The magician predicts a card mentally chosen.

How It Looks: A large sealed envelope is shown and set against a stand or perhaps is given to a spectator. The magician now has a pack of cards shuffled thoroughly and replaced in the card box. It is handed to another member of the audience, who removes the top nine cards and gives them to the magician. He shows a large clipboard with three clips along its edge. Each clip is on a different color surface, for the clipboard is painted or covered with three equal horizontal sections of colored paper, perhaps red, yellow, and green. The magician attaches three cards back out to a clip on the red section, a second trio of cards to the clip on the yellow section, and the last three cards to the green section's clip. Asking for random choice of colors from the audience, the magician eliminates the six cards attached to the clips whose colors have been called out. The last three cards are separated, and one each is put beneath the clips. Again the audience calls out colors, and all but one card is eliminated. It is placed under the top clip in the back-out position (sticking up so the magician glimpses its identity) and the large envelope is unsealed. Inside is a smaller envelope, which holds a third smaller one holding a pay envelope, and the large envelope is unsealed. Inside is a smaller envelope, which when opened reveals a playing card placed there before the show. Its identity is exactly the same as the one the audience freely picked—the one attached to the clipboard!

How It Works: The audience is forced to choose from nine preselected cards, and the envelope contains an index of all nine choices.

What You Need: Two decks of cards with the same back design. A clipboard with three equal thirds painted or paper-covered with three different colors. Three large clips which can be fixed to the clipboard and cards. One card box. Nine pay envelopes. Three of the next larger size envelopes. One of the next larger size envelopes. One of the next larger size envelopes.

Preparations: Select nine cards from ace to nine in denomination, and mix up the suits. Take the same cards from a second deck. Place one each of the sequence into the pay envelopes and seal them, making sure you know which rank is in each envelope. Take the ace to three—remembering which is where—and place them in one of the next size envelopes. Repeat with the four through six, and the seven through nine. Inside the next size envelope, place the three smaller-size envelopes that contain three cards each. Make sure you can tell which holds the ace to three, the four to six, and the seven to nine. Seal the whole thing in the largest envelope. Now place the other set of nine cards in mixed order in the card box and stick the box flap over them. Push the rest of one deck *partway* in the box with the box flap separating it from the nine cards.

How to Do It: Show the envelope and set it aside, but in plain view. Take the pack of cards out of the box, leaving the nine others behind. After the deck is shuffled, replace it behind the nine cards, which should be at the top. The box flap has been drawn forth and the box is closed in normal manner. The nine cards now have been forced onto the top of the pack and will be the ones the audience member removes. No matter which he selects mentally, you will be able to produce it from the nest of envelopes, simply by unsealing the proper envelopes and leaving the others inside.

Tips for Presentation: 1. Opening the several envelopes is an excellent misdirective detail (repetition). After a couple have been opened, the audience ceases to attach importance to the envelopes, so the magician is able to draw forth the proper card from his filing system without suspicion. To heighten the effect, it is wise to have an audience member open the first envelope and draw forth the one inside. Then the magician proceeds casually to open the rest, handing the used envelopes to the volunteer to hold. Once the card is produced, it should be handed to someone in the audience to draw forth, while the magician turns the chosen one on the clipboard just before the card in the envelope is revealed.

2. This effect uses a variation on a marketed trick called the Mystic Three. (A wonderful addition using a changing bag or dye box is outlined in the book *Tommy Windsor's Dye Box*. However, this variation turns the trick into magic rather than mentalism, and is consequently not used in the present context.)

3. Card tricks have limited appeal and effectiveness on platform and stage, but this one will be a fine feature in any program. It probably should be the last or next to last effect on the program; it is a strong one and will be hard to top with anything else short of a full-size illusion. It should play about five minutes.

Though this chapter has dealt with a few tricks that can be done on larger stages and in longer shows, no full-size illusions have been included, since they are beyond the ability of most performers. Anyone interested in staging large illusions should read up on the subject thoroughly, and also ought to have considerable experience directing regular theatrical plays, since an illusion requires a director's talent for blocking and timing. Sometimes an illusion can be staged inexpensively if the performer has a thorough grasp of various magic principles. For instance, a levitation of a woman can be presented in convincing manner simply by constructing a dead-black portion of the stage set and putting a velvet-covered table in front of it. The woman may be picked up by a strong man dressed head to toe in black and "floated" onto the table. But such illusions must be carefully rehearsed and viewed from every angle to make sure they are convincing.

MORE TRICKS

Some of the most interesting tricks available today vary greatly in size of equipment employed. In general, stage and platform effects should utilize large equipment. Yet there are some legitimate exceptions, and these are noted below.

Astrosphere: This lovely floating ball effect requires plenty of practice to do well. The ball is secured on thin thread, which is temporarily hooked to the trousers. A sheer cloth that intervenes between ball and pants gives the performer control over the sphere.

Blow-Van: This is a useful, easy method of vanishing a silk in a showy manner. The silk is stuffed in a paper tube, which is corked with Kleenex wads. Putting the tube to the lips, the volunteer blows the wads out—the silk is gone.

Clatter Box: This is my favorite audience-participation trick. A silk is vanished. It reappears in the box—after the spectator has "broken" all the equipment.

Copenetro: Though this apparatus involves a coin penetration, the actual trick involves loud clinking of the coins—so that even at a distance the sound convinces the audience of the magic. A wooden stand holds four coins, and is so built to vanish the coins while the magician pretends to take them in his hand. Another wooden stand holds a whiskey glass over which a larger glass is inverted. The coins appear to penetrate the larger glass and land in the whiskey glass. The duplicate coins are shot up with great force from below, with four levers easily controlled by the hand holding the glass-holder apparatus.

French Arm Chopper: There is no more startling guillotine effect on the market. When the blade chops down, the arm actually falls into the basket. It's quite shocking, but entirely safe.

Jumbo Cards to Pocket: This is a simple way to perform a trick that looks like pure manipulation. Several large cards "vanish" from the hands to appear in pockets that have been shown empty.

Professor's Nightmare: This is a lovely rope effect in which three ropes of different lengths are apparently changed to all one length. It works by a simple sleight.

Rainbow Symphony: This is a pretty trick in which several phonograph records change color to match silks threaded through their center holes. There is a cheap paper version which is quite effective, but the trick can also be done with more expensive apparatus that employs real records.

Seance: Also known as the Full-light Spirit Seance, this is a well-made one-man method of making bells ring, horns toot, and objects move as if by spirits.

Super Bill Tube: Though a small piece of equipment, this involves currency and can hold the attention of a large group. A brass tube is padlocked, a bill is borrowed and vanished; it reappears in the locked tube. The secret compartment which admits the bill is precision made and cannot be detected once it is closed.

Super Chain Cuff: This is the finest escape equipment I have ever seen, and it is not expensive. A solid chain is padlocked around one wrist, then a second padlock locks the other end around the other wrist. The magician, employing a hidden pick, releases himself in seconds.

Thumb Strap: The thumb-tie trick—in which the magician can pass his bound hands through various solid objects—is a cinch with this well-made and inexpensive equipment. A wrist-size version is also available for more conventional escape work, and the old Siberian Chain Escape repeats the principle in metal.

Zombie: Though this is the classic floating-ball trick, I prefer the cheaper Miracle Ball, which does the same thing—a ball floats behind and on top of a cloth—a bit more easily for the magician. Each employs a wire gimmick, but the lighter weight of the Miracle Ball gives the magician easier control.

REFERENCES

There is plenty of available literature on stage shows. At random, I would recommend Ken and Roberta Griffin's *Illusion Show Know-how* for its practical advice on logistics. Also Grant's *Victory Carton Illusions* and *Bodies in Orbit* show inexpensive ways of duplicating various full-scale illusions with the use of packing cartons. I am also very fond of Grant's *Challenge Magic Act,* in which the magician is able to announce that he will perform several tricks with *any* objects borrowed from the audience. *Situation Comedy for Magicians,* by Clettis V. Musson, contains numerous amusing gags, many of them involving standard props that most magicians own.

16

Performing for Children

Entertaining children with magic is at once the most rewarding and the most harrowing of experiences. It is a branch of conjuring that should not be attempted until the performer is an expert showman.

Unfortunately, nearly every magician seems to think he knows how to put on children's shows. "Oh, it's impossible to keep the little monsters under control," one may tell you, "but a kid's party or stage show is an easy way to pick up a few extra bucks, so it's worth the headaches."

Let's put it bluntly. Most children's magicians, amateurs and professionals alike, are failures because they do not understand children's psychology. Nor do they realize that the first priority of a children's magician must be to exert a strong control over the audience. The magic must be secondary to the careful orchestration of actions and reactions which the performer intends to elicit from his juvenile spectators.

Anyone who attempts a children's magic show should have at least an intellectual comprehension of the principles of children's theater staging. Preferably, the wizard's knowledge should also include plenty of experience working with children's audiences. If it is impossible to get personal experience, the magician should at least observe as many good children's plays as possible. (Finding a good one is no easy task in itself.)

The things that are most important to note at children's plays are:

1. *Broadness of gesture.* All hand movements should be larger than life, and often are quite graceful. Veteran children's actors employ a kind of pantomimic hand play, so that the important points are visually underscored, and physical action in the text is suggested in space. Thus, a character who claims to have recently climbed a mountain will outline the shape of the peak as he speaks the noun; the activity of climbing may be suggested by the feet and the rest of the body. A good children's entertainer may be quite as accomplished in mime and dance as in histrionics.

2. *Continuity.* All ideas developed must follow in an A-B-C progression, with little complication, so the young mind can follow what is happening.

3. *Vivacity.* A good children's play wastes no time in capturing the audience's attention and keeping it. The opening lines must be projected and articulated well, and a high energy level must be maintained throughout to prevent the children's attention from wandering. The polarization process is extremely important. Once lost, polarization is extremely difficult to reachieve.

4. *Diversity.* Novel ideas, characters, settings, and plot complications must be carefully engineered into a children's play to keep the audience alert.

All of these points are pertinent to the presentation of a children's magic act. When they are observed, a children's magic show may become the most rewarding theatrical event a performer can experience. Wonder in the eyes and laughter in the mouths of children is a splendid dividend for the hard work that goes into a children's magic show.

It is of paramount importance to respect the children's audience. It more than makes up for its lack of sophistication in its ability to discern between the genuine and the phony. When its intelligence is insulted, the children's audience is quick to react; when its attention is artfully engaged, it is just as fast to show enjoyment. If the performer does not know how to choose tricks, build patter, or routine for a children's show—or, worse, if he *condescends* to the audience—he will find the children inattentive, if not rude or belligerent.

Children love magic, yet few of them like to watch it passively for its own sake, as an adult audience might. Youngsters see magic as a game of wits, a contest of wills between performer and spectator. Will the magician be able to get away with his tricks, or will the children see what he is doing? Even children who are highly entertained by conjuring and convinced of the genuineness of the sorcery think they could do quite as well if only they could get their hands on the equipment.

Taking this perennial cockiness into account, the veteran performer will try to keep the kids occupied with what he wishes them to observe—and he will *program* their reactions as if they comprised an orchestra. When they talk back and try to tell him how he is doing a trick, the performer must be prepared. He must know the points in his act where shows of resistance are likely to occur. Sometimes it will even be possible to deliberately elicit cockiness, in order to stifle it. This is the basic effect of all so-called sucker tricks.

The magician should, however, resign himself to the fact that there will always be some children who claim to know how a trick is done, no matter how wrong they really are. Kids do not have a fully developed sense of logic; they will call out "trapdoor," "secret compartment," or "mirror" when an adult would instantly realize such a device could not possibly work under the circumstances.

The children's magician might as well forget about all clever devices and stage-size illusions. In a sense, it almost does not matter what tricks you show children, as long as their reactions are carefully orchestrated for the duration of the whole act. In every trick, the magician must provide opportunities for the kids to shout, clap, make funny noises, flap their arms, shout the magic word, and so on. Children have huge amounts of energy, and the performer must provide outlets for it. In fact, when I take out a full stage show as Count Emkay the Miraculous, I often begin the second act by telling the kids to get on their feet and stretch, hop up and down, and do other simple exercises, in order to burn up a little of the energy they may have acquired eating candy bars at the intermission.

Another important consideration concerning child psychology: many children are not at all theater-sophisticated, and know little about the custom of applause. The magician must learn to seek satisfaction instead in sounds of wonder and laughter. Sometimes the adult audience will lead the applause, but if there is a sponsor in the front office who must be impressed by the sound of frequent hand-clapping, it is wise to get lots of volunteers onstage and, when each returns to his or her seat, ask for a round of applause and lead it yourself. The sponsor won't know the applause is not for you, and even if he does, he may be impressed by the calculated show-manship of the technique.

In general, the tricks that can be performed for youngsters include anything with color, humor, and visual appeal. There are few tricks that cannot somehow be adapted to a kiddie show. Card, billiard-ball, and other manipulations would probably bore most children (such movements show an adult's dexterity, and the kids get tired of all the evidence around them of grownups' superior abilities). There are ways to work in some fingerwork, if an interesting theme is provided. One text suggests doing the Mul-tiplying Billiard Balls trick by disguising the balls as snowballs and pattering about winter snowball fights.

Mentalism is more or less beyond the comprehension of a juvenile audience, but there are a very few mental effects on the market which can be employed. (See references at end of next chapter.) "Torture" tricks also must not be attempted. Razor-blade effects, knives through throats, guillotines—these do not belong in a kids' show, for they may be dangerously imitated. I have often wrestled with my conscience about programing the Wrist Chopper into a children's show, since some kids are bloodthirsty little crit-ters—but I have always decided against it. *One* accident is enough to haunt the conscience for life. Fortunately, there is an excellent variation on the guillotine trick named Safari, in which the child puts his hand into a "tiger's mouth." The tiger's "teeth" bite down upon the hand without harm. Once, though, I asked for a volunteer and before I could call the child I had mentally decided on earlier, a small boy in the first row scooted onstage. There was no way to avoid using him, but I was worried that he was too young, and that the ferocious look of the tiger prop, together with the loud noise the apparatus made when the teeth "bit," might reduce the tot to tears.

So I played the trick very slowly and offered many reassurances to the child. "Now you're not afraid, are you?" I asked at last, and he vigorously shook his head. Unfortunately, I then overheard his father in the first row remark to a friend, "But my kid doesn't know what the word 'afraid' means!"

Also forbidden in children's shows are tricks that require placing a nonedible prop in the magician's mouth. Further, I doubt that anyone would perform a "drunk" trick for kids. This rule should be broadened to include tobacco (I use *no* smoking tricks of any kind for any audience).

When planning his act, the magician must take the age of the audience into account. Younger children are usually easier to control, politer, more attentive, and more open to wonder than older ones. However, many children's shows involve a wide spread of ages, and this sort of occasion ought to be avoided whenever possible. The tricks which appeal to the younger children will probably be too simple for the older ones—or at least the older ones will feel obliged to pretend this is so. When shows before children of varying ages cannot be avoided, the only recourse is to program certain effects for each age group and routine them to minimize the restlessness as much as possible. At any rate, never permit a sponsor to invite teen-agers *en masse* to a magic show primarily planned for younger children. Teen-age audiences are notoriously hard to please, and I would turn down such a show under almost any circumstances.

In planning patter and blocking for children, remember that clever word play is probably beyond their vocabulary level. Some atrocious puns may be suitable, and corny jokes are often acceptable, but witty gag lines are generally out of place. Strive instead for broad farce, slapstick humor, obvious sight gags, and unmistakable jokes. I have a dragon puppet named Melville who sometimes joins me for this immortal dialogue:

MELVILLE: I just had lunch.

COUNT EMKAY: What did you eat?

MELVILLE: I ate seven hundred and forty hot dogs!

COUNT EMKAY: Seven hundred and forty hot dogs!? You ate them *all alone?*

MELVILLE (*deprecatingly*): No-o-o! With mustard and relish!

Terrible, I know—but it gets a big laugh from five- to eight-year-olds.

Breakaway props are also good tools to have on hand. Fans and wands that come apart in a volunteer's hands not only are reliable comedy devices but also allow the magician to portray his frustration humorously as the materials misbehave.

An entertaining children's show positively must have numerous opportunities for the youngsters to act and react vigorously. The opening of the show is particularly important, and a variation on the formula below will aid the performer to meld the group into a homogeneous mass:

> Hello, boys and girls, I am Count Emkay, and I want everyone who wants to see a magic show to call out "Hello, Count Emkay" when I come onstage and say hello to you!

This is delivered, if possible, with the head of the performer jutting through the curtains. He withdraws, then appears on the side of the stage and calls out "Hello, boys and girls." The reply is usually disorganized and sporadic, so with a disapproving glare, the Count says, "That is not loud enough. We try again!" and he exits. Returning twice more, the performer repeats the business until the children are screaming the desired response—and have, in the process, become knit into an audience.

In similar fashion, the magician should teach a magic word to the kids so they can shout it whenever some important magical effect is to take place. If there is a sponsoring organization, its name or initials may be a good word to have the kids shout. When I did a show for a leading game firm, I asked the children to call the company name aloud every few minutes. The public-relations official for the company was in ecstasy, and I got several return engagements out of that show.

Many other important do's and don'ts are outlined in the already mentioned Easley-Wilson book on children's magic, and anyone who desires to entertain children magically *must* obtain a copy. Meanwhile, I have listed below several important rules, drawn both from that text and from my own experience as a children's entertainer. Any magician who ignores any of these suggestions is taking a great risk!

1. Forget the adults.

A children's show is no time to try to make the grownups snigger. If the children are well pleased, the parents will be, too. Ignore the adults in planning the routine and ignore them during the actual playing of the show. Of course, some adults are impossible to ignore. I have heard groups of parents gabbling so loud in the back of an auditorium that the children in front had to strain to hear the performer. The only solutions in such a situation is to project the voice and ignore the adults, or else tell the people in back in no uncertain manner to be quiet. The second course will surely make enemies, but who would want to be asked back under such conditions? Besides, if you are stern with the offenders, you may make conditions easier for the next performer who plays there.

2. Radiate fun.

Make it clear that you enjoy your job. If you really don't, then forget about kids' shows. They will spot the phoniness and make you suffer for it.

3. Take the audience's limited experience into account.

Try to choose effects that employ materials and situations familiar to the child. A trick involving playing cards will probably have less impact than one that uses eggs, since the egg is usually a more common object to the youngster.

4. Emphasize visual appeal.

Try to fill the playing space with intriguing, colorful props that strike the children with wonder when they first see the stage setting. A lot of mystical paraphernalia is also sound psychology; it suggests that the magician is a good one *because* he has all that magic at his disposal! Another advantage in having lots of equipment is that it may be spread out to dress up the full stage. If the magician cannot afford elaborate tricks, he can at least give the illusion of prosperity by filling the scenic space with many properties. However, if you show a piece of equipment, you must use it during the show, or some youngster will feel cheated out of part of the performance. If you are not sure precisely how long the act is going to play, it may be wise to have an extra closing trick out of sight. This is not a suggestion to leave the time of an act open. But because each audience differs, and because children's shows have a large number of audience reactions, it is quite possible that a show may play five minutes longer or shorter than planned. A wise performer will guard against such contingencies when timing—as in a school assembly show—is a crucial consideration. If a show looks as if it will run too long, it may be necessary to cut a portion of some trick, and to play some effects at a faster pace than usual.

5. Personify props.

Give them names whenever possible to make them more identifiable to the children. If there is a chance for the children to select a name, let them—but do not be surprised at some of the suggestions you will get. (It is wise to cultivate a deaf ear during kiddie shows; some precocious children are best ignored.)

6. Forget about subtleties of routining.

It is more important to keep the effects varied and the pace lively than to work toward unification of theme and effect. If a silk is needed, it may not be necessary to produce it from the air. If it slows down the pace, just pick up the prop from a table or stand. The most simple unification of theme I have ever employed is vanishing a prop at the start of a show to be produced at the end. This gives the children something to keep in mind ("Don't forget to remind me later to find the egg!") and also draws on a basic psychological characteristic of children's audiences: they want to see a vanished object brought back. Otherwise, they feel that half the trick has not been done.

7. Keep shows short.

A good children's show rarely runs longer than twenty-five to thirty minutes. If the occasion absolutely requires a much longer show, keep in mind that a child's attention span is rarely capable of extending beyond fifty minutes. (Hence the length of many class periods in public schools.) If the show has to run longer, plan an intermission; it will allow the kids to return refreshed for a new focus of concentration. I have toured an hour-and-a-quarter show with assistants, but I also included a fifteen-minute intermission. Furthermore, I never gave a juvenile audience magic alone during that period, but broke up the routine with comic dialogue with a dragon puppet, a paper-cutting race (with a slightly magical climax), and a drawing for prizes.

8. Consider sucker tricks and standard effects carefully.

If a magic trick has recently been done on TV, I would not use it, for every child will know what is about to happen. But the fact that an effect was done when you were young should not deter you from performing it. So-called standard tricks may be old hat to adults, but they are new to the child. Some of the finest sucker tricks—the Die Box and the Stop Lite Trick in particular—have been done countless times over the years, yet they are almost always a hit. However, I have occasionally had distressing experiences with sucker tricks. Once, I was performing the Stop Lite Trick before a group of ghetto children. In this effect, the magician shows three large cards, each with a different color circle on its face. The magician covers them, then removes two of the cards. The one remaining turns out to have the word "WRONG" on it rather than the circle the children expected. At this point, most children yell out, "Turn it around," and after some comedy byplay, the entertainer turns it only to reveal the word "WRONG AGAIN" on the opposite side. But when the ghetto children saw the trick not one child suggested that the card be turned around. All were amazed at the appearance of the first "WRONG" and were satisfied! I completed the trick by suggesting myself that the other color circle might be on the other side, then turned it around to reveal the second gag. But after the show, a counselor for the group suggested to me that the reason the children did not react in the usual manner was because they had never before had the chance to see a live entertainer. They were so overjoyed at the experience that they never thought of questioning the wizard's authority.

9. Select assistants carefully.

Just as in adult shows, the volunteers ought to be mentally chosen beforehand if possible. Repeated engagements will teach the magician which children to ask onstage and which to avoid. Often, the shyest ones are the best to recruit. Meek children often give fine reactions without trying to be clowns in their own right. The smart performer uses the child's earnestness and sincerity as part of the act, and if his equipment is scanty, he will often find he can give the illusion of a "big" show by using several assistants onstage at one time. Three is my limit, but with enough professional assistants I would certainly get quite a few more involved. Try to use an equal number of boys and girls during the course of the show, as children are quick to take offense at sexual favoritism. (I always keep one trick aside "for the girls" and tell the boys they will have one "especially for you later on.") If it is financially feasible, plan to give some small prize to each volunteer, *but do not award anything edible* unless it has been cleared beforehand with some adult in charge. If a child becomes sick because of something that was given by the magician, a lawsuit may be in the offing!

10. Be suspicious of magic tricks that dealers label "for children."

Some children's tricks include equipment made to look like bunny rabbits, dwarves, princesses, and so on. These are fine for the very young, but fairytale patter may bring outraged hoots from older children. Furthermore, *cutesy* trick equipment that is clearly made "for children" seldom permits the magician to bring much of his own style to the effect; he must perform the routine and patter that the equipment dictates. I have always found it more fruitful to buy basic magic equipment that can be used for miscellaneous vanishes, appearances, transpositions, and so forth, and build a highly personalized routine around it. (Examples may be seen in the next chapter.)

When performing a children's show, one must consider the possibility of using livestock. I have never had the facilities to house a rabbit or other small animal, and renting an animal from a pet shop does not allow enough time to develop ease of handling. If I ever used an animal in a children's act, it would only be because I could keep it between shows as a pet.

It is possible to buy very lifelike animal puppets from several magic stores. One beautifully made inexpensive white rabbit can easily fool children into thinking it is real. There is a fine routine using this puppet in one of the *Kid Stuff* children's books written by Frances Ireland Marshall. Though the routine clearly shows that the puppet is not a real creature, it invests the prop with considerable personal appeal.

Eventually, every discussion of children's shows returns to the problem of discipline. We have stressed the necessity of anticipating reactions and using up available energy so that the children's rambunctiousness is channeled to the performer's advantage. A new set of problems can arise when a child is asked onstage to assist. The youngster may talk back, try to handle forbidden props, or simply act silly and unresponsive.

No matter how irksome the child's behavior, remember that he is your guest and is supposed to be enjoying himself. Try to use the behavior to good advantage. If he acts silly, pretend to be serious and let him run down. If he talks back, give him something ridiculous to do that will take the edge off his cleverness. But do not embarrass him! Instead, use him in a sucker trick, or try some standard gag that will draw laughter yet leave his self-respect intact.

For instance, if a trick is not working because of a child's contrariness, you might suggest that he is not tall enough to make it work. Then have him stand on a piece of newspaper, and warn him not to step off if he wants the magic to work. In most cases, a firm but friendly manner will get the child to cooperate. After all, he is smaller than you, and he is out of his element, while the stage ought to be the magician's home.

Avoid ordering a child in negatives ("Don't touch that"), for this is the sort of sour experience he must undergo constantly. Give positive commands in a pleasant manner that still brooks no contradiction. "Stand right here," you might tell a child, while steering him into position.

A few words about logistics. Try to select tricks for a children's show which require little in the way of setting up. The performance of a children's magic exhibition requires plenty of energy on the part of the magician; it must not be sapped by a tedious session of prop setup beforehand.

When a long show is planned—and especially if it is necessary to give a second program later the same day—it is vital to plan the setup, breakdown, and resetting of each show to eliminate waste movement. At Sharon Playhouse in Connecticut, I had to do two hour-and-a-quarter performances on the same day, and there was very little time between shows. It was essential for every member of the troupe to know just which duties had to be performed by each during intermission and after the first show. Even so, we had to warn the house committee not to let the second audience into the theater until they had checked with us to be sure that all our props were reset.

Be sure, too, that there is enough space for all the props to be taken apart and put back together. Check the physical facilities carefully beforehand. Finally, be certain that the stage is policed before and after each show. Otherwise, there may be a surge of eager youngsters onstage when the show is over, and needed props may be spirited off.

17

Magic for Children's Shows

It is not easy to give advice on routining children's magic shows. I have always found this the most difficult part of getting ready for a scheduled children's date; sometimes I spend hours or even days trying to decide which tricks to perform, and in what order.

The Easley-Wilson book, *Doing Magic for Youngsters and The Art of Conjuring to Children,* offers a sensible model for preparing a forty-five-minute show, even though it does not take every variable into account. The book suggests beginning with a new and snappy opening trick; following with a sucker trick; then something small; a "time-waster" that can play short or long and that involves considerable noise and laughter; a quiet item to contrast with the previous; a "special trick for the girls" which emphasizes daintiness and/or color; a major mystifier (I call this the "real magic" number); a boys' trick with much humor involved; a small trick; another "time-waster," which can be stretched or compressed, depending on how fast the program is running; and a major production effect to close.

In my children's act, I cut the number of tricks down to nine for a twenty-five-minute show or, in the case of a longer program, for each of two acts of the same duration. The order I try to follow is: opener; small effect with some color involved; sucker trick; noisy, funny audience-participation trick; quiet item; girls' trick; real magic; boys' trick; and closer.

The purpose of the routining should be to get the show off to a lively start; to insert a sucker effect early to catch the smart alecks right away; to manipulate the energy of the group by alternating passive, quiet effects with loud ones that require audience participation; and to build up to an unusual closing number, whether it is a production or some other illusion.

In general, I try to keep the audience-participation tricks spaced far enough apart to highlight each group of volunteers, and also to contrast with the solo numbers. If I must do more than one act, I try to save the more elaborate equipment for later, especially if the end of a trick leaves a mess of used props onstage. (Using such effects in the second act cuts down on the clean-up work during intermission.)

If the show is being given in a theater that sells soft drinks and confections during intermission, it is wise to program tricks that involve such materials shortly before the act break. This will increase the concessionaire's business, and make your act rate high with the theater manager when you point out your strategy to him. In addition, tricks involving liquids had better be programed shortly before intermission or near the end of the show. The reason should be obvious.

Let us turn now to some sample tricks and routines I have used in my own magic act for children. I have set down a hypothetical eleven-trick act as if it were being played by Count Emkay the Miraculous, the humorous character I portray.

"Count Emkay" appears in black suit, red tie, and bowler hat (the kind worn by Laurel and Hardy), and has black-framed glasses, flared nostrils, and black lips, so that his initial entrance makes the children both laugh and shiver. He is a broad lampoon of Bela Lugosi. This description is given not as an invitation to copy this characterization, but to indicate the broad approach one should use in selecting a role for entertaining children with magic.

Though the act outlined below is too long for most purposes, it underscores various important points pertaining to children's magic. In practice, a slightly more compact act would be preferable. Here is a rundown of the effects:

TRICK	DESCRIPTION
Miser's Dream	Opener, with audience participation.
Melville the Dragon	Interlude with puppet.
Egg Routine	Noisy time-waster that sets up close of show.
Rings on Rope	Quiet effect, with introduction of magic word.
Acrobatic Silks	Sucker trick.
Afghan Bands Contest	Adapted from *Kid Stuff* routine, this is a time-waster with audience volunteers.
Rainbow Ropes	Girls' trick, with a volunteer.
Forgetful Freddie	Real magic: the only trick in the routine to employ a prop obviously aimed at children.
Coin Flight	A humorous boys' trick with volunteers.
E-Z Hat Loader	Novel production routine, linking up with earlier egg effect.
Bullet Catch	Humorous, "illusion-size" close.

SAMPLE COUNT EMKAY ROUTINE (45–50 Minutes)

(The lights dim. The Count puts his head through the center curtain. When he speaks, it is with a broad Hungarian accent.)

COUNT: Hallo, boys and girls, I am Count Emkay the Miraculous, and I want everyone who wants to see a magic show to shout out, "Hallo, Count Emkay," when I come onstage and say hello to you! *(He pulls back his head, then enters from stage right.)*

FANFARE: *Beginning of Triumphal March from* Aida.

COUNT: Hallo, boys and girls!

(Response)

COUNT *(scowling):* That is not loud enough! We try again! *(He exits.)*

FANFARE: *Second trumpet blast from* Aida. *He reenters.*

COUNT: Hallo, boys and girls!

(Response)

COUNT: That's better! I heard you with this ear *(he points)* but not that one! *(He gestures.)* Once more, please! *(He exits at a run.)*

FANFARE: *Third trumpet blast. He reenters at a run.*

COUNT: Hallo, boys and girls!

(Response: he is "blown" against the back curtain by its power.)

COUNT: That's better—now I can hear you! *(He peers at audience suspiciously.)* Oh, hallo, grownups. Listen, this show is for the boys and girls. The grownups can stay and watch on one condition. They have to promise to behave and be good!

I have to apologize, boys and girls, for getting started a little late, but I was supposed to meet my friend Melville the Dragon before the show, and he hasn't gotten here yet. But I'll tell you what—while we're waiting for Melville to arrive, I notice something funny about this theater *(place, school—whatever is appropriate)*. Have you noticed it?

(Sporadic response)

The thing I've noticed is there's a lot of loose change floating around. You must be a very rich group of boys and girls! I'll show you . . . *(He picks up a beaten brass flower planter, reaches into the air, and produces a coin, which he drops into the pot. The Count proceeds to take several coins out of the air. Then he goes down to the first row of seats and very quickly moves along it, plucking coins from children's shirts, pockets, hair, noses, and so on, until he gets about two thirds of the way across the front row. Then he runs back to one child near the beginning of the row, claiming to have missed one, and plucks another coin from nowhere. Returning to stage, the magician requests that the last child come onstage. Circling him with the brass pot, the magician plucks a myriad of coins from pockets, arms, head. At last, the magician sends the child back to his seat with a prize. But when the child is halfway down, the performer stops him.)*

COUNT: Wait a minute. You didn't keep any of the coins, did you? By accident? *(Child answers negatively.)*

COUNT: Are you sure? *(Child repeats his answer.)*

COUNT: You'd better check all your pockets and make sure. *(The child looks through his pockets, and finds a coin in one of them, which he returns—usually with a marvelous expression of wonder on his face.)*

What You Need: A brass planter, such as may be bought inexpensively in any five and ten. A coin holder with hook. Numerous palming coins. Coin "steals."

Preparation: Fill the coin holder with coins and hang it over the rim of the planter with the feeder inside. *(Fig. 58)* Fill the coin "steals" with coins and pin one on each side of the body just under the hem of the jacket. Have two or three coins ready to be palmed in the hand.

How to Do It: There are many pieces of excellent equipment on the market for performing this effect easily. The coin holder is available from most well-stocked magic dealers, and can be hung inside the planter and grasped with the hand so that the palm holds the planter from its lip while simultaneously concealing the holder. The "steals" come in various styles and prices; basically, they are clasps that hold a store of coins by pressure. Pins on top allow the apparatus to be attached beneath the bottom edge of the jacket

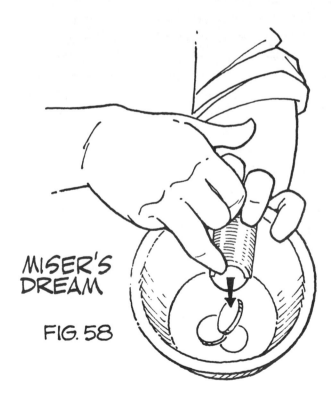

MISER'S
DREAM

FIG. 58

where the fingertips can easily curl upward, grasp the coins, and pull them out in palmed position. Using them, the magician is able to get hold of several coins prior to producing them. In this example, the "steals" are used at the end of the routine. First, the magician produces one coin from the air by manipulating one of the two or three hand-palmed ones to the fingertips. He repeats this action with the next coin and, if desired, does it again. But the last coin in the hand is not put into the bucket. Instead it is thumb-palmed, and at the same time, the forefinger of the hand that is pretending to throw the coin in the bucket hits the first coin in the holder and slides it downward so it falls into the bucket. It makes a sound which the audience naturally assumes is made by the coin they saw.

This dodge is repeated again and again while the magician walks swiftly along the front row of the audience, plucking coins everywhere. When the load of coins in the holder has been exhausted, the magician produces a final coin and really drops it into the bucket. He should do this with a flourish, so that the coin is clearly seen falling from some distance from the hand to the con-tainer—a move that reinforces the belief that all the coins really were thrown from the conjurer's hand. (Throughout this trick, the performer naturally will take care to hold the planter high enough so that the children cannot see into it.) As he turns and steps back onstage, the magician obtains the coins in the "steal" pinned on the upstage side of his jacket. He is then able to produce them rapidly, dropping them into the bucket with great clatter, from the pockets and person of the child brought onstage. During this process, the magician steals the second suspended group of coins and proceeds to produce more coins from the volunteer's person. As he reaches in to take a coin out of the child's pocket, the magician *drops* another coin in, and this is the one the child finds by himself at the end of the trick.

COUNT: Let's have a big hand for our volunteer!

(*Applause. The child takes his seat. Meanwhile, magician pours the coins noisily out of the bucket into another container, thus showing that he really did produce a vast quantity of money.*)

COUNT: Now if my friend Melville the Dragon would only show up, we could get started with the magic show . . .

(Melville pokes his head through the break in the curtain.)

COUNT: I don't know where he is. He was supposed to show up by now, and I promised I wouldn't begin until he could get here and watch . . . *(By this time, the audience is trying to draw the magician's attention to the fact that Melville has arrived. At first, the performer ignores the noise and continues to ad lib about Melville's tardiness. But at length he listens to the children and, after some misunderstanding, gets the message that Melville is in the theater.)*

COUNT: But where is he?

(Response)

COUNT: Where? *(He walks one way, and Melville tries to get his attention, but the Count walks right past him. This business is repeated in the other direction, the performer being constantly distracted by the noise of the children, who stridently attempt to make him aware of Melville. At last, the magician walks directly into Melville. The dragon does a "pullback" from him, and the magician bounces back a step or two, simultaneously emitting a surprised shout.)*

COUNT: Aaak! So there you are! What kept you so long?

MELVILLE: Sorry I'm late, but I was out fishing.

COUNT: Fishing? *(He remembers the audience and turns to them.)* Oh, boys and girls, this is Melville the Dragon. Say hello to the boys and girls, Melville.

MELVILLE: Hello, boys and girls!

(Response)

COUNT: Now—you say you were fishing?

MELVILLE: That's right.

COUNT: Catch anything?

(Melville sneezes.)

COUNT: Besides a cold?

MELVILLE: I caught a great big fish!

COUNT: How big?

MELVILLE: This big— *(He opens his mouth as wide as he can.)*

COUNT *(suspiciously)*: How big?

MELVILLE: We-e-ell . . . *(He closes his mouth partway.)*

COUNT: *How* big?

(Melville closes his mouth a bit more.)

COUNT: You know, Melville, it's only ——— months to Christmas.

(Melville ruefully closes his jaws until there is only a small gap between them.)

COUNT: That's more like it! Say, Melville, I understand you just started going to school.

MELVILLE: That's right.

COUNT: What do you like best?

MELVILLE: Recess.

COUNT: Besides that.

MELVILLE: Lunch period is nice.

COUNT: I mean, what do you like to learn about?

MELVILLE: Oh—'rithmetic.

COUNT: Oh? You know how to add and subtract?

MELVILLE *(proudly)*: Uh-huh.

COUNT: Would you like to show the boys and girls how well you can add?

(Melville eagerly nods his head.)

COUNT: All right, Melville, how much is one and one?

(Melville starts to answer, then looks confused.)

COUNT: One and one. How much is one and one?

(Melville does not answer, but hangs his head.)

COUNT: Oh, Melville! You don't know?

(Melville shakes his head.)

COUNT: Boys and girls, can you tell Melville how much is one and one?

(Response)

COUNT: Melville, I'm surprised at you! I thought you knew how to add, and here you don't even know one and one!

MELVILLE: One and one what?

COUNT *(starts to answer, then stops with mouth opened)*: What?! What do you mean, one and one *what*?

MELVILLE: One and one apple? One and one orange?

COUNT: O-o-oh, I see! *(He turns to the audience.)* Boys and girls, I forgot! Melville is a very little dragon, and he's only just starting in school. He only knows how to add if it's done in things! (*He turns back to Melville.*) All right, Melville, how much are one and one orange?

Melville (*brightly*): Two oranges!

COUNT: Two orange and two orange?

MELVILLE: Four oranges!

COUNT: Four orange and four orange?

MELVILLE: No oranges!

COUNT (*not sure he heard correctly*): Four orange and four orange?

MELVILLE: No oranges!

COUNT: Wait a minute! Let's try this again! How much are two orange and two orange?

MELVILLE: Four oranges.

COUNT: Four orange and two orange?

MELVILLE: Six oranges.

COUNT: Six orange and one orange?

MELVILLE: Seven oranges.

COUNT: Seven orange and one orange?

MELVILLE: *No* oranges!

COUNT: Aak!

(*The audience laughs.*)

COUNT: Look, shtupid dragon! Seven orange and one orange is eight orange! Eight orange! The oranges are eight!

MELVILLE (*positively*): If they're ate, there's *no oranges!*

COUNT: Aaak! (*He hops about in rage.*)

(*The audience laughs.*)

COUNT: I think it's about time for you to get a seat and watch the show! Unless—would you like to sing a song?

MELVILLE (*eagerly*): I thought you'd never ask!

COUNT: What would you like to sing?

MELVILLE: I know a brand-new song that I think everyone will like. It's called "Happy Birthday!"

COUNT: A *new* song?! (*He looks at the audience with surprise.*)

MELVILLE: Yes, I'm going to sing "Happy Birthday!"

COUNT (*taking a step to the audience and whispering a theatrical aside*): Now here's where he makes a fool of himself, boys and girls!

You can't sing "Happy Birthday!" unless you have somebody to sing it to! *(He turns to Melville.)* All right, Melville, go ahead! *(He clears his throat.)* Melville the Dragon now will sing "Happy Birthday!"

MELVILLE *(clears throat):* Happy birthday— *(He has started too high, so he clears his throat again and starts over; as he sings, he opens his mouth wide and sings with great animation.)* Happy birthday to you-oo! Happy birthday to you-oo! Happy birthday, dear— *(Melville stops for a moment, stuck.)* Dear . . . dea—a-a-ar . . . er-r-r . . . *(He nods his head vigorously and sings on one pitch.)* Substitute-the-name! Happy birthday to you! Applause, please! *(He bows as the audience reacts.)*

COUNT: That's shtupid! Come on, Melville, do it right! You have to have the name of someone in order to sing "Happy Birthday!"

MELVILLE: But who?

COUNT: We-e-ell— *(He surveys the audience.)* I'll bet there are some boys and girls right here who are having a birthday today . . .

(The performer solicits the information from the audience, finding out the names of several children with birthdays that day. Melville then sings with the Count and the entire audience, putting in as many names as necessary in the appropriate place.)

COUNT *(at end of song; very quickly):* That was wonderful, boys and girls! Give yourselves a hand!

(The audience applauds.)

MELVILLE: Goodbye, boys and girls!

(Response)

(Melville quickly pulls his head back through the curtains.)

Tips for Presentation: 1. This kind of puppet routine can be managed in either of two ways: the conjurer may do the puppet's voice himself if he is a ventriloquist, or he may have the assistant who works the puppet supply the voice. In the latter case, it might be necessary for the assistant to use a microphone, since the curtain might muffle the voice. But a mike should be avoided, if possible, because of the disparity between an electronically reproduced tone and the performer's live projection.

2. Keep the puppet cute, young, and sympathetic. One year Melville was portrayed a few years older and fresher, and the kids

did not like the character nearly so much. In fact, after one of Melville's remarks, a child shouted, "Don't take that from him, Count! Punch him in the nose!"

3. Back-and-forth patter such as that outlined above should be timed meticulously. The sequence about "no oranges" must build in rapidity until the unexpected answers stop the performer cold. His yelps of confused annoyance bring out the laughs set up by the rapid back-and-forth dialogue. But the lines do not get the laughs so much as the sudden break in rhythm. As far as I am concerned, there is only one source that can be studied profitably for this sort of lightning-timing comedy, and that is the films and (scarce) recordings of the vaudeville routines of Abbott and Costello, particularly the classic "Who's on First" routine.

4. The song is no problem. There are always a number of people in any medium-size group having a birthday. But if the one-in-a-million chance should ever occur, and no one responds, all the magician needs to do is to ask who is *about* to have a birthday. There will always be someone in that category.

COUNT *(after Melville has drawn back his head):* Now, for my first trick I need an egg. Does anyone have an egg in his or her pocket? No? Well, that's okay, because my invisible hen, Murgatroyd, is around here somewhere . . . *(Intoning.)*

> Murgatroyd, Murgatroyd,
> Hear me, I beg!
> Do me a favor and lay me an egg!

(He looks up, but nothing happens.) Maybe she didn't hear me. I'll try again. *(He repeats the jingle, but nothing happens.)* Murgatroyd, you're *not* listening! *(A pause. The performer pretends to listen.)* Oh! That's why?! *(He turns to the audience.)* Murgatroyd is afraid that the egg will break unless I catch it. That's no problem . . . *(The performer produces a cloth bag with a clear front and puts his hand in it to show there is nothing inside; the hand is seen through the transparent mesh front.)* Now Murgatroyd can lay the egg in here. Here we go . . . *(He holds up the bag.)* Maybe we should all ask Murgatroyd this time. *(He leads the entire audience in saying the*

jingle, line by line. When the final line is shouted out, an egg drops mysteriously into the bag.) Here we are! *(Reaching inside, he takes out the egg and holds it up for all to see.)* Now if I put this egg in *this* bag . . . *(Putting down the first bag, the performer picks up a second.)* And I wave my hand twice, I can make the egg twice as large as before! *(He reaches into the bag and takes out a lemon. Mystified, he searches the bag, but cannot find the egg; the bag is now empty.)* How do you like that?! First my act lays an egg *(he holds up the lemon)* and now it goes sour!

(The audience will probably groan here.)

COUNT: Well, never mind, we'll have to find the egg later, so I can give it back to Murgatroyd. But, boys and girls, will you please remind me to find the egg later on, all right? Don't forget to remind me to find the egg!

What You Need: A wooden egg. A Mesh Egg Bag. A hollow rubber lemon. A change bag (the kind without a handle).

Preparation: Place the egg in the pocket of the Mesh Egg Bag and have it ready to be picked up without prematurely revealing the egg. Place the lemon in one of the compartments of the change bag and switch the compartment so that the empty one is ready to use.

How to Do It: Like most of the children's magic I prefer, this effect is extremely simple to execute technically. The demands come in the playing. A group activity (the jingle) is essential at this point in the show, and it establishes the character of Count Emkay as something of a wizardly bungler, a characteristic that will be further developed in the routine.

The Mesh Egg Bag is a standard piece of equipment that employs the black-art principle (materials made from deep black cloth and other substances mask objects concealed with matching black). The egg is tucked into a pocket slashed across the middle of the black back of the bag. Though the audience is able to look right at the slash through the mesh front of the bag, it cannot see the opening. When the egg is released and the bag shaken, the white egg will drop through the opening into the bottom of the bag. It appears as if it had dropped from nowhere.

The change bag is a small purselike affair with a metal ring on top that holds the opening rigid. Inside is a cloth partition that may be pushed in either direction; it divides the bag into two distinct pockets, but when it is shoved one way, the other pocket cannot be seen even when the bag is turned inside out. (There are change bags with a long handle attached; I would avoid them, as they look too suspicious.) The lemon is placed in one pocket and the pocket is closed. The magician may now turn the bag inside out, and show that it looks empty. The egg is placed in the empty pocket and the partition is shoved over to close the egg pocket and open the lemon pocket. The lemon is removed and the bag once more shown "empty." A real lemon may be used, but the hollow rubber variety stocked by many magic stores can be collapsed into a very small space. With a collapsible lemon, the bag may be crushed in the hands to convince the children that it is empty.

COUNT: Now, boys and girls, I want you all to use your imaginations in the next trick. First of all, I will show you six large rings, three of them red, and three of them green. Let's take a closer look. Here are two green rings. I'll turn them over and you can see that they are green on both sides. Now here is the third green ring and one of the red ones. I'll turn these over, so you can see they are the same colors on the other side. And here are the other two red rings, which are red on both sides. (*During this speech, the magician holds up the rings two at a time and puts them down in the same order as he displayed them: two green rings on the right of the table, two red on the left, and the set of one red and one green ring in the middle.*) I'd also like to show you this rope. (*The rope, which is held up, has six bulldog-clamp paper clips along its length, evenly spaced.*) Now I will ask you all to imagine the green rings are sheep. What kind of noise do sheep make?

(*Response*)

COUNT: I also want you to imagine that the red rings are goats. What kind of noise do goats make?

(*Response*)

(*During this speech, the magician takes one of the right-hand green rings and attaches it to the rope with the farthest right clamp.*

Then he takes the middle green ring and puts it on second, moving to the next clamp to the left. Now the third green ring is put on the rope. Next: one of the right-hand red rings. Next: the middle red ring. Finally, the right-hand remaining red ring is attached. Though this order is deliberate, it should appear to be random.)

COUNT: Very Good. So, now if I hold up the rope, you will see that there are three green rings on one side and three red on the other. Remember, the green ones are sheep, and the red ones are goats. Now let us also pretend that the rope is a park or a meadow. So we can see that the sheep are on one side of the park, and the goats on the other. Now we'll mix them up . . . *(The performer puts both rope ends in one hand, then draws them apart again. There is no change in the order of the rings. He looks perplexed.)* That's funny . . . Oh! I know what's wrong! We forgot to say the magic word. *(At this point, the performer teaches the audience the magic word for the day, which ought to be the name of the theater or the sponsor or some other name of practical value to the magician. He must rehearse the children in calling out the word before he continues, much in the manner of the opening of the act when he got them to shout out his own name—which, of course, in addition to polarizing the group, also helped to fix the magician's name in the audience's mind.)* Now remember, boys and girls, the green rings are the sheep and the red, the goats. Anytime I say "magic word" from now on, be sure to call it out as loud as you can! *(He puts both rope ends in one hand again.)* Magic word!

(Response)

COUNT: And you can see just how easy it is to separate the sheep from the goats! *(The magician takes a rope end in each hand again. The order of the rings is green, red, green, red, green, red.)*

What You Need: The Rings on Rope trick.

How to Do It: This routine exactly follows the mechanical working of this fine trick, obtainable from many magic dealers. The secret: two of the rings are prepared, red on one side and green on the other. These are positioned third and fourth and the rings are stacked before first being shown. When the detailed layout is followed and the rings are put on the rope as explained, the trick will work automatically simply by exchanging rope ends and turning the whole line of rings around.

Tips for Presentation: A more elaborate but effective manner of introducing the magic word may be constructed by having a printer prepare a phony newspaper front page with a huge two-line headline which reads:

THE MAGIC WORD IS
(whatever it is)

Have at least three copies of this headline made, and set one aside in case it is examined at the end of the show. (It may be given as a souvenir to the sponsor.) The other two newspapers must be prepared so that one of the headlines is cut out, and the magic word scrambled when pasted back together. A flap then must be made of this false headline, and it should be taped over the second, unprepared, paper's headline. It will appear as if the magic word is unpronounceable. Example:

THE MAGIC WORD IS
UNKATEM COY

When the flap is quickly flipped back to show the correct headline, the magic word is revealed. (THE MAGIC WORD IS COUNT EMKAY.)

COUNT: I want to show you these three silk scarves. This yellow one on the end is named P-riscilla. *(He emphasizes the first letter humorously.)* The yellow one in the middle is named P-runella. You can see they both are threaded through the holes in this long bar, while the rings knotted on top keep the scarves from falling all the way through. You can see there is also a blue scarf on the end opposite P-riscilla. The blue scarf does not have a name, so we'll have to think one up, all right? Does anyone have any suggestions? *(Several suggestions will be called out; the performer eventually selects one. For the sake of the example, we will call the blue scarf Alvin.)* Now, P-riscilla is very quiet and never does much but hang on the bar, and P-runella is just about the same. But Alvin is an acrobat, and can jump and change places with P-riscilla here on the end—just like this. *(The performer places the bar behind his back momentarily; when he brings it forth, the blue and yellow silks have changed places, obviously because the magician turned the bar around behind his back. This business is repeated once or twice, until the children are screaming that they know what the magician is really doing. The performer ignores what they say at first, or pretends he does not understand them. He tries to explain that the children did not understand what kind of miracle they have witnessed, and proceeds to repeat the insulting trick.)*

COUNT *(at last):* Oh, you think I turned it around? Would you rather see Alvin jump and change places with P-runella in the middle?

(Positive response)

COUNT: Well, say the magic word!

(Response)

COUNT: Louder!

(Response. This time the magician passes his hand along the silks and they visibly jump and change places.)

Acrobatic Silks is a standard piece of equipment that relies on a careful twisting of the silks so that it *appears* as if the blue were on the end and the yellow in the middle, while in reality they are just the opposite. Note the personification of props in the above routine.

COUNT: At this point, I need two volunteers from the audience. *(After choosing them, the magician has one stand on downstage left, the other downstage right. It is necessary to use an onstage professional assistant for this effect.)* We are going to have a little contest, a kind of race. Let me show you what to do . . . *(He takes a strip of newspaper pasted into a loop and begins cutting along its length with a scissors until he has divided it into two loops, each half as wide as the first.)* I'm going to give each of you much larger loops of newspaper, and I want you to cut them the same way that I did, until you are holding two separate loops. The first one to finish without tearing or cutting the paper incorrectly wins. But even when one contestant completes his cut, the other must continue until his is all cut, because if the first one makes a mistake, the second will win *if* he has not done anything wrong . . . All right? Ready? Get set . . . go!

(The magician picks up one of the loops of paper and guides it in the proper path for one child's scissors. The assistant must guide the other's loop. The audience naturally will cheer the contestants on, but to better fill the time, music ought to be played during the cutting, which can take a little while. I have used the "Sabre Dance" to good effect. Once both children have completed cutting their loops, the magician calls for the music to stop, then goes to the child who finished cutting first.)

COUNT: We have a winner, unless—let's see— *(He holds up the loop. Instead of being in two, it is now a giant loop, twice as large as it was before it was cut.)* Sorry, this one didn't turn out quite right. Maybe the other one? *(He holds up the second loop. It has somehow turned into two small loops, linked together.)* There's something strange about this! I think we'd better give a prize to both of my contestants! *(He sends them to their seats with a round of applause.)*

This is the old Afghan Bands, or Moebius Strip, principle. One loop—the one the magician cuts—is unprepared. The strip of newspaper is merely pasted together at the ends. But one of the other strips is given a half twist before the ends are pasted. The other strip is given a full twist before the ends are pasted. If large loops of newspaper (each at least a few inches wide) are used, the twists will be too loose to be discerned. The trick then works itself. (See Fig. 59 for an outline of the way in which the papers are twisted.)

COUNT: Next I have a special trick for the girls in the audience. Don't worry, boys, I've got one for you later on! May I have a young lady come onstage to assist? *(A volunteer is selected.)* Hello, Mary, what's your name? *(Once in a great while, the name is Mary, in which case the magician plays it as if he really knew it all along.)* Your name is ———? Boys and girls, this is Mary-who-calls-herself-———. And what is your maiden name? *(The volunteer will most likely act confused; do not wait for an answer but proceed with patter.)* Now Mary-who-calls-herself-———, I'm going to tell a story about a little girl and a magic genie. I'll play the magic genie and you pretend to be the little girl. Once upon a time, there was a magic genie. He was walking down the street when he ran into a little girl who was crying. Can you cry?

(Response from volunteer)

COUNT: The magic genie asked, "What's the matter, little girl?" and she said, "I want to jump rope but this is all I've got . . ." *(The magician shows three ropes colored red, white, and blue—they are double-knotted together.)* Three ropes all cut up and tied in knots. *(He turns to the volunteer.)* You could not jump rope with this, could you?

(Response from volunteer)

COUNT: The genie said, "Here, let me take a look at that," and he untied one rope . . . *(He lets the red rope fall so that it is tied only at one end to the white rope. He addresses a question to the volunteer.)* What color rope is this?

VOLUNTEER: Blue.

COUNT *(indicating middle rope):* And this?

VOLUNTEER: White.

AFGHAN BANDS

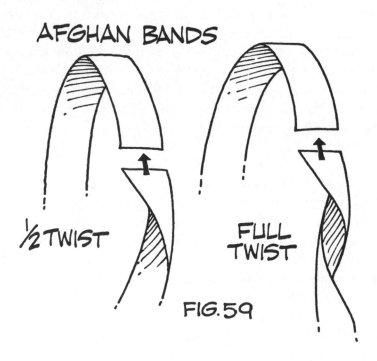

½ TWIST   FULL TWIST

FIG. 59

COUNT: White—right! And, boys and girls, what color is this? *(He unties one end of the blue rope and lets it hang suspended from a knot on the white rope. There are now apparently three ropes, tied so there is a red rope on one end, a white in the middle, and the blue on the other end.)*

AUDIENCE: Blue!

COUNT *(peering)*: Who said *green!* Blue—true! Well, the genie examined the ropes and said, "No, little girl, you could not jump rope with this *(the magician has given one end of the rope to the volunteer to hold and retains the other himself; standing a few feet apart, he lets the rope stretch wide between them)* because the knots might pull apart on you, or you might even trip on them while jumping, and you could fall and get hurt. But I think I can fix this—" And with that, the genie wrapped the ropes around his hand. *(The magician does so, coiling them about the clenched fist so the ropes run over the knuckles.)* And he got some magic woofle dust out of his pocket. *(The magician produces a handful of confetti from his pocket and sprinkles it over the ropes in his hand.)* "And now, little girl," he said *(the magician gives the girl the end of the rope to hold again)*, "if you hold on tight to this end of rope, you can jump rope with a single red, white, and blue rope!" *(The magician uncoils the rope and stretches it wide; it has turned into a single rope with three colored segments: red, white, and blue.)*

What You Need: A set of Rainbow Ropes, available from many magic dealers. Some confetti.

Preparation: Tie ropes in the fashion suggested in the Rainbow Ropes instruction sheet. Put confetti in a jacket pocket.

How to Do It: The Rainbow Ropes trick is a lovely and inexpensive piece of apparatus that depends on disguising a single tritinted rope by putting two false knots on it. This gives the appearance of three distinct ropes. The working is as described, and the use of a volunteer turns this small effect into a stage-size routine. At the climax, the hand wraps the ropes around the knuckles, and in the process the false knots are slipped off the rope and palmed. They are left inside the pocket when the confetti is brought forth. At the conclusion of the effect, present the child with a giveaway and return her to her seat with a round of applause.

COUNT: Boys and girls, I want you to meet a friend of mine whose name is Freddie. People always called him Forgetful Freddie because he never remembered where he put his books or his toys. And one day he even forgot—his head! *(The magician has shown a large wooden figure of a boy and removes the cutout's head.)* Well, he couldn't go to school without a head, so his mother blew up a balloon *(the magician does so)* and attached it to his neck and tied it to his collar. *The Figure now has a large balloon where the head was. It is knotted and pulled through a hoop and attached to the figure's tie, where there is a hook.)* But this made Freddie very unhappy, and do you know why? Because all the kids at school started to call him something. Do you know what?

AUDIENCE: Balloon-head.

COUNT: That's right! Well, one night the same magic genie I just told you about appeared to Freddie in a dream and said, "Freddie, I know what happened to your head—one day you were blowing your nose" *(the magician takes a large, loud handkerchief and tucks the head into it)* "and you forgot your head and left it there, and the handkerchief went to the laundry, and your head was left there." *(The magician spreads the cloth open with a flourish; the head is gone.)* "But I think I can help you get your head back. I will have all the winds of the world blow your head to you." Now, boys and girls, in order to show you what happened, I will have to ask you to pretend to be all the winds of the world. When I say "Blow!" I want you all to blow as hard as you can at the balloon! Ready? Blow! Now the genie said the magic word! *(The audience repeats the "magic word" and the balloon bursts; the head is back in place.)* And no one ever called him balloon-head again!

What You Need: A Forgetful Freddie outfit. Several balloons to fit the apparatus. A Devil's Handkerchief.

Preparation: Set up Forgetful Freddie as in the instructions, with a nail in the head, which is secured by a clamp in a position behind the upright figure. A second head is slotted into the neck.

How to Do It: This is the only effect in this routine which uses apparatus obviously designed for children. Forgetful Freddie is available from many magic suppliers; the design is not nearly so cloying as other children's magic props, and the effect is a knockout. The working is simple enough: an identical second head is mounted on a powerful spring which, when released, shoots the head up into position; a nail in the second head bursts the balloon. The Devil's Handkerchief is a standard piece of equipment with a pocket inside to conceal objects and make them apparently disappear. Do not be deceived at the short patter: this effect plays between four and five minutes, partly because it takes time to attach the balloon. It must be practiced plenty beforehand and executed slowly in performance. Use of an assistant in this effect is valuable, because an assistant on stage right and the magician on stage left fill up the scenic space. But when the assistant springs the second head, she should be stage center. Two tips: 1) Have several extra balloons handy, in case the lights are hot enough to accidentally break the first one. 2) Gently rub the top of the balloon and position it upright just before the assistant releases the spring; otherwise the nail may not break the balloon but simply push it forward. Note the patter at the end of the routine: "And they never called him balloon-head again!" This is one of those unimportant throwaway lines that nevertheless tell the audience clearly that the trick is over and applause is in order.

COUNT: I have a special trick for the boys, just as I promised. I need several volunteers. *(The magician drafts three assistants from the audience and has them stand stage left, stage right, and center.)* What's your name, young man? *(He asks the boy stage left, then repeats it for the one stage right. The magician approaches the one standing center last.)* All right, what's your name, George?

(Volunteer responds.)

COUNT: This is George-who-calls-himself-____. Now Geo—uh—____, I have a quarter which I want you to look at and read the date. Good. Please make a mark on it with this pen. I want you to put it in this box. *(The magician holds up a cylindrical container with a slot on top; he raps it smartly with the pen to prove its solidity.)* Boys and girls, you can see this box is solid with no holes except for this slot. *(He gives the box and quarter to the boy stage left.)* Would you please drop the coin inside? *(The boy does so, and the magician rattles the box so everyone can hear the coin.)* I want you to hold this box high up in the air—better put it on top of your head and hold it with both hands so nobody can get near it. *(The performer crosses to the child stage right, meanwhile taking a small red box with rubber bands wrapped around it out of his pocket; he immediately holds the box at arm's length as he crosses the stage.)* Here is a small red box. The lid is closed. Can you see what's holding it together?

CHILD: Rubber bands.

COUNT: Hold it with both hands as tight as you can. *(He crosses to the volunteer stage center, standing to left of him.)* Now, ____ alias George, you are going to make this trick work. Do you remember the magic word?

(The volunteer replies. If he remembers the word, fine; if not, drill everyone in it once more.)

COUNT: All you have to do is take this magic fan *(the magician shows the fan, which he waves back and forth)* and wave it at the two boxes, one at a time. All right, take the fan and wave it at the boxes! *(The performer raises his voice at the last phrase and gestures to the two boxes, looking away from the boy stage center. The fan breaks into several segments. There is laughter, but the entertainer pretends he has not seen what has happened.)* Very good! Now we'll take the rubber bands off the box, and open the lid *and we find* (surprised) another box? *(There is a smaller red box fitting snugly inside the first. The performer discards the first and gives the smaller one back to the stage-right boy to hold.)* Something's wrong! *(He sees the fan.)* Aah, that's it! You didn't wave the fan right! Let me have it—see? You wave it like this . . . now *you* try. Open the fan and wave it at the box. *(The child does so; the fan breaks again.)* You don't understand, ____ alias George. You're letting in too much air through here! *(He waves his hand between any two fan segments.)* Well, let's see if the trick worked anyway. *(He opens the lid and finds a smaller box inside.)* Another box? We'll have to try it again. Here—open the fan, like this, and wave it at the box! Take it—now wave it at the box. *(The fan breaks again; the magician reacts accordingly.)* Young man, what will your wife say about this? *(Leaning down to the child, the magician pretends that the child has said something.)* You say you left your wife at home? *(He repeats the leaning-listening business.)* Oh, you haven't got a wife! *(He turns to audience.)* But he's looking! All right, let's see whether the trick worked *this* time. *(He opens the lid; there is a smaller box inside.)* *Another box!* You know, I think you're a little short to do this trick well, young man. But that's all right, I can fix *that!* *(The magician gets a piece of newspaper, puts it on the floor, and has the child stand on it. After thinking for a moment, the performer has the child step off. Picking up the newspaper, the magician folds it in half, then has the child step on it again.)* Now we'll have you wave the fan like this *(he demonstrates)* and—here we are—wave it at the box . . . *(The fan breaks again.)* Well. *(The magician acts resigned.)* I suppose I know what we'll find. *(He opens the box, and there is still another, smaller, one inside.)* Another box! *(Very often, at this point, the audience will repeat this with the magician without any coaxing. If this occurs, the performer naturally plays his line to the audience with a knowing nod.)* You know, I finally realized what's wrong! You've been forgetting to say the magic word. Remember what it was? Does everyone remember? *Magic word!*

(Response)

COUNT: All right, now open the fan and wave it at the box, while saying the magic word.

(The child does so. This time the fan works.)

COUNT: Now let's see how we've done. *(He turns to the stage-left volunteer.)* Would you take the other box down and get the quarter?

(The child does so but, shaking the cylinder, discovers it is empty.)

COUNT: Ah-hah, now let's open the red box. *(The magician does so, leaving the bottom half in the child's hand.)* What's in the box now? *(He asks the stage-right child to reply. The child says, "A quarter." The magician should have him repeat this louder for effect.)* There you are—the very same quarter has flown all the way across the stage from that box to this one with the aid of the magic fan. Let's have a hand for these three fine magical helpers!

What You Need: A Devil's Coin Box. A quarter. A pen. A Breakaway Fan. A Coin in Nest of Boxes trick.

Preparation: Set up the Coin in Nest of Boxes according to the trick's instruction sheet, and place it in a jacket pocket.

How to Do It: This is a prime example of how to perform a big effect with equipment marketed for close-up use. Filling the scenic space with three assistants from the audience and implying that the coin flight has occurred invisibly across the entire width of the stage makes this a full-size stage routine. The byplay with the fan, of course, is really more important than the magic itself, and the constant breaking of the implement, together with the succession of ever smaller boxes, makes for excellent comedy for the youngsters. The Devil's Coin Box is an extremely inexpensive trick consisting of a cylinder with a slot in one end and a false bottom on the other. When the coin is rattled during the effect, the false bottom slides out a bit, permitting the magician to tilt the coin into the palm of his hand. Afterward, the hand squeezes the box and the bottom is shoved back flush with the rest of the cylinder. The Coin in Nest of Boxes has been described in Chapter 3 in the trick entitled the Traveling Coin. It works by means of a metal slide that guides the coin into the nest of boxes; when the slide is removed, the rubber bands snap the boxes snugly shut. The Breakaway Fan is simplicity itself: opened the logical way, it breaks; but if it is opened by the magician in what would seem to be the wrong direction, it "stays together." Note at the end of this routine that no provision is made to check the date and pen marking on the coin. I feel this verification merely slows the trick down when the climax clearly has been reached. However, the performer is welcome to verify the coin if he really feels obliged to. But if he plays it both ways a few times, he will probably decide that the lag in timing is not worth the conscientiousness.

COUNT: Well, boys and girls, it looks like it is about time for my final trick. But first, it seems to me that there was something else I was supposed to do. What could it have been? (*He tries to remember.*) I can't recall. Wasn't there something you were supposed to remind me to do?

(Response)

COUNT: The egg! That's right—I have to find Murgatroyd's egg! Well, when a magician wants to find something he has lost, do you know where he usually looks first? His hat! *(The magician's assistant enters with the hat the performer wore at the beginning of the act.)* This is my hat, and you can see it is empty. *(The assistant holds it upside down, shows the inside of it, then holds the hat with the opening inverted so it faces upward.)* The hat is empty, and some people say it always was, but I don't like them, either. Now in order to find an egg inside my hat, I will have to use not just a little bit of woofle dust, but a whole canful of woofle dust. *(The magician picks up a colorful cylinder filled to the top with confetti. He approaches the hat and, holding the can above it, begins to drop a few grains of confetti in it. Suddenly he gets a thought and drops the can in the hat and holds up his index finger.)* You know, boys and girls, I just remembered that woofle dust works best when it is very, very, wet—so I am going to moisten the woofle dust a little bit. *(The magician picks up a pitcher of milk from the table and approaches the hat to pour in a few drops. But as he crosses, he pretends to trip and the pitcher's lip tilts into the hat. When he straightens up, the magician finds that nearly all the milk has apparently poured into the hat, for the liquid level in the pitcher has dropped way down.)* Well *(with a sour face)*, that woofle dust is *very, very* wet. Oh, well, I'll look for the egg, anyway. *(Removing the canister, he sets it aside. Then, standing next to the hat, he reaches out his arm sideways and dips into the hat with his fingertips. This position permits the performer to keep his face toward the audience and allow the audience to see his expressions in what follows.)* Now I reach into the hat and find Murgatroyd's egg. *(He removes his hand and a white silk is seen dangling from the fingertips. He stares at it, looks at the audience, looks back at the silk, and drapes it over the hat.)* Now I reach into the hat and find Murgatroyd's egg. *(He pulls out his hand. There is a red silk dangling from the fingertips. This time he seems a bit uncomfortable. Smiling wanly at the audience, he drapes the silk over the hat and reaches back inside.)* Now I *really* reach into the hat and pulls out the egg! *(But out comes a bouquet of flowers. This makes him angry. Tossing them back into the hat, where they still remain visible, the magician yelps in rage.)* Aak! This is ridiculous! Now I find the egg! *(He pulls out a long, colorful paper streamer, tossing it high into the air as he does. At the same time, he steps back, startled, and shouts in fright, as if the streamer were a snake about to leap on him. Then he recovers and, furious, dives inside the hat only to yank out another streamer which dangles down almost to the floor.)* Where is that egg! *(He stamps his feet up and down in rage like a child having a tantrum. At last he stops, exhausted, panting. Then he turns to the audience, calm once more.)* You know, boys and girls, I think that egg is embarrassed to come out. It must be bashful. Maybe if we make a lot of noise like a mother hen, we can fool the egg into thinking that its mother, Murgatroyd, is out here. I'll tell you what—all the girls in the audience make a noise like a hen. Go cluck, cluck, cluck!"

(Response)

COUNT: Now, boys, maybe you can make a noise like a rooster. Go "Cock-a-doodle-doo!"

(Response)

COUNT *(looks inside the hat, then shakes his head):* It didn't work. Let's try it again, louder, and all at the same time. Girls go "Cluck, cluck, cluck"; boys, "Cock-a-doodle-doo!" Ready? Now!

(Response)

COUNT *(peers in the hat, shakes his head):* Still didn't work. I tell you what—let's all try it once more, even louder. Girls, "Cluck, cluck, cluck!"; boys, "Cock-a-doodle-doo!"—but this time, to make it more realistic, I want all the boys to stretch up their necks like a rooster—just like this—and I want all the girls to flap their wings like chickens—like this. Ready? One, two, three, *go!*

(Response.)

(The magician, standing sideways to the hat once more, smiles and during the cacophony, reaches into the hat and takes out an egg.)

COUNT: You did it! *(He places the egg down, then reaches back into the hat.)* By the way, boys and girls, in case you were worried about the milk I spilled, don't let it bother you, because here it is— *(and he removes a glass of milk, which he brings to his lips as the curtain falls.)*

What You Need: A hat. An assistant. A bouquet of spring flowers. Two silks. An E-Z Hat Loader set. A Vanishing Milk Pitcher.

Preparation: Plan a way to get the hat offstage early in the act. I hand it to my assistant, who takes it backstage. Since I wear my hair as the Count straight back, the removal of the hat gets a laugh. Backstage, she drops the folded bouquet of flowers into the hat. Set up the E-Z Hat Loader as per the trick's instruction sheet, and put the two silks on top of the load that comes with the equipment as purchased. Fill the milk pitcher with "milk" made from water and Oil of Milk, available from magic shops.

How to Do It: The E-Z Hat Loader is simple to use. It consists of a glass painted white to resemble milk, inside of which is stored a wooden egg, two folded paper streamers, and whatever other objects the magician cares to produce. The "load" is covered with the cylinder which has a false shallow top on which are scattered a few inches of confetti. When the cylinder is lifted from the hat, the "load" remains behind. The Spring Flowers are paper (sometimes leather-reinforced) with watch springs in the petals so that when released, they spring open into a bouquet. It is held together by folding each flower, then slipping a clamp or rubber band around the packet. The assistant, when bringing the hat on, has the folded bouquet resting on the upstage inside of the brim, with the hand that holds the hat concealing the flowers. After the hat has been shown empty and inverted, the assistant raises it fairly high. At this time, the bouquet is released so that it drops into the hat, still folded. The Vanishing Milk Pitcher works automatically. It has a false wall inside the glass exterior, and a very small quantity of the fake milk is poured into this compartment. Since the wall surrounds the pitcher, the small quantity of liquid seems to fill the pitcher. When the pitcher is tilted, the liquid flows into the central cavity of the pitcher, thus lowering the level in the compartment. It appears as if the milk were being poured out. The working of the effect now should be apparent. When the magician reaches in to obtain the flowers, he slips off the clamp or rubber band and takes the bouquet out by the strings that fasten the flowers to one another. The clamp or rubber band is left in the hat with the rest of the items.

Tips for Presentation: 1. Many other objects may be produced. The only limitation is the capacity of the glass or the maximum time the effect should take; the magician may actually palm and sneak in objects to be pulled out of the hat *while reaching in* to remove other objects.

2. It might be neater to place the produced objects on the table, but it is better showmanship to leave them in the hat. Though a bit messy, the latter procedure quickly fills the hat to over-flowing—which heightens the effect, since it seems clear that so much junk never could have come out of that small hat in the first place.

3. It is not necessary to drop the cylinder in the hat. This is the easiest method of "loading," but it is perhaps a bit more artistic merely to hold the cylinder just above the hat, then let the "load" slide in from that position. I prefer the easier method myself, perhaps because of laziness; it does not at all sacrifice the effect. For one thing, the audience does not yet know what is going to happen. For another, the milk pitcher business is a strong misdirective device.

4. When the milk is "accidentally" spilled, the magician should keep the pitcher tilted as he straightens up so that a few drops of the liquid really drip from the lip of the container. This reinforces the impression that there is a lot of milk in the hat.

5. No one should attempt an effect of this sort unless he has considerable experience in comedic timing. While it is important to build the character's embarrassment, confusion, and anger at the situation, the humor of the trick depends even more on the steady increase of tempo as the unintended objects are produced.

At the end of the last trick, it was suggested that the curtain be lowered. This enables the assistant to set down the hat and its contents, and the magician to obtain the props for the final trick. If no curtain is available, the lights may be lowered. If this cannot be done, then the business must be executed unobtrusively in full sight of the audience.

COUNT: I will now perform one of the most famous—one of the most difficult—one of the most *dangerous* tricks in all magic history—*The Great Bullet-catching Trick!* *(The assistant is now down-stage right; the magician is behind his table.)* The Great Bullet-catching Trick involves a silver coin. *(He shows a half-dollar-size palming coin held between thumb and fingertips of one hand. He raps it against the table or perhaps the milk pitcher a few times, thus proving it solid.)* I will give this coin to my assistant to hold between the clenched fingers of one hand. *(He flips the coin from hand to hand a few times, then gives it to the assistant, who closes her hand on it. Her downstage hand is stretched out straight at arm's length and the fingers curl about the coin, with the opening toward the magician.)* Meanwhile I take my pistol from my pocket. *(He takes out a brightly colored water pistol. The audience quickly reacts to this.)* What? What did you say?

(Response)

COUNT: A water pistol? Don't be silly! *(But he sprays a stream of water in his own face. Sputtering, he then grins sheepishly at the group.)* Heh-heh . . . wrong pistol. *(He puts it down and picks up a deadly-looking revolver from the table.)* *This* is the one I wanted! Now I am going to aim it at my assistant, and fire right past her clenched fingers and imbed the bullet in the middle of the coin—without hurting my assistant . . . I hope. *(The assistant has been looking confident up to this point, but now some doubt begins to register.)* But to make the feat more difficult I am going to do it—*blindfolded!* *(At this point, nervous music plays until the end of the act, and the performer speaks above the music. I have sometimes used a live pianist, but recently I have employed a tape recording of the delightful piano tone poem, "Rage for a Lost Penny" by Beethoven.)* And now, I aim at my assistant. *(But the performer, being blindfolded, has bumped into the table and subsequently nearly falls off the stage. In the process, he becomes confused in his directions and, when he says the line, aims offstage in the opposite direction from the assistant. The audience will, of course, loudly call out his mistake.)* What? I'm aiming in the wrong direction? All right . . . *now* I aim at my assistant! *(He squirms around so that he faces upstage and begins to point the gun. The audience again shouts.)* Still the wrong way? *(He turns again and faces the audience, aiming in their direction.)*

(Important: Aim above *their heads. They will, of course, scream*

"No!" at this point. The magician lowers the pistol, and motions for silence.)

COUNT: You see, the trouble is that I can't see. I'm blindfolded. But I can fix that! Just a minute! *(He scurries up to the table and behind it, feeling his way. At the table, he lowers his head for a second. When he comes up, he is wearing a gigantic pair of Super Specs, the oversize novelty eyeglasses, over the blindfold.)* There! *(With a broad smile.)* Now I can find the right way! *(He marches down to a position stage left that complements the assistant's location.)* Now I aim at my assistant! *(Taking his time, he begins to aim the gun at the assistant's clenched fist. For dramatic impact, the arm should be crooked at the elbow, gun pointed up, then slowly stretched straight forward as far as it will reach. When the arm is fully extended, the magician suddenly relaxes and turns to the audience.)* I hope this works! I never tried it before. *(Striking the firing attitude again, he slowly aims the pistol a second time. But just when it seems that he will fire, he breaks the attitude to sneeze spectacularly, perhaps hopping a few inches as he does. He turns to the audience, embarrassed.)* Excuse me! *(Once more, he begins to aim at his assistant. When he has stretched the business as much as possible, he drops the arm again, turns to the audience, and addresses it with a new urgency in his voice.)* Boys and girls, before I fire, I need a little more magic help from you! I am going to count three, and when I say "Three," I want you to shout out the magic word as loud as you can! Ready? *(He aims. Then he barks out the numbers with great force.)* One . . . two . . . three!

(Response. The performer stamps his foot and fires. At the same time, the assistant screams. The magician immediately tears off his blindfold and speaks rapidly and loudly.)

COUNT: There you are, boys and girls, the bullet is right in the middle of the coin! *(The assistant holds it up to show it, then runs into the audience and up the aisle, holding the coin with the bullet through it high so all can see as she runs past.)* You can see that at the box office *(or lobby)* on the way out! *(The magician comes forward. If there is a curtain, it closes and he puts his head through it as at the beginning. He speaks even more rapidly and urgently.)* Boys and girls, I want you to do one more thing for me before you go. I want you to call out, "Goodbye, Count Emkay," when I say goodbye to you. Goodbye, boys and girls!

(Response. The performer immediately pulls his head back through the curtain. The lights come up.)

What You Need: A Bullet-catching trick outfit. A larger cap gun than is used in that equipment. Round, plastic caps. A magician's blindfold. Water pistol. A pair of Super Specs.

Preparation: Load the gun with a round of caps. Lay the specs on the table and cover with the blindfold, on which are placed the two coins supplied in the Bullet-catching apparatus. Fill the water pistol partially and place in jacket pocket; if necessary, line the pocket with oilcloth or plastic wrap.

How to Do It: This routine is all buildup, with practically no climax at all, magically speaking. When the several noises take place at the time of the shot, the effect really is at an end. Showing the coin with the bullet through it is anticlimax; it is imperative that the last lines be played at breathtaking speed. The children should be caught unprepared for the rapidity with which the act ends, thus leaving them wanting just a little more. However, by allowing them to see the coin in the lobby on the way out, it is possible to satisfy their curiosity.

It is also possible to sell magic tricks or books of magic at a table set up in the lobby. My assistant has often done so, placing the coin with bullet on the table in front of the merchandise. One could flip the coin out to the audience at the end—a nice gesture, but hard on the budget, since it is then necessary to buy a new Bullet-catching outfit to replace the coin.

Not only is the change of tempo important at the end, but the final change of tone of the performer's voice ought clearly to tell the audience that the laughs are over and the serious and dangerous part of the trick is about to take place.

The actual working of this effect is simple. There is an unprepared coin and another with the bullet stuck through it; they are picked up at one and the same time, the prepared coin in the palm of the hand. During the flipping from hand to hand, the prepared coin is substituted for the unprepared one and is immediately given to the assistant, who conceals it by closing her hand over it. (For details of this coin flip movement, see Coin Flip at the beginning of Chapter 7.) The unprepared coin is left in the pocket when the water pistol is withdrawn from the same place. The blindfold must be a fake one so the magician can see through it. The rest of the trick depends on the performer's comedic and timing skills.

In the above routine, it should be noted that the entire impact can only be suggested, since neither inflection nor accent can be accurately rendered; besides, they change with every performance. But the student performer should examine the various psychological techniques pointed out, and notice the vocabulary chosen and the repetitions of important phrases. Rarely is there any word used that will not be immediately understood by every child present.

Equipment tricks fill the bulk of the routine, and only the simplest fingerwork is used. It is far more important to concentrate on the timing and orchestration of audience responses.

The reader may find it profitable to draw a diagram of a stage and attempt to construct a physical setting for the above routine that will provide maximum use of the scenic space. Then the detailed blocking pattern for the act can be worked out.

REFERENCES

In addition to the Easley-Wilson text on children's entertaining mentioned before (see bibliography), the student is directed to the four-volume *Kid Stuff* series published by Frances Ireland Marshall. There are some splendid routines in this series, including the Afghan Bands race, as well as one I perform occasionally called Thought Camera. It is one of the few mental effects I have ever found that work well for children.

Clown Act Omnibus: This large handbook has hundreds of ideas for clown acts, simple and complicated. It has a wealth of material and lots of good comedy that can be used in children's magic acts.

Napkin Folding, by Tom Osborne. This delightful, well-illustrated booklet explains how to make numerous figures from a table napkin. It is a valuable tool for the children's magician who wishes to pass a few minutes of nonmagical time.

MORE TRICKS

Card Ducky "Jo Ann": This splendidly made prop consists of a wooden duck which can reach into a houlette and select a chosen card from a deck therein. It is an appealing child's prop; although card effects are not suitable for most children's audiences, alphabet or number cards may be substituted.

Chapeaugraphy: This circle of felt can be molded into a variety of hats. Once a foolish magician told me he played ten minutes of his act with this prop. I can imagine the kind of attentiveness he commanded. I would use this prop as a running gag myself, putting it on whenever a behatted character is needed during a patter story.

Dot's-a-Dandy: A pleasant opening trick, involving a board with a colored circle drawn on it. It changes positions mystically and finally changes color.

Egg Bag: This old chestnut still plays well for children and can be used in a great variety of routines. The small bag conceals an egg that the children are led to believe has been palmed and removed.

Fraidy Cat Rabbit: One of the few good tricks with a children's look to the apparatus. This is a good closing trick on a short show. A black rabbit turns white, then black again. The children are sure the surface on which the bunnies are drawn has been simply turned around, but the magician proves they are mistaken.

Journey Through Space: A large cutout wooden rocket ship vanishes, flies "invisibly" through space, and is found on the other side of stage. This transposition effect can be worked to great effect with an assistant.

Mental Miracle: This simple device is another of the few mental effects that children can appreciate. The magician shows a list of states painted on a board and puts an X on one of them. Then a child calls out the one he chose mentally. The board is turned around, and the X is found next to the appropriate state's name.

Paper Tearing: There are many varieties of paper tears on the market. In each, the magician creates some new figure with the papers torn. They all involve the simple substitution of an already constructed figure for the torn pieces.

Run Rabbit Run: This, I believe, is the greatest sucker trick for children ever made. Though it uses a rabbit prop, it is not at all cutesy. A rabbit figure hides in a house and when the door is opened it has evidently vanished. But the audience sees the bunny scurry to the other side of the prop in the old Sucker Die Box manner. Yet at the climax, it vanishes to reappear elsewhere.

Spelling Lesson: This is a cute audience-participation stunt in which the children spell the names of objects and turn up a picture of the things spelled as they do. One child is kidded throughout by turning up a "dunce" picture repeatedly because he forgets to say the magic word.

Visible Walking Through Ribbon: This is a fine boys' trick when the Bullet Catch is not on the same program. Ribbons are circled around the magician's assistant's waist and are pulled through when two boys yank on them. The routine may be played with patter similar to the Bullet Catch.

18

Other Special Audiences

In a way, the title of this chapter is misleading. Every audience a magician encounters is special, and should be treated as such. However, as we have seen in the two previous chapters, some shows require a major reordering of technique to fit the peculiar needs and limitations of the audience.

Dariel Fitzkee has classified spectators into several groups, each of which he delineates by interest and attention span:

1. One individual seeing a pocket trick.
2. A small group of people at an informal get-together or in a home.
3. A family audience of mixed adults and children.
4. A mixed audience of adults of average intelligence. (By "mixed," he means of both sexes.)
5. Same as 4, but of very high intelligence.
6. Adults who have been drinking.
7. Men only at a smoker, banquet, or business meeting.
8. Women only at a ladies' club or similar function.

I think there is little practical difference between the first two classifications—an individual or a small group watching magic at an informal gathering—and such shows have been discussed earlier. Likewise, I find that differentiating between a family audience and one of mixed adults of whatever intelligence is of little practical value in deciding what sort of show to perform. If one knows there will be children in the audience, one might have to decide whether to aim the show specifically at them or to include only one or two children's tricks in a routine aimed primarily at adults. But as for differences in intelligence of an adult audience, it is very hard to draw conclusions that are not stereotypical. Classifying an audience by intelligence also presupposes that the magician is capable of judging whether or not they are cleverer than he is. I would suggest ignoring such divisions and concentrating on putting on a well-timed, entertaining show; that should be sufficient for any audience.

Fitzkee's latter classifications, I believe, have greater merit. A drinking adult group, such as one encounters at a social affair or in a nightclub, is indeed a special audience, even a problem one. Adults who are drinking are harder to please than children. Their attention span is shorter, their manners are abridged, and it is much harder to polarize them at the outset and keep them attentive. When one must perform on such occasions, it is wise to keep the act even shorter than usual if the sponsor will allow it. Patter should be greatly reduced, and flash effects ought to be relied upon heavily. Here, if anywhere, a "silent" act may spare the performer from dealing with hecklers.

A group of all women, says Fitzkee, is seldom receptive to magic. I do not know whether this generalization was accurate when he wrote it or whether it is valid today, but I do believe that a magician performing for a women's club must carefully review every word of his patter and each effect. There is never an excuse for poor taste, but the latitudes of taste probably are a trifle wider at mixed shows and at smokers.

In smokers and other all-male shows, the inclusion of so-called blue material is probably a cliché left over from vaudeville days. I have found that most business conferences and other all-male events tend to be just as conservative as any women's club. A group of men may enjoy, or at least tolerate, bathroom humor at a nightclub, but it rarely goes over at their commercial lunches or banquets. For one thing, they may be playing host to some straitlaced businessman from out of town. Or there may be members of the press covering the function, and that may make the hosts (perhaps unduly) sensitive to the image they project.

Whenever I perform for a business dinner or similar affair, I try to do two things, if permitted. First, I restrict the act to mental effects. Mentalism has a "quality" appearance that overcomes any hesitation the sponsor might feel about booking a magician. Second, I try to adapt each trick to the nature of the industry for which I am performing. For example, I entertained at the eighty-fifth anniversary party of Parker Brothers, the game-manufacturing firm, shortly after the firm was purchased by General Mills. The first effect I did was a marketed trick called Supersonic Card Prediction, predicting which one of ten cards would be "freely" selected by an audience volunteer. I pattered that each card might represent a different toy or game company, but that the astute General Mills management could not help selecting Parker Brothers. Then, presenting an envelope with a sealed prediction in it, I explained that before the show, I had decided that one of the ten cards would represent Parker. I called on a General Mills executive to make the "free" selection of card—and it turned out, of course, that he had picked the very card I had written down in the sealed prediction. For every trick in the ensuing routine, I adopted the patter to some aspect of the toy or game business. The extra effort was greatly appreciated by the sponsor.

In general, I would classify special audiences in a manner somewhat different from Fitzkee. To me the essential criteria are the degrees of attentiveness, comprehension, and good manners in each group.

We have dealt with children's audiences at some length. In my experience, there are at least three other major special-audience situations which today's magician may frequently encounter. The rest of this chapter will be devoted to these "problem" shows.

SHOWS FOR THE UNDERPRIVILEGED

I have performed many shows in underprivileged neighborhoods, for the Police Athletic League, for Operation Head Start, and—during a tour of the South and Midwest—at Job Corps camps for the State Department. In each, I have found the degree of success of the act depends principally on choice of material, size of stage and group, and the disciplinary customs of the sponsoring organization.

Shows for the underprivileged are difficult for several reasons. The audiences are seldom aware of the courtesy required during live shows in order for the performer to be heard and seen; they frequently have preconceptions about what is entertaining and what is not, and magic tends to rate low on the scale; often they have a great distrust of any person of a different social scale than theirs. This last point is quite understandable: not only is the entertainer probably in a more attractive economic position than theirs, but appearing before them may be interpreted as a type of condescension. When calling volunteers onstage, treat them the same way as any juvenile volunteers—with respect, patience, and kindness. Even so, the performer will meet with trying times and frequent suspicion.

The only way around this is to genuinely dedicate oneself to the work. It should be a *privilege* to perform such shows, for magical entertainment, however modest a mode of culture, at least contributes to the enrichment of audiences suffering from a paucity of experience.

Shows for the underprivileged are not so difficult if the audience consists of young children. But by the time the youngsters approach age nine or thereabouts, they tend to be unruly. At Job Corps shows, the performer generally faces a group of boys who may have attained maturity of years, but whose background makes them behave almost like children. A State Department representative booking one such tour suggested that I play the shows as if they were children's programs. This attitude was a bit condescending—but not overmuch. I found it necessary to perform children's tricks but with adult patter—a strange hybrid of material and presentation.

Stage size and the size of the group will determine the effectiveness of the program to a large extent. The bigger the audience, the more likely it will be for its members to be rambunctious. The talking, laughing, and wisecracks will be thicker and faster simply because of the audience's size. Should such be the situation, do not try to match the volume and smart-aleckiness; competing with the audience is never a good policy, but even worse in this instance. Trading quips with the group will merely spur it on. The contest can become quite an ego problem for the audience, and rightly so. The last thing an underprivileged audience needs is a middle-class "dude" coming on as if he were superior to them.

But large audiences do not have to be unruly. Their behavior really depends on the degree to which the sponsors control the group. Yet I would rather smile and talk louder for a difficult audience clearly enjoying itself than work smoothly for a group policed by an authoritarian band of counselors.

A magician who undertakes shows for the underprivileged will eventually face every variety of audience and disciplinary problem. He must be prepared to adapt greatly to the circumstances, if necessary, shortening the performance by several minutes to prevent restlessness from growing into belligerence. But in all cases, the magician should remember that there are all too legitimate reasons for any problems he may encounter in such shows; it is his job to minimize, not maximize, them.

One particular difficulty that often faces the performer in such shows is language: sometimes English is not well understood, and in most cases fancy vocabulary is out of place except possibly for humorous effect.

When comprehension is a factor, be especially careful to use simple-to-understand patter. But more important, choose tricks whose effects are perfectly plain because of visual impact. Color-changing silks, productions and disappearances, transpositions—these tricks are reliable. Mind reading is obviously out of the question, as, for that matter, is any effect which uses a prop with printed words upon it.

GERIATRIC WARDS AND OLD-AGE HOMES

Performing for the elderly has problems similar to those discussed in the previous section. Language is frequently a consideration, either because some old-age homes cater to particular ethnic groups or because hearing is difficult for many members of the audience. The solution to this is the same as before: choose visual material and don't rely on clever patter unless you are sure that the group will be capable of comprehending it.

The elderly are frequently encountered at hospital shows, but the general problems of the latter will be deferred till the next section. For now it should be noted that older audiences in homes or wards are virtually prisoners in their environments. They are extremely happy to be visited by anyone, and are most appreciative of any efforts on the part of the entertainer. I doubt that one will find any more rewarding shows to give than an act performed in a geriatric ward; however, the experience is also frequently a melancholy one, and the artist should be prepared to be depressed—though, of course, he must never let such an attitude show. The last thing the elderly (or for that matter any special audiences) need is pity. The role of the entertainer must be to lighten their burden for a time, and to divert their minds with new thoughts or pleasantries.

Choice of material ought to reflect this. A geriatric ward or old-age home is no place to bring a themed act centering around one kind of property. I would never do an all-ropes routine at such an occasion; it is important to vary the physical properties to include different textures, colors, shapes, etc. The audience has been used to seeing drab hospital corridors every day; a riot of hues can provide pure sensuous delight.

There is one special decision each magician must make before routining an act for the elderly. Should mind reading be included?

This is a tough choice to make. In a geriatrics ward, the chief work of the hospital staff is often simply to prevent the patients' minds from further regression. There is almost no hope of reversing the ravages of senility—at least, so I have been told by geriatrics specialists. As a result, the performance of a mental effect faces a high risk of failure. If it requires the volunteer to retain a thought for later divulgence, it is quite possible that he or she will simply be unable to remember it.

To guard against this, it is wise to have a volunteer confide the thought to another member of the audience, or perhaps write it down. Even so, there may be an uncomfortable lag in timing while the thought is recalled and produced. Is such a problem worth incurring?

In answer, I can only offer an experience I have often had at such shows. After nervously awaiting the revelation of the volunteer's thought, and finding, to my relief, that he or she has been able to bring it to mind once more, I have later been told by hospital workers that the volunteer showed greater concentration in that moment than in weeks of staff-conducted recreational projects.

Said one specialist to me at New York's Elmhurst Hospital: "That old man really enjoyed being the focus of attention for a few moments, and he made an amazing effort to remember his card. This experience was better for him than a month of therapy!"

HOSPITAL SHOWS

Professional comics, singers, and magicians frequently lament the death of vaudeville because there is no longer any place to try out new material and to perfect showmanship technique. But I have found the hospital circuit an excellent place to break in new material and polish timing and patter.

However, I have also seen perfectly awful performers subject bedridden patients to condescending "put-down" jokes. I have heard of magicians who go on for hours, even when the audience disgustedly begins to wheel itself out of the room. I have seen shows where the booker has thrown together a miscellany of unrelated acts that go on too long, perform unsuitable material, and bombard the poor convalescents with one hard rock song after another.

In New York, there are many agents who send acts out on hospital shows. They rarely audition these performers beforehand,

and they almost never routine the shows. To these agents, hospitals seem to be composed of beggars who will gratefully accept whatever alleged entertainment is thrown at them. Such bookers are nothing more than cynical opportunists who use hospital shows to bolster their reputations as community-minded citizens.

The only hospital troupe I have ever worked for is the Florence Duray touring company. Its shows are kept to about an hour in length and a careful routining of various acts is always presented: usually a singer or two, a dancer, a magician, and a comic—not necessarily in that order, but presented in a carefully programed and pleasing arrangement. Every act is auditioned.

But the most pleasing thing about the Duray troupe is the attitude of the performers toward the hospital audiences. Never is there any condescension. The mere fact that the show is free is no reason to disdain the occasion.

A condescending attitude toward free shows is self-indulgent and unprofessional. As a matter of fact, the nonpaying audience is likely to be harder to please than the ticket-buying one. Free tickets are often viewed with disdain, as Robert-Houdin once observed; for one thing, he says, the person admitted free tends to think the rest of the audience is nonpaying, too, and that the whole group is doing the performer a huge favor just by donating its time.

Personal proof is vital at hospital shows. No matter what the group thinks of the magician's tricks, it should genuinely like him or her. This is of great practical importance in wards, where the sight lines are frequently terrible. I have had to give shows in fracture wards where the patients are in traction and unable to see. Sometimes the beds extend down impossible vistas, and once, at New York's Beekman Hospital, I had audience members seated *behind* me.

Sight lines are crucial, and unless the magician is aware beforehand that he will be playing on a stage or platform, he had better pick angleproof illusions. What is more, he may have to stand up on a chair just to enable everyone to see the props. I had to do so once at Bellevue Hospital at great personal risk (being somewhat of a klutz even when standing on the floor) and had to hold each prop over my head before and during each effect.

The same guideline mentioned in the previous section holds for all hospital shows: a variety of colorful props should be routined. If you experiment with new material in the act, put it in the number two spot (right after the start of the act). If there is any problem with it, at least a good initial impression will already have been made and there will still be time to rectify the misfire during the remainder of the performance.

In a hospital show, it is nearly impossible to rely on tricks that require borrowing money or some small object. Hospital patients are usually in robes and can carry very few personal effects with them. If a trick calls for a coin to be borrowed, you can ask for it but should have one on the table just in case.

Similarly, audience participation may be severely limited in certain wards. At the children's shows I do for New York's Institute of Physical Medicine, I cannot include any trick that requires a child to come onstage. They are all in wheelchairs, and may have dwarfed or missing limbs. Since audience participation is essential in children's shows, I simply double the usual verbal byplay whenever I perform at this hospital.

If you are engaged to give a hospital show, select your material carefully and never, never exceed ten to twelve minutes of playing time if you are appearing with many acts. If you are on a smaller bill, or are playing a solo date, the act may last perhaps twenty-five to thirty minutes, but that is, to my mind, the very longest one should plan to perform. If you intend to include edible giveaways for children in such a show, always clear it ahead of time with the recreational supervisor for the hospital. (Some patients might have restricted diets.)

Hospital shows are—as all magic performances ought to be —opportunities to bring diversion and joy to the world. The magician who submerges himself to such a goal will reap a reward that will never be equaled by his most lucrative performances.

19

Do's and Don'ts
of Magical Entertainment

Other magic books are chock full of do's and don'ts, which are usually more concerned with preserving the fraternity of magicians than with advancing the conjuring art.

For instance, there is the basic axiom of nearly all prestidigitators: *never reveal secrets.* Naturally no performer in his right mind will tell an audience how he just worked a trick. But I believe this hush-hush mystery business reaches a limit if keeping the secret would offend or hurt a close friend. The limit has also been passed if a magician gives an audience the impression that he really has occult powers. There are indeed untutored individuals capable of being hoodwinked by the misrepresentations of charlatans. Before such audiences, disclosure and debunking may be a moral duty.

There is another old chestnut: *never repeat a trick.* The basic philosophy of this rule is sound enough: the immediate repetition of an effect (perhaps because the audience has requested it) suffers because the audience knows what to look for. Discovery of the secret may be more likely on a second viewing. At the least, the structure and pacing of the act may be sacrificed.

On the other hand, there are some tricks which not only can be repeated but may gain by a second showing. Certain mental effects might be attributed to chance on a first viewing, but repetition will strengthen their impact. I suppose one might argue that the initial effect and its repetition together make one combined trick, but that is quibbling. The point I wish to underscore is that there may be legitimate occasions for repeating a trick provided that the second viewing enhances the mystery and entertainment value of the performance.

There is another self-serving don't bandied about by some magicians: *don't knock other magicians*—in other words, don't deride the work of your fellow performers. Naturally, it creates a poor impression if a performer remarks to the sponsor that so-and-so is a wretched entertainer. It looks like a case of jealousy, or perhaps sour grapes.

But if you read some magic books and magazines you see a perversion of this principle to the point where nothing the least bit negative (even if constructive in tone) can be said or written about the work of any conjurer. Perhaps we should refrain from volunteering opinions on fellow magicians in public, but if a sponsor solicits our opinion, it would be less than honest to praise blunderers.

If I were to draw up a list of do's and don'ts for magicians, it would certainly echo the major points stressed in this book:

Do be original.

Do use improvisational patter.

Do not copy another's act or patter.

Do not perform shows longer than the time requested.

I might also throw in a don't pertaining to ethics:

Don't assume a magician you have never met would be thrilled at the honor!

Local magicians seem to think they are obliged to play host backstage whenever a guest wizard pays a call. In Sharon, Connecticut, a man dropped in on me backstage during intermission, when many props had to be set up for the next act. He seemed to think I had nothing else to do but explain all my apparatus on the spot. I suffered him graciously, but I would have liked to pitch him out bodily.

Perhaps the only traditional magical don't I would wholeheartedly endorse is: *Don't do a trick until it has been practiced to perfection.* Beyond that I would add the ultimate do for any serious artist:

Do continue to study your own art and that of others. Constantly analyze the results in order to improve.

Only through honest self-appraisal and a quest for perfection will we continue to grow as entertainers.

Supply Sources of Magic Tricks and Literature

Many dealers in magic apparatus and books may be found in the United States by checking the Yellow Pages in the telephone directory. Another excellent supply source is *Genii*, probably the slickest magazine for magicians generally circulated at magic shops in this country. Subscription information may be obtained by writing to 4200 Wisconsin Avenue, NW, Suite 106-384, Washington, D.C. 20016, genii@geniimagazine.com, http://www.geniimagazine.com.

Many dealers issue catalogs that include merchandise locally invented, as well as that produced by some of the principal manufacturing concerns in the country. Some catalogs are free, while others cost from a few cents to a few dollars. Some of the more expensive listings come from Abbott's in Colon, Michigan and Tannen's in New York. The Tannen's catalog is especially valuable for every serious magician to have; it contains hundreds of pages of generally reliable descriptions of tricks classified by type of materials used (cards, rope, liquid, etc.), as well as, to some extent, by audience and size of room.

Suppliers listed below are ones with whom I am most familiar. The list is by no means exhaustive, but most of those omitted can be found in the pages of *Genii*.

ABBOTT'S MAGIC CO., 124 St. Joseph Street, Colon, Michigan 49040. This is one of the largest manufacturers in the country, producing everything from pocket-size tricks to illusions, which generally have to be specially ordered and commissioned, then made to order. If you order the larger effects, plan to wait some time before receiving the apparatus, as the equipment may have to

be programmed into the firm's work schedule.
  1-800-92-MAGIC
  amagic@net-link.net
  http://www.abbott-magic.com

EAGLE MAGIC AND JOKE STORE, 708 Portland Avenue, Minneapolis, Minnesota 55415. This is an absolutely charming little store with a handsome layout of magical equipment. The staff is very friendly, and from time to time offers some tempting second-hand pieces of equipment on sale.
  612-333-4702

FLOSSO HORNMANN MAGIC CO. This venerable institution, billed as America's oldest magic store, closed its doors on September 30, 2000, ending its long presence on Manhattan's West Side. For the time being, the company will continue to do business via the Internet and mail order.
  http://www.martinka.com

MAGIC, INC., 5082 North Lincoln Avenue, Chicago, Illinois 60625. This firm produces both a tricks catalog with some interesting-looking customized merchandise in it and a book catalog. Its prices are reasonable.
  773-334-2855

LOUIS TANNEN, INC., 24 West 25th Street, 2nd Floor, New York, New York 10010. This is, without doubt, the Mecca of magic supply in America. The store is clean and well lit with a friendly and helpful staff—but avoid the busy hours if you can help it. Tannen's catalog is a must and has a higher percentage of reliable copy than most.
  212-929-4500
  info@tannenmagic.com
  http://www.tannenmagic.com

D. ROBBINS & CO., INC., 70 Washington Street, Brooklyn, New York, 11201. Producers of a large range of smaller magic, Robbins primarily deals through wholesalers but will fill orders for anyone located in a town without a local magic dealership.
  718-625-1804
  http://www.ezmagic.com

Glossary

Anticipation: A way of fooling the audience by making it think the secret move or magic trickery has not yet taken place, although it really has. See Misdirection; Chapter 9.

Assistant: A person who appears onstage with the magician and aids during the act. The audience realizes that the assistant is part of the magician's show. Compare Confederate; Volunteer. See Chapter 14.

Attention control: The channeling of an audience's interest to the sights and sounds it must observe in order to understand and enjoy a magic show, or any kind of entertainment. Attention control includes misdirection, the diversion of audience notice from secret maneuvers, but is not limited to it. It encompasses *all* the action that takes place in a show. Compare Misdirection. See Chapter 9.

Audience: A person or a group, no matter how large or small, whose attention has been successfully directed to the "playing area" of a show.

Billet: A small piece of paper, sometimes written upon, used in mental effects.

Blocking: A technical term derived from the theater. It refers to the patterns of movement a performer follows during a show.

Breakaway: A term referring to certain magic comedy props, such as the breakaway fan or breakaway wand, which seem to come undone in a spectator's hands, to his embarrassment.

Center tear: A maneuver that enables the magician to discover the contents of a secretly written message. For details on working, see Chapter 7.

Close-up magic: Magic using smaller equipment, which requires the audience to be quite close to the magician to appreciate what he is doing. Compare Parlor magic.

Confederate: A secret assistant who aids the magician in performing some desired trick. The audience is never aware that a confederate is being employed; frequently, the confederate pretends to be an audience volunteer. Compare Assistant; Volunteer.

Confusion: A way of fooling an audience by presenting so many details that it cannot tell the important secret moves from the innocent ones. See Misdirection; Chapter 9.

Conjuring: The calling up (conjuration) of demons to gain supernatural aid in performing miracles. "Conjuring" is synonymous with "magic." One who performs magic, therefore, is a conjurer.

Creative flow: The linkage of points of focus so that the audience's attention is smoothly drawn along from trick to trick. See Points of focus; Chapter 9.

Dealing seconds: A sleight that permits the magician to retain the top card of the pack and deal cards below it as if they were uppermost. The term derives from the world of gambling and often connotes cheating. The move may be accomplished by using the Glide. See Chapter 6.

Dissimulation: A way of fooling the audience by pretending something is not so when it is. See Misdirection; Chapter 9.

Distraction: A violent way of taking an audience's attention away from something it should not notice. Compare Diversion. See Misdirection; Chapter 9.

Diversion: A way of fooling the audience by taking their attention away from something they should not notice. See Misdirection; Chapter 9.

Double lift: A sleight that enables the magician to pick two or more cards from the pack as if they were one. The move can be performed easily with the aid of a Svengali, or Stripper, Deck.

Dressing movement: A theater term pertaining to the subtle balancing movement an actor makes to keep the stage picture pleasing to the eye when another actor crosses in front of him and moves elsewhere.

Effect: A technical term often employed by magicians to refer to the

302 / *The Creative Magician's Handbook*

apparent magic witnessed by the audience in any given trick. Example: The effect in the Nonburning Handkerchief is that flammable cloth resists flame.

False cut: A move that enables the magician to cut the cards and still keep them in the same order. See Chapter 6.

False shuffle: A move that allows the magician to shuffle the cards and retain the whole pack or certain cards in a desired order. See Chapter 6.

Flash effect: A magic trick whose climax is fast and highly visible. Example: The magician twirls a silk in the air and it instantly changes to a cane.

Foo can: A magic device that enables a container to be shown empty even though it holds liquid. A partition keeps the liquid inside when the can is tilted one way, but a reverse tilt will allow the liquid to pour out.

Force: A technical term referring to a ploy for making a spectator select a prearranged card or other object, even though the audience believes the choice is free. See Chapter 6.

French drop: A sleight that enables the magician to retain a small object in one hand while pretending to pass it on to the other hand. See Chapter 6.

Gimmick: Any secret device employed to accomplish a trick.

Glide: A sleight that allows the magician to retain the bottom card of the pack and deal the second from bottom as if it were the lower-most card. Also may be used in "dealing seconds." See Chapter 6.

Illusion: Any trick may be called an illusion, since the magician is pretending that an impossibility is real. But magicians often use the term *illusion* specifically to refer to bigger effects generally performed onstage in front of a theater audience. An illusion in this sense often requires large, expensive, bulky apparatus—such as Sawing a Woman in Half with a Buzz Saw. However, it is sometimes possible to present a full-scale illusion with little in the way of costly equipment. See, for example, the bullet-catching routine for children in Chapter 17.

Key cards: Any secretly noted cards used to locate a selected one of unknown identity. See Chapter 7.

Legerdemain: Literally, "light of hand." This term is a fancy way of referring to manual manipulation. By extension, it has been taken to mean any kind of performed magic. Compare Sleight of hand.

Levitation: A trick in which a person or large object "floats" upward from the floor and seems to hang in the air. Compare Suspension.

Load: A technical term referring to a packet or bundle of objects to be magically produced. A "load" often must be put into the production apparatus in an unobtrusive manner after the same apparatus has been shown to be empty.

Lota bowl: A piece of magical apparatus which appears to be empty or filled with liquid, at the magician's whim.

Magician's choice: A force technique in which two or more objects are supposedly offered for free selection by the spectator, but a predetermined one actually is foisted off on him. See Chapter 7.

Magician's rope: Very soft cotton rope with a removable core, available from most magic dealers. It is unusually pliable and easy to work with in cut-and-restored tricks and rope escapes.

Magician's wax: A substance sold by magic dealers. It is useful in making small objects "float" in air (see the Floating Pencil, in Chapter 3) and has a variety of other applications.

Misdirection: Any technique used by a magician to divert the audience's attention from noticing some secret maneuver or device involved in making a trick work. Compare Attention control. See Chapter 9.

One ahead: A mental magic system for discovering the written thoughts of several audience members by finding out the contents of each message before the audience realizes the magician is doing so. For details, see Chapter 12.

OOM: An oily substance which, when added to water, results in a liquid which resembles milk. Also known as Oil of Milk or Magician's Milk.

Pace: The deliberate alteration of tempo in order to achieve stronger presentations of tricks. Compare Tempo. See Chapter 11.

Palm, or palming: A sleight that enables the magician to conceal a card, coin, or other small object undetected in the palm or another portion of the hand. See Chapter 6.

Parlor magic: In the past century, the room where guests were entertained was known as the parlor. Since amateur magicians frequently gave their shows in this room when visitors dropped by, the term *parlor magic* became commonly used to describe magic shows given in intimate surroundings for a small audience. Parlor magic, as the term is now used, generally refers to tricks with small props, such as cards, coins, thimbles, and so on. See Close-up magic.

Patter: A technical term referring to anything the magician says while performing. Patter often helps misdirect the audience's attention, provide transitions from one trick to the next, afford comic relief, and so on. See Chapter 4.

Personal proof: A quality of assurance and an aura of pleasantness which a performer should communicate on his first entrance to make the audience like him as soon as it sees him.

Plant: A term sometimes employed to refer to a secret assistant. See Confederate.

Platform tricks: Magic that must be performed on a platform or stage for best effect because of the size of the equipment and/or the necessity of keeping the audience at some distance to prevent detection of the secret. Compare Close-up Parlor magic: magic

Playing area: The portion of a room or stage in which a performance is to take place is the "playing area."

Plot trick: A magic effect on which the magician can pattern a story when devising his patter. (Example: The Floating Pencil, Chapter 3.) Compare Process trick.

Pointing: A technique for focusing the audience's attention by direct physical indication of the point to be focused upon. See Attention control; Misdirection; Chapter 9.

Point of focus: The place where the audience's attention is supposed to be at any given instant during a performance. See Creative flow; Chapter 9.

Polarization: A mechanical and psychological process by which a group of people is turned into an audience. Polarization takes place before the magic show begins and focuses the attention of the group to the front of the stage or room, or wherever the show is about to take place. See Chapter 2.

Premature consummation: A way of fooling the audience by making it think a trick is over before it really is. See Misdirection; Chapter 9.

Prestidigitation: Literally "rapid fingerwork," this jawbreaking word specifically refers to hand movements, but has come to mean magic of all kinds. One who performs magic, therefore, is a prestidigitator.

Process trick: A magic effect that involves a process complicated enough to be interesting in its own right. (Example: A Chronological Prediction, Chapter 3.) Contrast Plot trick.

Production: A technical term that refers to a magic trick in which an object or person appears from nowhere.

Props: Short for *properties,* this technical term is derived from the language of the theater and refers to any objects handled by the magician in the course of performing a trick. *Props* may refer both to equipment which the audience sees and to secret devices which help bring about an effect.

Question-and-answer act: A kind of mental magic performance in which the mentalist appears to divine answers to queries written down by many audience members. See Chapter 12.

Repeater: A magic trick whose dramatic effect is enhanced by repetition.

Repetition: A way of fooling the audience by doing an innocent action often enough so no attention is given it when it is changed into a secret move. See Misdirection; Chapter 9.

Roughing fluid: A substance available from magic dealers. Coated on playing cards, it causes them to adhere slightly to one another, which makes it possible for the magician to show two cards as one.

Routine: A sequence of tricks which flow easily into one another. Also, an extended arrangement of tricks which have been merged into a single trick plot. (Example: The Drunken Magician, in Chapter 15.) To *routine* is to arrange a sequence of tricks into a unified whole comprising a show. See Chapter 11.

Ruse: A way of fooling an audience by doing something openly which at the same time covers up a secret move or action. See Misdirection; Chapter 9.

Setup: A secret way of arranging a deck of cards to accomplish a specific trick or sequence of tricks. Compare System; Chapter 8.

Silent act: A performance in which pantomime substitutes for the spoken word. A silent act is usually performed to music and/or sound effects.

Silk: A technical term for the extremely sheer handkerchiefs which magicians use in productions and vanishes. The thin material makes the cloth easier to handle. Silks are available in many colors and sizes from most dealers.

Simulation: A way of fooling the audience by pretending something is so which is not. See Misdirection; Chapter 9.

Sleight, or Sleight of hand: The term commonly used among magicians to refer to various secret hand maneuvers employed in manipulating cards, coins, and other small objects. See Chapters 6 and 7.

Spelling trick: A card trick in which the chosen card is located by "spelling" a word or words while simultaneously turning cards over from the pack with each letter. When the last letter is spelled, the card turned over is the selected one.

Spring flowers: Artificial flowers that can be hidden in a small space. Springs inside open them up when they are removed from the compact place in which they were stored.

Steal: A technical term for a packet of small objects (such as cards or coins) that is attached to the body in a concealed position, so the magician can secretly obtain them during the act.

Stripper deck: A deck of cards whose sides or ends have been planed on a taper so that if a card is reversed, it can be located by feeling the protruding edges. Also called a wizard deck.

Sucker trick: A magic trick in which the spectator thinks he has figured out the secret or caught the performer in an error—only to be proven wrong. (Example: The Wise Guy Turnover, in Chapter 3.)

Suggestion: A way of fooling an audience by intimating something is so which is not, or vice versa. See Misdirection; Chapter 9.

Suspension: A trick in which a person or large object is placed in the air, where it remains unsupported. Compare Levitation.

Svengali deck: A versatile trick deck useful in forcing a card and capable of many miraculous effects. Every other card is the same and is cut short, making it possible to execute easy double lifts and other maneuvers.

System: In card magic, a secret way of arranging the pack so the magician can perform various effects. Compare Setup. See Chapter 8.

Tempo: The speed of speech, movement, and physical activity which a magician sets while doing a trick. Compare Pace. See Chapter 11.

Timing: The art of pacing a performance to make it appeal to the audience by virtue of the overall length and variety of tempo. See Pace; Tempo; Chapter 11.

Transposition: A magic trick in which two or more objects or persons mysteriously change place.

Vanish: A technical term for a trick in which an object or person disappears.

Volunteer: An audience member drafted by the magician to help during a trick. Compare Assistant; Confederate. See Chapter 14.

Wizard deck: See Stripper deck.

Bibliography

Sources consulted range from contemporary books in print to obscure mimeographed manuscripts turned up in dusty back rooms of magic shops, and complete publication information is not always available. In addition to the following books and pamphlets, the author is indebted to various issues of conjuring periodicals such as *Genii, Jinx, Linking Ring, Magic Handbook, Magic Is Fun, M-U-M, The Phoenix,* and *The Sphinx.*

ANNEMANN, T., *Practical Mental Effects* (Louis Tannen, 1963).
———, *202 Methods of Forcing.*
BLACKSTONE, H., *Blackstone's Modern Card Tricks and Secrets of Magic* (Garden City Publishing Co., 1941).
———, *Blackstone's Tricks Anyone Can Do* (Garden City Publishing Co., 1948).
BURLINGAME, H. J., *Magician's Handbook* (Wilcox & Follett Co., 1942).
CHRISTOPHER, M., *ESP, Secrets and Psychics* (T. Y. Crowell).
CORINDA, T., *13 Steps to Mentalism* (Louis Tannen, 1968).
CRIMMINS, J., ed., *Annemann's Miracles of Card Magic* (Max Holden, 1948).
———, *Ted Annemann's Full Deck of Impromptu Card Tricks* (Max Holden, 1943).
CURRY, P., *Magician's Magic* (Franklin Watts, Inc., 1965).
DEXTER, W., *131 Magic Tricks for Amateurs* (Arco, 1958).
DUNNINGER, J., *Dunninger's Complete Encyclopedia of Magic* (Spring Books).
EASLEY, B., *Doing Magic for Youngsters,* and WILSON, E. P., *The Art of*

Conjuring to Children, two books bound as one (Louis Tannen, 1948).

ELLIOTT, B., *Classic Secrets of Magic* (Collier Books, 1962).

FITZKEE, D., *Magic by Misdirection* (Magic Ltd., 1945).

———, *Rope Eternal* (Louis Tannen).

———, *Showmanship for Magicians* (Magic Ltd., 1945).

GIBSON, W. B., *The Complete Illustrated Book of Card Magic* (Doubleday & Company, Inc., 1969).

———, and YOUNG, M. N. (eds.), *Houdini on Magic* (Dover, 1953).

GILBERT, A. C., *Handkerchief Tricks* (A. C. Gilbert Co., 1920).

———, *Knots and Splices with Rope Tying Tricks* (same).

GRAHAM, W. B. (comp.), *Magic Secrets from the Seven Circles* (Modern Litho Inc.)

GRANT, U. F., *The Challenge Magic Act* (U. F. Grant).

———, *25 One Man Mind Reading Tricks* (U. F. Grant).

———, *Valuable Information for Magicians* (U. F. Grant).

GRIFFIN, K. and R., *Illusion Show Know-how* (Abbott Magic Manufacturing Co., 1972).

HILLIAR, W. J., *Modern Magicians Handbook* (F. J. Drake, 1902).

HOFFMAN, PROFESSOR (Angelo Lewis), *Modern Magic* (George Routledge & Sons).

———, *Later Magic* (E. P. Dutton & Co., Inc., 1935).

HOY, D., *Psychic and other ESP Party Games* (Doubleday & Company, Inc., 1965).

HUGARD, J. and BRAUE, F., *Expert Card Technique* (George Starke, 1950).

———, *The Royal Road to Card Magic* (Faber & Faber, 1949).

JONSON, W., *Magic Tricks and Card Tricks* (Dover, 1954).

KELLAR, *Kellar's Wizard's Manual* (Wm. W. Delaney).

MARSHALL F I *V'd Stuff,* Volumes 1–4 (Ireland Magic Co., 1954–68).

"THE GREAT MASONI, *Showmanship Out of a Hat* (The Supreme Magic Co.).

MAURICE, E., *Showmanship and Presentation* (Goodliffe, 1946).

MULHOLLAND, J., *The Early Magic Shows* (Office of John Mulholland, 1945).

———, *Quicker Than the Eye* (The Bobbs-Merrill Co., 1932).

MUSSEY, B., *Magic* (A. S. Barnes & Co., 1942).

NELMS, H., *Magic and Showmanship: A Handbook for Conjurers* (Dover, 1969).

POSGATE, B., *Kid-Show Showmanship* (Abbott's Magic Manufacturing Co., 1961).

PRICE, H., *Confessions of a Ghost Hunter* (Putnam & Co., 1936).

RENEAUX, J., *The Professional Technique for Magicians* (Abbott's Magic Manufacturing Co., 1968).

RICE, H., *More Naughty Silks* (Silk King Studios, 1947).

ROBBINS, D. (ed.), *Practical Magic* (David Robbins & Co., Inc., 1953).

ROBERT-HOUDIN, *King of the Conjurers* (translation of *Memoirs of Robert-Houdin* with a new introduction and notes by Milbourne Christopher, Dover Publications Inc., 1964).

SEVERN, B., *Magic and Magicians* (David McKay Co., Inc., 1958).

SHIELS, T., *13!!!*

———, *Something Strange* (The Supreme Magic Co.).

———, *Daemons, Darklings, and Doppelgangers* (The Supreme Magic Co.).

STEVENSON, A., *75 Tricks with a Svengali Deck* (The Wizard's Workshop, 1964).

———, *75 Tricks with a Wizard Deck* (Wizard Books, 1962).

TANNER, D., *Grant's Fabulous Feats of Mental Magic* (U. F. Grant).

THURSTON, H., *300 Tricks You Can Do* (Pocket Books, Inc., 1948).

TURNER, B., *How to Do Tricks with Cards* (Collier Books, 1963).

VOLKMANN, K., *The Oldest Deception* (Carl W. Jones, 1956).